STEVE MAC

THE MIGHT

MY LIFE INSIDE TH   CENTRE

First published 2016 by 2000 AD
an imprint of Rebellion Publishing Ltd,
Riverside House, Osney Mead,
Oxford, OX2 0ES, UK

www.2000adonline.com

UK ISBN: 978 1 78108 475 5

10 9 8 7 6 5 4 3 2

A CIP catalogue record for this book is available from the
British Library.

Designed & typeset by Rebellion Publishing

Printed in Denmark

STEVE MACMANUS

THE MIGHTY ONE

MY LIFE INSIDE THE NERVE CENTRE

INTRODUCTION

HEAVY WEIGHS THE Rosette of Sirius on the head that wears it. He who would be Tharg the Mighty must not only manage and maintain the reserves of Thrill-power that the readers of the Galaxy's Greatest Comic demand but he must also keep in line a small army of surly art and story droids, both inside and outside the Nerve Centre. As if that wasn't enough, he occasionally has to dress up in a motorcycle suit and gauntlets, put on a rubber Neanderthal mask, and make sure that the aforementioned Rosette of Sirius remains glued to his forehead throughout a gruelling photo-session.

As someone who was once persuaded to don equally outlandish garb and pretend to be the superheroic editor of another comic, I feel uniquely qualified to declare that Steve MacManus could wear that weighty Rosette like no other Earthlet before or since.

I feel further kinship in that Steve and I both began in comics in the age of Cow Gum, scalpels, typesetting, and editors that wore leather-elbowed sports jackets and smoked pipes whilst leaning against the office fireplace, reminiscing about the Second World War. Not quite as distant as the Neanderthal Age, but close.

In our time at *2000 AD*, I was always struck by Steve's quietly spoken and affable temperament, although he was no push-over, as I discovered when I arrogantly gave him an 'either the writer goes or I go' ultimatum.

I went.

Over the years, not only with *2000 AD* but with *Battle*, *Starlord*, *Crisis*, *Revolver*, *Diceman*, the *Judge Dredd Megazine* and many others, Steve has overwhelmingly proved that he knows how to edit. With this honest and engaging autobiography, he's now proved that he can write too.

Wearing the Rosette of Sirius or not, and modest though he might be, he is unquestionably a Mighty One.

Dave Gibbons
May 2016

1973: COMIC CHARACTERS

'HOW DO YOU spell *"harass"*?' The question was shot at me by the editor of *Valiant*, one of Britain's top adventure comics with weekly sales in excess of 100,000 copies. I was standing in the offices of Fleetway Publications in London and was hoping to be hired in the role of sub-editor in the Juvenile Group. To my left sat the present sub, who was leaving to join a new magazine called *Football Star*. This title's unique selling point was meant to be its mix of football and pop, but in fact this proved to be its downfall and *Football Star* closed within six issues of its launch. Also in the room were the art editor and the art assistant, making an editorial team of four. This was the staffing ratio for each of the weekly comics published by Fleetway; the scripts, artwork and lettering being created on a 'work for hire' basis by a host of freelancers based in Britain, Europe and South America. I answered, nervously, spelling *'harass'* with one *r*, only to be corrected by the sub, who was sure that it had two. Fortunately, I was proved right when the editor burst into laughter and mocked his sub's poor spelling. The whole room began to chortle (that's what comics folk do) and I was told to come back on Monday to meet the deputy managing editor.

Going home along Fleet Street, aboard a bus bound for Pimlico, I mused on the events that had led me to Fleetway Publications. Leaving school early to spend six months in Sicily, and then scraping three A-Levels at Plymouth Tech, I had returned to London eager to get a job. It was a wage that I wanted, not a university degree, and so I joined the Alfred Marks employment agency. After temping as a linen porter at the Cumberland hotel (changing the live-in maids' bedding, but never being invited into a bed, nor even tickled with a feather duster), I next found myself sent to the Swan and Edgar department store in Piccadilly Circus. On arrival, I was dispatched to the basement – there to crush used packaging that cascaded with terrifying speed from a chute outlet in the ceiling. Following two weeks of near death by cardboard, I decided to try my luck at journalism, parleying my three A-levels into a meeting with an HR person at IPC Magazines. I must have made an impression of sorts because interviews were arranged for me. After a calamitous ten-minute audience with the publisher of *New Scientist* I applied for a post on *Shoot* magazine, armed with the inducement that my silky skills on the football pitch had made me vice-captain of the first team at the tender age of fourteen, only to be told firmly that the position had been filled. As a consolation, I was informed there was a job going on 'one of the comics' if I wanted to apply, which is how I had come to be standing in the *Valiant* office. My thinking was if I could just get into Fleetway then I could apply internally at a later date for another, more prestigious job. My time on *Valiant* would be merely a temporary stopover. After all, comics were for kids, weren't they?

The Juvenile Group had a boys' department, girls' department, nursery department and humour department.

Each was run by a managing editor, who reported to the group publisher. The man I met on the Monday was named Sid Bicknell. He more or less made it clear to me that had he not been on holiday the previous week I would have had a lot more trouble getting hired. What had happened was that Sid's boss, the exotically named Jack Le Grand, had interviewed me in Sid's absence and seemed quite happy to hire me. I didn't mind Sid's initial ire and managed to impress him by being able to recall my eight-digit bank account number, which he needed for the payroll department. Both Jack and Sid were veterans of World War II, Jack as a glider pilot and Sid on the landing craft on D-Day. Sid used to joke that it was all right for the troops being unloaded on to the beaches, they could hightail it to the nearest cover, but he and his landing crew colleagues had to remain exposed to incoming fire until they could turn about and head back to the mothership. Jack for his part survived the Arnhem debacle even though his glider, like so many others in that operation, crash-landed. They were an unlikely combination: Sid was the stickler for detail with a grasp of grammar that extended to the assertion that *lay-byes* should actually be called *lie-byes*, while Jack was the expansive, chain-smoking, larger than life character, always up for a drink after work. After one such drinking session I tried to put him in a Mercedes mini-cab to take him home, but he declined saying, 'I can't be seen arriving home in an effing wedding car, chum!'

And so my career in comics began. I was twenty years old and found myself working on the very comic that I used to read every week in my youth. *Valiant* was an anthology title, like most of its stablemates, and I was amazed to find it featured the same characters that I had followed a decade earlier. The lead strip was called *Captain Hurricane*, featuring a World War II Marine Commando whose gimmick was to have to a 'raging fury' at a key point in each weekly episode. These furies, usually caused by a build-up of irritations in the story, gave Captain Hurricane enormous strength, which he then used to pick up enemy tanks and hurl them back at the approaching 'Westphalian warmongers!' (his words not mine) to save the day. His long-suffering batman Maggot Malone witnessed such acts. The strip was drawn in a slightly cartoony style and it was *Valiant*'s most popular story, which says a lot about the needs of the audience at the time. *The Wild Wonders* were a pair of Hebridean heroes who were able to pull off prodigious but unlikely feats of athletics due to their arduous upbringing. Under the guidance of their guardian they were brought to London, from where many a long-running adventure was launched. Again the art was in a slightly cartoony style, communicating the comedy-drama nature of the strip. *The House of Dolmann* featured a master puppeteer who had created a fantastic army of mechanical warriors with which to fight crime. Using ventriloquism Dolmann gave his dolls personalities, such as Togo, the manic, wrestler puppet, and Mole, the myopic digger equipped with drill hands. *Raven on the Wing* was introduced as 'A gypsy boy named Raven', who displayed uncanny, barefoot ball skills on the football pitch but was always at the beck and call of Morag, his tribe's wise woman. Dark and moody, *Raven* was a prototype for a television football soap opera. Completing the line-up were *Kelly's Eye* (man protected by life-giving Eye of Zoltec), *Jason Hyde* (from whose eyes streamed coloured, mind-reading rays) and my favourite *The Steel Claw*, who gained invisibility by plugging his prosthetic hand into any local power supply. As I perused the pages of *Valiant* once more I realised that nothing had changed in this cosy, albeit fictional world, in stark contrast to events unfolding outside the office window, where the three-day week was in full force, and across the Atlantic the Watergate scandal was about to bring down the President.

I can't say there was much on-the-job training, although I was advised to make myself scarce if I ever saw the publisher coming towards me wearing dark glasses. *Valiant*'s editor, my first editor for that matter, was named Stewart Wales. He and I made up the editorial team, supported by an art editor and an art assistant or 'bodger' as they were more commonly known. In true *Mad Men* style, everyone smoked. Stewart, like Sid, was unsure of my ability to do the job and effectively I was on trial, although I did not know it. One of my duties was to check the artwork for each strip to ensure the artist had correctly followed that episode's picture instructions as detailed in the script (a comic script consists of scene directions for each picture with accompanying dialogue for the characters in the picture). The dialogue would then be subbed, if necessary, and the art and script handed to a freelance letterer, whose role was to letter the script dialogue onto the artwork and draw a tail to the character speaking. The first artwork I had to sub was three pages of *Captain Hurricane*. The big shock for me was the size of the artwork. As I unrolled the art it just kept on unrolling, like an infinite piece of wallpaper. By the time I had managed to wrestle the pages flat on my desk I was looking at artwork that was twice as large as the story in the printed comic. That was my first learning in comics: that the artists drew pages that were at least half as big again as the printed page and sometimes, in the case of Charles Roylance (the artist on *Captain Hurricane*) twice as big. Roylance had an agency to represent him, like most of the artists working for Fleetway. He lived in Spain and the process was that the agent would come in to the office to pick up the script and then return a week later with the drawn artwork. For his labours Roylance was paid £33.00 a page, which gave him an income of £100 a week, good money at the time. Naturally his agent took a cut, but that seemed to be the routine everyone followed. In fact the only artist I saw come in who did not have an agent was Leo Baxendale, renowned creator of *The Bash Street Kids* and other classic British comic characters. Legend had it that Leo had once come into the office with a brown parcel in which, it was assumed, was his latest artwork. But inside was merely a pair of corduroy trousers. 'Oh dear,' he is said to have announced, 'I must have sent the artwork to the dry cleaners!'

Another of my duties involved opening the readers' mail and selecting their jokes and missives for the letters page. The widespread belief that reader correspondence printed in comics (and magazines for that matter) is invented is actually a misapprehension. *Valiant*'s postbag was huge; everybody wanted to win the £1 postal order prize offered for each entry published. Often I had to take the post home and open it whilst watching *The Sweeney*, being careful to make sure I tallied the voting coupons on which each reader had diligently named his or her top three characters in the comic. These votes were transferred onto a popularity chart, which hung in the office and was worshipped by the staff with the same reverence as if it were a religious icon. *Captain Hurricane* was always the most popular character and his strip appeared at the front of the comic. Each editor determined the line-up of who appeared where in their thirty-two page publication and the accepted wisdom was to lead with your most popular character and end with your second-most popular. Least-liked heroes would be marked for the chop in an end-of-term edition in which all the current serials concluded. As a reader, it was a calamity if you happened to miss this particular issue with its explanations to mysteries that had kept you hooked for the past six months and vanquishing of villains who had had the upper hand over your heroes for far too long. And it was no use asking for enlightenment, as the accepted practice among friends who also read comics was that each person followed a particular title. These competitor titles would be borrowed and then returned, sometimes scornfully, jeering at jokes that had clearly been copied from one's own title or laughing at the ridiculous hero fighting on the North-West Frontier armed only with an ancient cricket bat, even if the item had once been used to score a test century at Lord's.

Of course all thoughts of what had happened to whom and how would be swept away in the excited expectation of the next issue. This would contain new stories for the evergreen heroes, introduce debuts from 'exciting new' characters and promise a 'free gift for every reader!' Of all these giveaways, the free spud gun has to rank as one of the most entertaining bits of plastic ever devised, its play value remaining unsurpassed to this day.

Another of my duties was to come up with the pithy phrases known as toplines. These bold announcements sat above the logo on the front cover and proudly proclaimed the title's rich cast of characters. For example: 'Amazing Thrills With The Steel Claw Inside.' Having composed several of these to last us the next few issues, I would mark them up for the typesetter to provide a proof. Once corrected, the typesetter would return a finished proof and the first topline would be cut out with a scalpel and pasted onto the front cover using a spirit-based adhesive called Cow Gum. My difficulty was that I could never get the toplines to come out at the right size; they had to be an exact width and mine were always too short or too long. When they were too long, the bodger could sometimes be cajoled into cutting a word out, but if they were too short the proof was useless and everybody's time had been wasted. No matter how hard I tried, for the life of me I could not get the lines to fit. Perhaps I was high from the fumes wafting out of the open Cow Gum tin; mixing with the clouds of cigarette smoke, these made a toxic concoction that hung in the air ready to clobber that rare specimen, the non-smoking visitor. One thing was for sure, as I peered over my typewriter through the smoke in the general direction of Stewart's desk, I began to sense that I was not making a good impression. I had already incurred Sid's wrath when I passed him an episode of *Raven on the Wing* in which a footballer, playing on the right wing, had the wrong number on his shirt. Sid was mortified by this glaring error on my behalf. I put up the shaky defence that rigid numbering of shirts had gone out of fashion after England had won the World Cup in 1966, but this had only irked him all the more. If he had been a referee I think I would have been sent off there and then. Clearly, my prospects of continued employment were receding faster than the hairline of the then England No. 9 Bobby Charlton.

Fleetway Publications' offices were in Farringdon Street, EC4, a stone's throw from Fleet Street and the national newspapers that were written and printed there. A multitude of historic pubs served the industry's workers, but all had to close on the dot at 2.00 p.m. with ten minutes for drinking-up time. The only two places you could get a drink after that were the Press Club or the City Golf Club. However, the only balls to be found inside the Golf Club's pitch-black basement venue were highballs, the golfing bit being merely a ruse to acquire club status and so be granted a licence to serve drinks in the afternoon. Stewart introduced me to the City Golf Club; we weren't members, we would just walk past the concierge with a cheery wave and descend into the Stygian gloom, groping our way along the bar rail until we found the welcome light of a beer pump. The only time I was asked for identification was one Christmas Eve. A sea of growling, thirsty journalists thronged the entrance area, clamouring to be let in. I fought my way to the front only to be confronted by a man with a Rolodex, who was checking members' names and addresses. He looked at me sourly, but I knew that my brother was a member and so gave his name and our home address, which thankfully matched the one on the card. My interrogator was about to question me further, but a sudden surge from the back of the throng propelled me past him like a champagne cork and I was in.

In Farringdon Street, the company occupied the whole of Fleetway House, which had been purpose-built in 1912 for the magazines division of the Amalgamated Press. Nothing appeared to have changed in the marbled reception and one had the sense of walking into a hotel each working day. There were old-fashioned lifts, manned by uniformed operators wearing bellhop- style hats. Each floor had a long, dark corridor illuminated only when a door to one of the floor's rooms was opened. Each of these rooms housed a magazine title and many had fireplaces, giving them a homely atmosphere, one that was occasionally enhanced by pipe-smoking editors standing round the mantelshelf musing on whether their innocent readers realised that the character

Buster was actually the spawn of *The Mirror*'s roaming cartoon lothario Andy Capp.

There wasn't much socialising in work time and you could go for months without meeting your neighbours. The only person who saw everyone was Flo, the tea lady, who wore a white hat and wheeled a tea trolley laden with a vast urn and tasty snacks up and down those dark halls twice a day. In a future move across the Thames, Flo was to be inadvertently left behind and we were never again to enjoy her comic comestibles.

Way down the hall on my floor resided the humour department, comprising a gaggle of titles with names such as *Shiver and Shake*, *Whoopee*, and *Knockout*. On my first day I had briefly met another new recruit, who disappeared into the gloom to work on one of these titles. He eventually left to become Bob Monkhouse's gag-writer, and I do believe Mr Monkhouse bequeathed him his treasured joke book containing 10,000 witty one-liners. Another staffer had recently left to launch *Men Only* for Paul Raymond. Then there was the colleague who took me aside one day and quietly informed me he was the reincarnation of Al Capone. He stepped back to get a good look at what was clearly supposed to be my utter astonishment. I did my best to mug shock and awe at this revelation and was able to respond by saying I had just returned from spending six months in Sicily, in the vicinity of Castellammare del Golfo, birthplace of many a future Don. This news seemed to go down well for the next thing he said was, 'Good, good. If anyone bothers you let me know.' This became his refrain any time we passed each other in the gloomy corridor. '*Ciao*, Stefano, anybody bothering you?' To which, I always replied, '*Non. Tutto va bene, grazie a lei.*' I had the feeling that had I ever answered in the affirmative then things would not have gone well for the culprit, with perhaps one of their vital organs being found shortly thereafter, floating disconsolately in a tin of Cow Gum.

High up in a garret lolled *Lion* comic, edited by a dyspeptic man named Geoff Kemp. *Lion*'s more energetic stablemate *Tiger* was next door. *Tiger*'s most popular character was *Roy of the Rovers,* who had been scoring goals for Melchester Rovers since 1954. Across the corridor from these two industry titans, a kindly chap named Ted Bensberg was single-handedly restaging the events of World War II. His job was to produce a couple of sixty-four-page *War Picture Library* titles every month. Even though they were pocket-sized I am reliably informed it took more than two thousand issues and twenty-six years to complete this lonely task.

One aspect of the job that delighted me was the encouragement to write scripts and features. Writing skills were valued as highly as the ability to spell. If you could master the technique of writing a picture strip, there was plenty of paid work on your title's annuals or summer specials and even freelance work on other titles. Not long after I started, Stewart commissioned me to write a two-page *Swots and Blots* strip for the *Valiant Summer Special.* I was also asked to caption a feature about giant-sized, earthmoving equipment for the *Valiant Annual.* Meanwhile, Sid had set me the fiendish task of cutting a fifty-page *Wild Wonders* adventure down to ten pages for reprinting in the same publication. It's probable that these three tasks were part of my trial, a triathlon designed to make or break me, but in an amazing comeback I was able to complete them all. My pithy captions for the earthmoving feature had Stewart regarding me in a different light. True, I had forgotten to caption one picture, which featured a machine with giant-sized wheels. When Stewart pointed out the omission, I offered from the top of my head the caption: 'This huge machine has wheels bigger than a man – and it's a man-sized job to change them!' Stewart looked impressed and from across the room Janet, the art editor, chirruped, 'Who's a clever little cock sparrow?' I got the feeling the tide was turning. Sid had already grudgingly acknowledged that I had done well to cut forty pages from the *Wild Wonders* and still retain the semblance of a story, complete with beginning, middle and end. I didn't tell him how at first I had struggled and struggled with this job. But then, suddenly I had seen that the writer, Tom Tully, had gone off on a lengthy detour halfway through the story and, Russian doll style, there was a mini-story within the main story. All I had to do was cut out the main story, add one small caption to introduce the mini-story, and I had completed the task. My *Swots and Blots* story was accepted, too, although the letterer, Johnny Aldrich, jokingly said that any more dialogue and the artwork would have been covered entirely by the word balloons. Shortly afterwards, I was informed my trial was over and I was to be hired permanently, becoming a fully fledged member of staff and compulsory new member of the National Union of Journalists to boot.

Naturally, I was delighted. However, little did I know that the whole cosy set-up of the industry I had just joined was about to be torn apart. A new wave of titles was coming, one that was to sweep me along with it for the next three decades and which would later become known as the 'Renaissance of British Comics'.

1974: A CALL TO ARMS

STEWART NOW ACCEPTED me and we became good friends. For Stewart a common criticism of a fellow staffer was that they 'did not know what day it was'. This was an expression I had never come across before, along with many other Fleetway colloquialisms I was to overhear as I navigated its lonely corridors. I was keen to impress Stewart, though, with my social life and one time used a Polaroid camera to take a picture of a model in a magazine. I showed him the picture, claiming the person in it was an intimate acquaintance. He believed me, given that the evidence was a Polaroid and I let him mull over my amazing social life for a good few hours before disclosing the deceit.

Stewart told me about his career, how he had recently returned to Fleetway from a stint on *Look-In*, a bestselling TV tie-in magazine for children. There his job had been to interview film and TV stars such as Roger Moore. It sounded very cool and I often wondered why he had decided to return to the less glamorous environs of the picture-strip industry. When Stewart wasn't acquainting me with new public houses, he was putting work my way. The front cover of *Valiant* had a feature called *The Rivals* and I was proud to be asked to write about the rivalry between the two train companies that built the USA's first transcontinental railroad. Another front-page series invited the reader to guess the celebrity in a feature called *Who Is It?* My subject was Bruce Forsyth, then hosting the television show *The Generation Game*. But Stewart wasn't pleased with my draft text at all. 'What Brucie is best known for,' he said tersely, 'is dropping plates on *Sunday Night at the London Palladium*.' So I rewrote the text and then went to Fleetway's in-house photo-library to ask for a photo of Forsyth dropping plates as reference for the intended artist. The photo-library was a large room crammed with filing cabinets, the remaining space being occupied by a single desk at which sat a stern-looking woman nearly hidden by piles of by 8" x 12" photographic prints. I could see no sign of the cabinets being catalogued or any evidence of an index system and didn't expect to have any success in my picture request. Sounding apologetic, as if I knew I was asking for the impossible, I enquired as to the remote possibility of there being a picture of Bruce Forsyth on the premises, preferably one showing him dropping plates at the London Palladium. My colleague considered my request and sucked thoughtfully on the cheroot she had been smoking when I entered. Then, pausing only to place the cheroot in an ashtray, she rose with a practised sigh, strode across the room to a particular cabinet, yanked open the second drawer and plunged both hands into its contents. A period of intense riffling then ensued before she retrieved three prints with a flourish and waved them in my direction. 'Bruce Forsyth, dropping plates at the London Palladium,' she barked, 'and mind you bring them back.'

Stewart introduced me to the three writers who scripted most of *Valiant* and a lot of the other boys' titles at that time: Angus Allan, Scott Goodall and Tom Tully. All in their forties, these hard-working freelancers would deliver a bunch of scripts by hand and then be taken by Stewart to The Old King Ludd on Ludgate Circus, there to talk about the declining state of the industry. Shots of whisky would be nursed while Stewart and I drank the new-fangled lager under the stony gaze of older bitter drinkers. On the rare days they were all in town together, the trio would retire to the pub and critique each other's work. As the drinks flowed the conversation would focus on the finer points of scripting, which generally concerned the correct use of sound effects. Effects like 'Wham' and 'Kapow' were derided for being redolent of American superhero comics. Between loud, head-turning burps, for which he was famous, Tully would proclaim the rectitude of good old-fashioned British sound effects such as *'Screeee!'*, *'Kraaak!'* and the ubiquitous *'Aaaaahhh!'*. Of the three, Tully was the one I got to know best and, indeed, I worked with him for most of my career. Although Goodall and Allan were known by their first names, Scott and Angus, Tully was always just 'Tully'. Maybe this was because he was thought to be big-headed; indeed the surname usage was often accompanied by a grimace as though to signify he was hard work. Perhaps the fact that he had once worked as a tallyman contributed to the picture. Despite this he was acknowledged as one of Fleetway's star writers, for he had developed a technique no one else could master, try as they might. Sure, all the writers made sure each episode would end on a cliffhanger, which had to be resolved at the start of the next episode, leaving just enough room to develop the story a little before introducing the next cliffhanger. Tully, however, infused his stories with a sense of realism that made their gimmicky nature just that little bit more believable, even if on closer inspection a completed Tully adventure would often turn out to be much less than the sum of its parts. This aside, no editor could afford to be without a Tully character in their title, be it a footballing hero like Roy of the Rovers, a suspense star like the Steel Claw or a historical figure such as Heros the Spartan. His crowning achievement was to come later with the creation of Johnny Red for *Battle*, superbly drawn by Joe Colquhoun.

As a young reader, two of my favourite artists on *Valiant* had been Mike Western and Eric Bradbury, but it was much harder to get to know them for the simple reason that they rarely came into the office, and when they did appear it was always a fleeting visit, with just time to drop off their artwork before disappearing back to the solitude of the Home Counties. Mike, a dapper man with a twinkle in his eye and a penchant for pork-pie hats, would sometimes share a joke with Stewart or Janet, while Eric was the quieter, more serious visitor. Like many of their fellow artists they had both seen action in World War II. I was told Eric had been an air-gunner on Wellington bombers. Situated alone at the rear of the plane, the gunner's job was to scan the night, searching anxiously for the deathly shape of an enemy night fighter. I can only assume it was these long missions spent peering into the dark that influenced Eric's unique style. Indeed, of all the artists I have known and admired, Eric has to be the one who used the most black in his work. This gave his art a scary, suffocating aura that made him highly sought after for the darker tales such as *Cursitor Doom* or *Doomlord*, not to mention his incomparable work on *Joe 2 Beans* for *Battle Picture Weekly*. In that strip, Joe 2 Beans is a US Marine and Blackfoot Chief, who initially does not speak. The strip begins with the rhetorical question, 'What goes on in the mind of Joe 2 Beans?' Eric's artwork showing Joe 2 Beans staring impassively out at the reader illustrates the question perfectly... leaving it unanswered, hanging in the air, as he himself was suspended in space during those desperate hours spent over enemy-occupied Europe.

Demand for artists always outstripped supply, so Fleetway had found studios in Italy that could take up the slack, and from there, contact with artists in Argentina had been made. The studio system meant that sometimes the famous artist you thought was drawing the whole strip would often only be drawing the protagonist's head, after his studio assistants had previously drawn the body. This is why in a studio-drawn strip like *Raven on the Wing*, for example, every picture of Raven shows him with an alarmingly small head in comparison to his body. That's comics folk for you, not averse to a bit of division of labour when needed.

Europe was a lucrative sales market for the company. Publishers on the continent were keen buyers of strips marketed to them by the syndication department. This was a great job to have, travelling to international book fairs such as Frankfurt and Bologna, meeting up with a local publisher and going out for dinner once the deal had been done. The Fleetway archive boasted some ten million or more pages of comics to buy, and demand was high, especially from Dutch and Spanish publishers. Being on work-for-hire contracts, though, neither artist nor writer would receive any secondary payments for this reuse use of their work. They didn't even get a payment if their work was reprinted in an annual at home. (The accepted rule of thumb was that a story could be reprinted five years after first publication. This was based on the calculation that the average customer life of a reader was five years, so no one would be any the wiser.) In terms of page rates, scriptwriters earned a quarter of the sum the artist received for each page of comics created. However, a good weekly output of scripts more than made up for this since the maximum an artist could comfortably produce was two to three pages, whilst a writer could generate three or four times that amount. In short, everyone was making good money, but the crunch was coming.

The first casualty occurred early in 1974. Stewart told me that a merger was to take place. *Valiant* was to 'join forces' with *Lion* to make the super new title *Valiant and Lion*. In theory this was good news for both sets of readers, as they would now get to enjoy the best of each title in one publication. That's how it was spun to them, anyway. The reality was a little different; after twenty years of publishing *Lion* was to cease and its staff would be given the choice of leaving, in the hope of forging a career as a freelance, or staying put, with nothing to do but pray for a new launch that might see them rescued from limbo. We *Valiant* staffers were safe, of course, and could live to edit another day, riding the sales boost provided by the transferring *Lion* readers. Quality-wise it was a different story. Three strips from *Lion* were inherited as part of the merger process, but only one could be deemed a success. This was *Spot the Clue With Zip Nolan* drawn by Joe Colquhoun. It featured ordinary crimes solved by a believable American Highway Patrolman riding the extraordinary Harley-Davidson Electra Glide. *Captain Hurricane,* however, had to team up with *The Steel Commando*, a pathetic pairing that tarnished the good Captain's reputation and changed his strip from being faintly ridiculous to just plain silly, disappointing the fans of both characters in the process. *Adam Eterno*, a time-travelling eternal wasn't much more popular, either; *Valiant* had plenty of lone-wolf heroes of its own, so Eterno did not bring anything new to the paper.

The closure of *Lion* was a blow for Sid and Jack. When I had joined the boys' department Jack had waved a dummy for a new publication at me but I never saw it launch. Meanwhile, the girls' department had been having notable success with new launches *Tammy* (1971) and *Jinty* (1974). The launch of *Tammy* had challenged *Bunty*, the market leading title published by DC Thomson in Dundee. *Tammy* was not a clone of *Bunty*. Bright and sassy, *Tammy* knew exactly which entertainment dramas its readers were watching on television and actively sought to emulate them. *Tammy*'s downtrodden yet gutsy protagonists were also put through darker, nastier trials than those endured by the heroines in *Bunty*. True, the traditional Cinderella plot principle was still evident, but that was no guarantee each serial would have a happy ending. This editorial ethos saw sales of *Tammy* soar to 200,000 copies a week. Reality fiction had become the name of the game and the girls' comics were targeting this new sweet spot with unerring accuracy, leaving the boys' adventure titles looking increasingly out of touch.

As it happened, soon after the merger, I found myself attending an in-house training course on scripting picture strips for girls. I've often wondered who put my name forward for the module, but whoever my benefactor was, their good deed was to prove instrumental in furthering my fledgling career. Our tutor was a small Scotsman called John Purdie and I took an instant liking to him and his clear passion for fiction writing. There were six of us in the room and under John's astute editorial direction we fleshed out a comic strip named *Beatty of the Baths*. We were then set the task of scripting the first six frames in the opening episode of our protagonist's story. Each of us had a typewriter and soon the room was alive with the clacking of keys. The course was actually part of a training programme run by Fleetway's parent company IPC and most of my colleagues were magazine staffers, hailing from posh titles such as *Woman* and *Woman's Own*. Nonetheless, as I actually worked on comics and spent most of my time working with scripts I felt I had a head start on the others. I found the picture descriptions and dialogue came naturally to me and I was soon lost in the turbulent world of our putative Olympic swimmer, for that was the dream we had chosen for Beatty. By picture six in my story Beatty had trodden on a rusty nail left by some lout at the swimming baths where she worked as an attendant, using the baths to train in when they were closed. Desperately in need of a tetanus shot, I had Beatty facing the dilemma that to go to the hospital would mean leaving her little brother alone with their brutal stepfather, who was soon to return home, skint from another fruitless afternoon spent at the bookies. As we typed, Purdie walked around the room looking over our shoulders at our work. When he came to read my effort he nodded approvingly before moving on with a word of encouragement. I was very pleased, but at the back of my mind I kept thinking I had seen him before. Then it suddenly clicked: he was the managing editor of the girls' department, their offices were located upstairs, somewhere I seldom ventured. This was the man who was responsible for the successful launch of *Tammy* and who would soon oversee the launch a range of bestselling photo-romance magazines with names such as *Mates*, *Oh Boy*, *Photo-Love*, *My Guy* and *Photo Secret Love*. What I didn't know was my script work that day had been noted and later a call would be put through to my superiors asking about my availability to work on a new title but, as I was to discover, one for boys not girls.

On my return to *Valiant*, Stewart was bursting with good news. We were to have a free gift. 'Somebody loves us,' he said happily. A free gift was a powerful promotional tool, guaranteed to bring in tens of thousands of new readers eager to get their hands on the paper dart that soared like a bird or the 'Thunderclap' that was sure to cause a commotion in the classroom. *Valiant*'s sales needed the boost, despite the recent merger, and the decision to invest in a free gift showed management still had faith in the title. Launched in 1962 it had become a mainstay of the industry and was held in high esteem by industry professionals. But my time on the title was drawing to a close and soon after I was called into Sid's office to be told that there was an offer of a sub-editor's job upstairs, working on a new title. He looked pained when he mentioned the words 'upstairs' and 'new title' and I gathered he was not in favour of either. I was told to report to the title's editor, David Hunt, straight away to learn more. Rather than navigate the murky corridors all the way back to the main staircase, I took the service lift. On my way up I realised I did not know David Hunt at all, other than that he had been the editor of *Scorcher*, a football comic that had launched in 1970 but recently closed. His appointment as editor at the time, though, had made him the youngest person ever to boss a title, so youthful talent was clearly something that was valued by our new masters in the girls' department.

Emerging on the next floor I found my way to the room where the new title was being produced, then knocked and entered, keen to learn more about it and David as my new editor. The room was large and bare, furnished solely with two desks, two chairs and two typewriters. The desks faced each other to make one large desk and on one side sat David, who welcomed me in and gestured for me to sit opposite him. As I did, I noticed he had been reviewing some artwork that appeared to feature events from World War II. David came straight to the point in a businesslike manner that suggested whatever the new title's theme, it had already been scheduled for publication. He asked me if I knew of a new war comic called *Warlord*. I had seen it, in fact, and I had admired its realistic coverage of World War II. Its lead strip featured a Royal Marine like Captain Hurricane, but there the similarity ended; realism was in, tank-throwing was out. The title had cool characters with names like Union Jack Jackson and Killer Kane and its launch had clearly dropped a hand grenade into the stagnant boys' market. David explained that *Warlord* had been a big success for its publishers DC Thomson. They were Fleetway's main rivals in the comics market and it was planned for Fleetway to launch a competitor as quickly as possible. This was the title we were to work on and it was to be called *Battle Picture Weekly*.

I was delighted, having had a keen interest in World War II since I was young. Growing up in the fifties and sixties you could not help but be enveloped by its legacy: fathers and uncles had fought and sometimes died in the damn thing, mothers had hidden under tables in the Blitz, grandfathers had enlisted in the Home Guard, and aged aunts had patrolled hospital wards bringing succour to the casualties of the night. Comics of the time were full of it and every boy was a reader of the *War Picture Library* and *Commando* pocket series. Miniature plastic toy soldiers were inherited from elder brothers and played with endlessly, and for those with generous pocket money, Airfix kits of every description were bought, assembled, painted and pimped with fanatical devotion. The war's grip on British culture had waned in the late 1960s, but now it was returning and I was more than ready to climb aboard the first tank into town.

David introduced me to the two other members of staff who had both been recruited from titles in the girls' department. They were located through a connecting door and they were art editor Norman Fletcher-Jones and art assistant Chris Dias. I must admit we seemed an unlikely choice of team to spearhead a counter-strike against the might of DC Thomson, although Norman was a veteran of the war and he had the silver moustache and furled black umbrella to prove it. David must have read my mind because that was when he let me into a secret. His disclosure shed light on a lot of things that had previously been unclear, not least the reason for the pained expressions in the boys' department downstairs.

He told me that two freelance writers had been brought in to be the creative force behind the new title, which would be produced under the auspices of the girls' department. The publisher had taken this decision and its effect would be to freeze Jack and Sid out of the title's development and launch process. David's job as editor was to ensure the paper got to press on time, blending his editorial skills with freelancers' creativity. I shook David's hand, saying I would be delighted to join his title. I had the feeling it was going to be the beginning of a beautiful partnership and I was not proved wrong.

I returned downstairs to say goodbye to my colleagues on *Valiant*. It had been decided that Stewart would absorb my duties into his role and he jokingly said, 'What is it you do over here anyway?' Glad that there was no animosity, I headed back upstairs… somewhere in Britain a printer's time had been booked and it would be my job to assist in getting the new title to them, with no ifs nor buts. After all, I was in the army now.

1975: BATTLE STATIONS

THE DECISION TO let the girls' department launch a title for boys cannot have been taken lightly, but its effect was to herald a new era in British comics publishing that would see the launches in quick succession of *Battle Picture Weekly*, *Action*, *2000 AD* and *Starlord*. The timing for *Battle*'s launch in 1975 was perfect. A new generation of schoolboys was into World War II, thanks to the release of stylish feature films such as *The Dirty Dozen*, *Where Eagles Dare*, and the quirky *Kelly's Heroes*. With repeats on television of big action classics such as *The Battle of Britain*, *Tora! Tora! Tora!* and *Patton: Lust for Glory* the war was fertile ground for a comic specialising in its world-shattering events. On my first day in the *Battle* office I learned that a dummy for the new title had already been created and David took me along the corridor to meet the two men responsible. We slipped discreetly into a room no larger than a broom cupboard and David introduced me to its occupants: their names were Pat Mills and John Wagner. Both were in their middle twenties. I knew Pat from afar as the writer of *Yellowknife of the Yard* for *Valiant*, but I had never met John before. He later told me he had previously worked at

Fleetway as the editor of *Sandie*. A telegram to Scotland had brought him south once more, this time to be reunited with Pat, his erstwhile writing partner. On their desk I noticed a list of freelance writers whom they presumably had chosen to script the new title. Above the writers' names were the words 'The Hack Pack'. I deduced that one of Pat and John's tasks was to turn this bunch of scripters into a crack team, one whose stories would make *Battle* an indispensable part of each schoolboy's weekly entertainment fix. This objective sounded like a wartime mission in itself and I felt honoured to have been chosen to work alongside them in the role of sub-editor.

As the weeks passed I would get to know Pat and John properly and learn from them some of the secrets of creating a successful comic character, be they hero, anti-hero, coward or villain; but for the moment I had my duties as the sub to get on with. The first task David assigned me was to create some letters for the new title's letters page, which promised a Polaroid camera for the writer of the star letter, and was titled *Battle Stations*. For the first issue of a magazine the letters do need to be invented, or at least solicited from compliant colleagues. In the case of *Battle*, David said I should ask Norman to tell me a few anecdotes from his time in the war and turn them into letters from readers. After talking to Norman I wrote the first letter which began: 'During the war...' and then went on to explain a funny event experienced by the writer's 'granddad'. When the first issue was published and the readers began writing in for themselves, they all began their letters with the same three words, substituting great-uncle or great-granddad for granddad, if necessary. I was struck by the power I appeared to wield. Supposing I had begun my false letter with the words, 'During our glorious war against the fascist Nazi warmongers...' would the readers have begun their letters in the same fashion? Either way, the weekly postbag was huge and I had no doubt the letters we received were genuine. As well as allowing readers to share their stories, the letters page added a pinch of human interest to *Battle*'s unashamed entertainment mix.

I had less success with the next task David gave me, which was to sub a text story that had been commissioned from a freelance to fill a page in *Battle* called *Daring War Tales*. I could tell the writer had written something pretty naff, but I had never subbed fiction before. What's more the author had not double-spaced his text so it was impossible to cross out words so as to insert new text. The whole thing was a turkey and it needed to be subbed and marked up for the typesetter that day. All I could think of was to retype the text there and then, which made nonsense of paying someone to write it in the first place. I shared my dilemma with David and he looked concerned. In the end the story ended up in the managing editor's lap and, despite the deadline, he gave it to the editor of *Mates* – 'The paper packed with pop and romance' – to rewrite overnight. The next day the editor popped in with a professionally presented, perfect rewrite of the story. 'Where did you learn your journalism skills, Les?' I asked and he replied, 'DC Thomson.' I began to see a pattern here; John Purdie was Scottish, presumably he had worked at DC Thomson, and was now bringing editorial talent down from Dundee to work on his new projects. I knew John and Pat had trained there, too, so who better to be given the opportunity to create a competitor to *Warlord*? It occurred to me that in terms of staff training, there was a huge difference between the approaches of Fleetway and

DC Thomson. What David and I were learning was that if something wasn't good enough it was now expected of us to take the time to rewrite it. Hopefully, the author would see what we wanted and do better the next time, if he hadn't already resigned in a huff at his precious fiction being rewritten in the first place. Since there wasn't time to do it in the office, David and I took the next two text stories home to rewrite. I don't think mine was much better than the original but David had done a great job on his and I was impressed. He wasn't happy, though, having had to write it on a Saturday morning at full speed while the junior football team he ran at the weekends sat outside in his estate car, restless and eager to get to their weekly match.

I came to see that the rewriting of freelancers' scripts was fundamental to Pat and John's development of *Battle Picture Weekly*. Their first mission had been to create memorable characters for the new title, characters that would outshine those in *Warlord*. This they had done with great flair and their troop of innovative heroes had then been farmed out to the Hack Pack to develop as serials. Pat and John were, for want of a better word, trying to instil a new ethos in the writers. I learnt several of its key points, the main one being: don't short-change the reader by writing episodes in a 'V'. This common technique involved starting an episode with last week's cliffhanger and resolving it (the top of the V), then doling out a smidgeon of plot development (the bottom of the V) before ending on another, often spurious, cliffhanger (the second top of the V). Instead, the writer was expected to pack more much more storyline into each episode, to the point where the episode was practically a story in itself, complete with beginning, middle and end. Pat explained to me that this followed the storytelling practice in the girls' department where, as he put it, a young protagonist might compete in a horse trial in the morning, appear in court in the afternoon, stable the horse at tea-time and then dash home to make tea for a coterie of siblings, all in the space of a single, twenty-two picture episode. Similarly, while *Battle* was not a violent comic, its writers were expected to ensure their protagonists endured the harsh realities of warfare, being careful, of course, not to get too carried away and cause upset to the readers' parents and guardians, not to mention the company's distributors and retailers. In all, the new guidelines were designed to help the writers create compelling stories that, once drawn, would grip the attention of the sophisticated 1970s schoolboy audience.

Unfortunately, the initial scripts submitted by the Hack Pack were patchy and often failed to excite. It was then the rewriting took place. Pat and John would read a script, agree on changes, and one or the other would bring out their subbing pen or, in extreme cases, a pair of scissors. By the time the smoke had cleared, there wasn't much left of the original script, but what was left was kept and used as the basis for the in-house rewrite. Normally, an editorial team would not have had time to do this, meaning a script that could be improved would often be sent to the artist untouched on the justification of time constraints. As such, the idea of hiring top-gun writers to work in-house alongside the editorial team was a neat piece of lateral thinking, which contributed hugely to the fiction in *Battle* being a cut above its rivals. The next stage in the process was for the rewritten scripts to be given to David to book out to the artists, complete with deadline, of course. A week or so later the artwork for the script would arrive from the artist and it would be taken down to Pat and John's office for review. There would then follow a period of intense scrutiny by each of them, punctuated by comments like, 'Och, he's drawn Dawson [the hero] with a fat arse again.' In short, the examination concerned how well the artist had captured the action and emotions in the script's scene descriptions. But, above all, the prime question was how visually exciting the pages were. The appraisal of the art was not the last stage in the editing process. What came next was the subbing of each slug of dialogue in the script against the corresponding picture in the artwork. Often, the artist would not have left enough space for the dialogue assigned to the picture. The sub was then left with the choice of cutting the dialogue to fit, or taking some of it into the next picture, which might only serve to postpone the problem. Alternatively, the artist might have added a small headshot that required the addition of a terse '*Jawohl*' or fearful '*Nein*'. But the real skill in subbing was to tweak the dialogue to match the dramatic 'beat' of the pictures so that the story flowed seamlessly for the reader, as if they were watching a film. Then and only then could David or I arrange for the speech and sound effects to be added to the artwork, using an IBM golfball typewriter.

The sum of all this hard work was the seven stories in the dummy. Today, a dummy is market researched and changed so that the first issue reflects the feedback of the consumer. Back then the company had no marketing department and Fleetway had to have the confidence to trust in its own consumer knowledge. In fact, most dummies were prepared purely to show the board so they could approve a publication's launch with an airy, postprandial wave of the hand. As such the *Battle* dummy was pretty much the first issue, prepped, polished and as ready for publication as it would ever be. The pre-launch mood seemed to be, 'Why should we let a bunch of marketeers mess up everyone's hard work?' The line-up of strips in the first issue was as follows:

D-DAY DAWSON

In the Hell of the D-Day landings, Sergeant Steve Dawson has just one thought – to shift his inexperienced squaddies off the bullet-strewn beachhead. But a stray shot brings him down and a medic informs him that the bullet has lodged near his heart. Dawson keeps the news to himself even though he could drop dead at any moment. Realising he is a man with nothing to lose, he vows to lead his boys safely all the way to Berlin, and Heaven help anyone in their way. Although the tone was similar to the 'straight bat' stories of the *War Picture Library* it was the gimmick of the dead man walking that made each three-page episode so powerful. *D-Day Dawson* quickly became *Battle*'s most popular strip.

THE BOOTNECK BOY

In this strip, young Danny Budd dreams of swapping the ill treatment handed out by his coarse, coal merchant uncle for the life of a Royal Marine Commando, the career followed by his late father. But he is turned down at the recruiting office on account of his small stature. After many trials and tribulations Danny does gain admission to the self-styled 'Bootnecks' and his story as *The Bootneck Boy* begins. Whereas *D-Day Dawson*'s exploits were presented in self-contained episodes, *The Bootneck Boy* was written as a gritty serial and its early episodes were more akin to a Catherine Cookson novel. (Indeed, writer Gerry Finley-Day was the deputy managing editor of the girls' comics at the time. As well as being a valuable sounding board for Pat and John he was also a gifted writer and went on to create many of the memorable characters in the comics revival of the 1970s.) Gerry's stories about Danny Budd became ever present in the pages of *Battle*, taking the reader to many of the actual theatres of World War II, a clever plot device that allowed the reader to travel the world, perhaps secretly believing they were the real Bootneck Boy.

RAT PACK

Meet the convict commandos known as *Rat Pack*. In this strip, four highly skilled but criminal soldiers are granted their freedom from imprisonment in return for undertaking suicide missions in enemy-occupied Europe. Their handler is Major Taggart, a man who knows that one false move on his behalf could lead to a knife in the back from any one of his untrustworthy charges. *Rat Pack* began with a two-part establishing episode. By issue three they were ready for action and immediately took and held the paper's centre pages, the prize being the full colour availability afforded by this key position. Each mission began with a film-poster splash visual and then hurtled through four more pages of furious action, laced with hardboiled dialogue. A large roster of writers and artists was required to fulfill the demands of the six-page slot and the quality was variable, but overall the readers loved the series for its exuberant anti-heroes and subversive undertones.

DAY OF THE EAGLE

Mike Nelson is an agent for the Special Operations Executive, a clandestine organisation set up by Churchill to wage guerilla warfare on mainland Europe during World War II. Codenamed 'Eagle', he is an ice-cold operator haunted by the deaths of his father and brother at Dunkirk.

In the opening episode, fate hands him a chance to strike back at the very heart of the Nazi war machine when his bosses give him the task of assassinating Adolf Hitler himself. A vital ingredient of the 1970s war comic was the secret-agent strip and SOE spy Mike Nelson fulfilled this role perfectly for *Battle Picture Weekly*. Suggested by the publisher ('Why don't you have a story about a man sent to kill Hitler?') the strip was notable for the photographic nature of the artwork and the real-time storytelling. Both combined to give the strip a documentary feel. Such was the success of the first story that the Nelson returned over the next six years in a series of missions with titles like *Return of the Eagle*, *Night of the Eagle*, *The Eagle Must Die* and *The Eagle Strikes Back*.

THE FLIGHT OF THE GOLDEN HINDE

The Flight of the Golden Hinde tells of a naval captain's vow to sail a replica of Sir Francis Drake's famous ship back to England from the Indian Ocean. Hunting them is the might of the German navy, and what a slap in the face it would be to the German High Command if the *Hinde* could be sailed home to the safety of its base in Plymouth Sound.

LOFTY'S ONE-MAN LUFTWAFFE

This interesting idea of a British pilot impersonating a German officer to fight the Luftwaffe from within was moderately popular, but in the end was perhaps a gimmick too far.

THE TERROR BEHIND THE BAMBOO CURTAIN

Set in a Japanese POW camp, *The Terror Behind the Bamboo Curtain* was a clever mix of mystery and horror.

However, its subject matter never really caught the imagination of the readers, despite a villain worthy of a role in a Bond movie, much intricate plotting, and some more than decent artwork.

We sent issue one to the printer in the last week of January 1975. Its market was the million or so boys aged 8-12 living in Britain at the time. The publication date was six weeks down the line, to allow for proofing, printing, distribution and the insertion of the free gift. This offering was a sheet of combat stickers of World War II (followed by a poster in issue two and some handy swap cards featuring weapons of World War II in issue three). I felt *Battle Picture Weekly* would give a good account of itself at the newsagents. To my mind it was not just the equal of *Warlord*; it had a steely glint in its eye that promised stories that were more edgy, and, dare I say it, more 'knowing' than those in *Warlord*. But we would have to wait six weeks to find out.

In the meantime we had work to do. *Battle* was a weekly title and as such followed a weekly schedule. Routine became our master and soon everyone got to know his job, just like in the army. The attention to detail was worthy of the then-recent *Apollo* programme to land a man on the moon. I discovered this late one evening, being still in the office, loath to go home in a thunderstorm that was raging around Farringdon Street. David had already rushed off to catch his train, having approved the issue we were working on as being ready to go to the printers, and I had thought I was alone when the office door opened revealing a shadowy figure, holding a scalpel. As the lightning flashed the thought crossed my mind that Fleet Street had been home to many murders down the years, so why would my demise be so unusual? Then I realised that the figure was John and that in his other hand he was holding a sheet of Letratone. This piece of artist's kit was widely used to add texture to line art. John sat down in David's chair opposite me and fished out a page of *The Terror Behind the Bamboo Curtain* from the package containing the issue ready to go to the printers. Then, he laid the Letratone over one of the pictures and used the scalpel to carefully cut round the outline of a figure in the foreground of the picture. When he had finished he pulled off the excess Letratone and smoothed the remaining piece down over the background. The visual effect of adding the Letratone to the background was to throw the foreground figure into sharp relief, giving the picture much more oomph. That's comics folk for you. We surely do dot the i's and cross the t's.

The work of training up the Hack Pack proceeded apace. One day, Pat offered me the chance to write an episode of *Rat Pack*. I spent the weekend carefully copying the plot of *Where Eagles Dare* and timidly handed him my thirty-picture script on the Monday morning. I think Pat felt there was something in it that could be rescued to form the basis of an in-house rewrite, but John was not so sure and my first effort as a member of the Hack Pack came to nothing. But my dialogue must have caught Pat's eye because occasionally he would bring a page of artwork he was subbing along the corridor to get my input. On one occasion it was a page of *Day of the Eagle*, in which Mike Nelson had been captured. Strapped to a torture chair, Nelson tells his inquisitor that he will 'die before he talks'. The next picture is a headshot of the inquisitor looking coldly out at the reader. Pat asked me what I thought the man was saying and I came up with the response, 'Oh, you'll die all right, Eagle, but not yet.' Pat seemed pleased with this and then he neatly finished the sentence by adding the words 'Increase the treatment!' In the next picture Nelson has passed out and you know that between the two pictures the voltage to the torture chair has indeed been increased. Staying with this episode, Nelson's ordeal is far from over and in the next picture he is injected with a truth drug to make him talk. As the drug takes effect, Nelson begins to hallucinate and his questioners assume the shapes of vultures and other grotesqueries. Pat Wright's artwork for this scene pulled no punches and the graphic pictures were something that those downstairs might have considered unsuitable for a schoolboy audience. But upstairs the episode was waved through with Hibernian gusto.

Before long our six weeks were up. David had done a sterling job of balancing Pat and John's creative input on the scripts (and late-night tweaking of the artwork) with the demands of the production schedule and he had shepherded six more issues down the publishing pipeline. D-Day was nigh and in-house expectations were high. There was a lot riding on the launch – not just the title's own future but the future of its creators. For myself there was no turning back, either. It was the smell of cordite that now filled my nostrils, not Cow Gum, and I was more than ready to hit the beaches.

Launching a new title can be compared to being forced to chuck a close pal off a cliff: you just hope they manage to catch hold of something before hitting the bottom. For a magazine this metaphor translates as the early issues selling enough copies to ensure it is economically viable to print further issues. Today, sales data can be gathered in hours from a common supermarket sales system called EPOS. But in the 1970s the best indicator of early sales was the new title's mailbag. The more sacks of mail you received in the week following the title going on sale the more people had clearly bought the first issue. The mail also contained the popularity voting coupons, so the two combined to give an approximate picture of a) how successful the title was and b) what were its most popular stories. Once the votes had been counted, the relative popularity of each character did not vary much from issue to issue. Knowing that the three least-liked stories were never going to climb out of their relegation position allowed the editor to plan their speedy replacement. For a new weekly title the soonest you could end a strip was around issue twelve. The next issue would introduce the replacement strips and soon enough their popularity (and fate) would be decided by the readers. At which point, the cycle of replacing the least popular strips with fresh ones would be repeated. Working to this pattern a weekly comic could have three or four 'relaunches' a year. Each time the trick was to plaster the front cover with the word 'NEW', in the hope of enticing unfamiliar readers into buying the issue (perhaps under the false assumption that it was a new title). In this sense the market was being researched on a weekly basis.

On Monday 10 March I walked into the office early and found several mailbags piled up against the fireplace. Our first post! As the sub-editor, it was my job to open the mail but I was quickly joined by the rest of the team and soon we were all tearing open the letters, counting the votes and getting our first feel for what the readers were thinking and saying about the title. Within half an hour *D-Day Dawson* and *Rat Pack* were fighting it out for the top spot in the popularity chart, with Danny Budd and Mike Nelson contesting third and fourth place. Lagging some way behind were *Lofty's One-Man Luftwaffe*, *The Terror Behind the Bamboo Curtain* and *Flight of the Golden*

Hinde. Despite the unpopularity of these three stories, *Battle Picture Weekly* itself seemed to have gone down well with the readers. Anecdotal evidence from the circulation department seemed to confirm this. By the end of the week, sales of issue one had reached 100,000 copies, and issue two came in at about the same figure. During a rare trip downstairs I had a conversation with Sid in which he teased me that perhaps sales weren't all they could have been. But my view was that the days of mass-circulation comics were gone and the future was going to be all about higher cover prices and smaller audiences, swapping the mass market for the specialist market.

Buoyed by our early success, we pressed on. The title had established a level of sales worth working with and now it was our job to build the readership. As editor David decided to finish the adventures of *Flight of the Golden Hinde* (for some reason war stories about the Royal Navy were never popular), *Lofty's One-Man Luftwaffe* and *The Terror Behind the Bamboo Curtain*. Three new stories would replace them in a 'second wave' scheduled for issue thirteen, on sale at the end of May. Those stories were: *Coward's Brand On Bradley*, *Battle Badge of Bravery* and *The Fortrose Falcon*. The first, *Coward's Brand on Bradley*, told the story of Ben Bradley fighting to clear his name of cowardice in Burma, 1942. The second, *Battle Badge of Bravery*, related factual acts of individual heroism from both world wars. The third, *The Fortrose Falcon*, followed the military fortunes of the Fortrose Clan over two centuries, from 1743 through to 1943. These three strips were, in fact, chosen from the original pool of stories that had been created for the dummy issue. As such, they could not be expected to cater for the tastes and preferences expressed by the readers in their letters to *Battle* and their voting coupons. Nonetheless, the new stories gave *Battle* breadth in terms of its fiction, if not exactly setting the voting chart on fire. In my experience the 'Pareto Principle' can be applied to a title's success, namely that eighty per cent of its sales are due to twenty per cent of its content, no matter how hard you try to deliver stories of equal appeal. To this extent the worship of the popularity chart was misguided. Either way, the new stories were accompanied by a *Battle* boardgame, a supplementary offer that was designed to retain new readers for the four weeks it took to collect.

Battle was famous for its supplements, many of which were the work of Doug Church. Doug was the group art editor, and he was able to parachute himself into any title that needed creative back-up. Naturally, as a new title *Battle* was an obvious choice in terms of helping it get up to speed but I'm sure David would have booked him in at an early stage anyway. Doug was tremendously energetic and talented, very knowledgeable about the war, and he worked tirelessly to design informative posters, diaries and pullouts for *Battle*'s readers, of whom he had a great understanding. These supplements added real value to the title, not least because they were accompanied by fabulous pieces of artwork that Doug would unearth from the fabled Fleetway art library; items that had originally been drawn for *Look and Learn* and other educational magazines of the 1960s. Doug was also a great layout man. This meant giving the artist a visual brief of how to layout the pictures on each page of artwork to be drawn from the script's scene descriptions. His contribution to *Battle*'s success cannot be underestimated. Doug always had a joke for you, told from behind spectacles that flashed with fire and with one hand on his trousers to prevent them falling down. He was also a hi-fi expert who loved music and lived in a specially soundproofed house. After dinner there one night he demonstrated his sound system to me. It was a sonic experience, to say the least.

Doug used to call me Stevie Wonder. Little did he know that at school I was, for a time, known less affectionately as Stevie Blunder. This sobriquet was given to me following an early experiment in electronics in which, whilst replacing a valve in my Dansette gramophone, I managed to send 240 volts of prime Devon current through my puny teenage physique. The force of the shock flung me across the room and against the wall. I was dazed and confused. In my stupor I feared that my actions had plunged the inhabitants of the nearby town of Totnes into darkness. But when I came round, revived by the sickly smell of burning hair, I realised 'Totters' had not tottered and the fairy lights on its grandly named but ever so cosy Seven Stars hotel would still be illuminated. I headed for its lounge bar immediately, in need of a more liquid jolt, stopping on the way to look in at the Queens Arms to 'loosen up the infield' as the Americans say. Thirty-five years later two young artists showed me their artwork at a Scottish comic convention and I was very impressed. Their names were Jock and Dom and it transpired they had hitched all the way to see me from their hometown of... Totnes. Today the town is a Transition Town and I sometimes wonder if my historic encounter with the local electricity supply had anything to do with the townspeople's current mission to imagine a life without oil.

Summer came and went, bringing with it steady sales. David had a problem, though, and it was getting serious. The truth was we were finding it harder and harder to meet the weekly production deadline: the date when the issue had to be sent to the printer. In fact the title was so late that there was a danger it might 'miss an issue'. Effectively this meant skipping a week's publishing in order to catch up with the production schedule and so get back on time. Financially this was unthinkable; such a choice would reduce the planned annual turnover by nearly two per cent. In short there is no worse crime for an editor to commit, apart from publishing material that might engender a costly lawsuit. As it happened, that year's other new launch, *Mates* magazine, was also late. So late, in fact, their tardiness brought a visit from the publisher. I witnessed it all one morning as I was hanging around the corridor in the forlorn hope of bumping into Flo and her tea trolley. I heard footsteps coming towards me and then, out of the gloom, the publisher appeared, like a gunfighter striding down Main Street. He was wearing dark glasses. I pressed myself into the shadows and saw him open the door to the *Mates* office. The normal hubbub of a teenage magazine filled the corridor for a brief second, and then the door closed and quiet was restored. I don't know what was said behind that closed door but I do know that soon after *Mates* was back on time and remained so for the rest of its illustrious publishing history.

I related this story somewhat breathlessly to David, but I think he already knew what he had to do. The fact was that the balancing of the creative input with the production schedule was becoming impractical. Shortly thereafter, and I imagined following a meeting between all concerned, it was announced that David would take overall responsibility for the title with Pat and John still consulting editorially but in a much less hands-on way. David brought me up to speed on the new process and then he reached for the make-up book, which listed the status of scripts and artwork for each issue going forward. 'Right, Stevie boy,' he said, 'let's get some scripts out to the artists.'

By the autumn it was clear that *Battle Picture Weekly* was a title with a solid readership and a bright future. The effects of its launch had definitely been felt in Dundee and as such were a validation of the decision to bring Pat and John in to create the dummy and oversee the title's initial development. The triumph at the newsstands led to Pat being asked to create a new boys' adventure title. I think this was an offer he couldn't refuse and he threw himself into the new project's development process with his customary passion and energy. John, in turn, was offered the job of trying to bring *Valiant* up to date. As it happened, the title had already introduced a realistic strip about a boy saving up week by week for a bike and this had challenged *Captain Hurricane* for the top spot in the popularity poll. John accepted and found himself overseeing my old colleague Stewart. They made a good editorial team, never afraid to have fun. Stewart related to me with great amusement the time he came to work and found John already at his desk, busily typing away... wearing a gorilla mask.

With Pat and John demobbed, David and I were left to carry on the circulation war with *Warlord*. We received a tremendous boost when Gerry Finley-Day said he would be keen to contribute stories for other strips in addition to *The Bootneck Boy*. As mentioned, Gerry was the deputy managing editor of the girls' comics and wrote many of its top scripts. For *Battle* I think of him as the third man alongside Pat and John in their role as the title's developers. Another good omen was that the work with the Hack Pack had been bearing fruit. One writer who graduated with honours was Alan Hebden. Alan was the son of Eric Hebden, a major in the war and regular contributor to *Battle*'s factual stories, like *Battle Badge of Bravery* and *The Fortrose Falcon*. Alan had been submitting *Rat Pack* scripts for a while and these had gone through the usual editing process. One morning, Pat had come round to the office carrying Alan's latest submission. I noticed it did not bear the usual signs of a heavily edited Hack Pack script. Pat handed it to David with words to the effect that Alan had come good. He had written a perfectly respectable *Rat Pack* script and there would be no need for his work to go through the editing process again. Alan soon became a mainstay of *Battle*'s scriptwriting team. We also had our secret weapon in the form of artist Carlos Ezquerra, who had first demonstrated his talents in issue one's episode of *Rat Pack*. Carlos was represented by the Bardon Art Agency, but he liked to deliver his pages in person when he could, travelling up from his UK base in Croydon. Whenever he appeared in the office all work would stop as we gathered to admire his amazing artwork. Carlos would stand by, smiling modestly and occasionally explaining why he had had to amend something in the script, ending his explanation with a deprecating laugh.

Backed by our band of writers and artists, it was up to us to take *Battle* forward, to break out from the bridgehead so to speak. We were bidding farewell to 1975 and looking forward to an action-packed 1976. As I turned my attention to the new year I had no idea that I was about to experience a different kind of action altogether, a gig that would see me featuring in *Action*: 'The explosive new comic of the 70s.'

1976: ACTION MAN

ACTION WAS LAUNCHED in February 1976: 'Read it and get caught in the blast' was its audacious calling card. Pat had put it together in a frenzy of activity since handing *Battle Picture Weekly* over to David a couple of months earlier. The short timescale can only have been to counter the launch of a similar adventure title from DC Thomson called *Bullet*. It was *Battle* versus *Warlord* again; only this time there was to be no happy ending. To begin with, though, everything went smoothly and I found myself playing a part in the title, even though I was still working for *Battle*. Pat had always been very generous in encouraging me to develop my writing skills and I was very gratified when, early in the development of *Action*, he described an idea for a fugitive story that I might like to develop under his tutelage. That story became *The Running Man*, a contemporary thriller in which a British athlete visiting New York is forcibly given plastic surgery to make him look like the son of a Mafia Don. The son it turns out is a wanted cop killer and our Brit hero has to go on the run whilst trying establish his innocence. We had several conversations about the story, which we saw as a road movie visiting all the famous American landmarks and places we could think of, then Pat sent me off to have a go at the first episode. I wrote it in a ten-hour stretch one Sunday and took it in to him on the Monday. He cut about six pictures from the ending and pronounced the script good to go, admiring a fake hospital scene in which loudspeaker announcements convince the recovering protagonist that he is in a hospital ward. A similar plot device in *The Ipcress File* film was my inspiration. Our artist was Horacio Lalia, a thirty-five-year-old Argentine, whose artwork captured perfectly the gritty realism we wanted for the visuals. Unfortunately, the readers failed to engage with the story, as the lead character appeared to be running away from his troubles rather than confronting them. All the same I had a great deal of fun working with Pat on the story, researching its locations in St Bride library, just off Fleet Street. The plan was that the story would end in San Francisco with the villain, Crazy Luigi, getting squashed between two cable cars travelling in opposite directions. (Some years later, I was able to check the likelihood of this happening and was pleased to find out that it is possible, so hang tight, fellow travellers.) A short while later, and perhaps impressed by my work on *The Running Man*, Pat suggested I might like to work on a story idea of his called *Sport's Not for Losers*. Again the arrangement was that I would work under his tutelage and I rapidly agreed. Aside from the pleasure of writing the scripts, the cheques for the freelance work Pat was putting my way were beginning to stack up. *Sport's Not For Losers* was never going to be a huge hit with the readers, but it was a neat idea involving a talented hurdler trying to train his indolent brother Len to take his place on the track. The artist Dudley Wynn adopted a scruffy style for the story that perfectly suited Len's unkempt appearance.

In the early days of its development, Pat fielded several suggestions of what to call the new title. Dropping in on the *Battle* office one day he told us the latest was *BOOTS* (as in bovver). He didn't seem that happy with the title so I suggested *ACTION '76*. The idea of the numerals was that they would increase with each calendar year, so if it was still going today it would be called *ACTION 2016*, bless its little bovver boots. This suggestion proved too complicated for the circulation department, who blocked it on the grounds that the newsagent would be confused when the title's name changed each year. But *Action* was accepted and I was chuffed to see my suggestion make the masthead.

As the 'Paper of the Seventies', *Action* was designed to reflect the big box-office movies of the decade: *Jaws*, *Rollerball*, *Cross of Iron* and *Dirty Harry* all provided fodder for the new title. For the readers of traditional adventure comics it was a case of saying 'Goodbye' to Kenneth More and issuing a big 'Howdy!' to Clint Eastwood. True, *Action* followed the traditional comic template of thirty-two pages with the usual eight stories, but there the similarity ended. Out were the pipe-smoking heroes of the 1950s, in were the cigar-chewing, taciturn anti-heroes of the 1970s.

The line-up of strips that appeared alongside my two efforts in the first issue was as follows:

HOOK JAW

This *Jaws*-like gorefest was introduced with the strapline: '*When Hook Jaw strikes, you only scream once!*' Although unashamedly inspired by *Jaws* the 'Man versus Nature' plot of the film is cleverly reversed so that the story is about 'Nature versus Man' and the audience's sympathies are very much drawn to the Great White shark. Beyond that, *Hook*

Jaw's sole purpose was to depict, with youthful glee, the effects of a Great White biting off a leg, an arm or even a head, all in glorious web offset colour. The quickfire scripts and visceral artwork took the readers by storm and the story quickly became *Action*'s number one-voted strip.

DREDGER

Action comic had not one but two secret agents. In this case 1+1 added up to trouble, especially if you were at the sharp end of Dredger's .44 Magnum. A man of few words, Dredger's CV did not make pleasant reading: five years in the Royal Commandos before being kicked out for brutality. He disappeared for a while then turned up in '69 as a mercenary working for an African despot. In short, Dredger was just the sort of man you wanted around if there was dirty business afoot and the British spy agency known only as DI6 had plenty of that to deal with. Partnering Dredger was public school-educated Simon Breed, just the man for a diplomatic function in Freetown but not so comfortable in a midnight shootout in downtown Santiago, where even the rats carry pistoleros. Dredger opened issue one of *Action* with three pages of dirty action that left four terrorists dead and one Boeing 747 crashlanded on Heathrow's runway number 3. He carried on in this fashion every week until the story was replaced by a less powerful version, following *Action*'s withdrawal from and return to the newsstands.

HELLMAN OF HAMMER FORCE

Among the many groundbreaking aspects of *Action* was Pat's decision to run a war strip featuring a German soldier as the protagonist. Enter Panzer commander Kurt Hellman. Naturally it had to be made clear that Hellman was a soldier of honour and had no love for Hitler or any of his Nazi party organs such as the SS and the Gestapo. Furthermore, Hellman was always given the opportunity to take prisoners instead of lives. He fought fairly and often said: 'I am a soldier, not a butcher.' Hammer Force was assigned a Gestapo Officer, Gauleiter Kastner, whose murderous actions helped the reader see the distinction between soldiering for one's country and racist fanaticism. Fans of this story, and there were many, followed Hellman on his travels as he swapped the push to Dunkirk for the sands of North Africa (*Hellman of the Afrika Korps*), then the horrors of the Russian Front (*Hellman*). Surviving the merger into *Battle Picture Weekly*, Hellman's backstory was related in *The Early Adventures of Hellmann*. Eventually, the series ended with the fall of Berlin and the capture of Hellman by the Red Army.

DEATH GAME 1999

Take the future-sport concept of the film *Rollerball*, then sprinkle elements of the arcade game *Pinball*, and you've got the recipe for *Death Game 1999*, or Spinball as it is known to its bloodthirsty television audience. In the game, two teams of seven use motorbikes and ice skates to attack and defend point-scoring pins with a steel ball. The protagonist is Joe Taggart, whose skill as a biker and a former football quarterback makes him an ideal replacement for the crocked captain of the Karson City Killers. Joe doesn't want to play ball, but he has no choice when he is falsely arrested and sent to prison. Convicts play Spinball as an alternative to the death penalty and now that Joe is a convict, he has no alternative. Readers up and down the UK lapped it up and were soon playing a variation of the game on their bikes after school.

THE COFFIN SUB

The crew of a British World War II submarine fear they are sailing in a coffin sub when their captain begins to display a death wish. Plagued by the loss of a previous ship's complement, Captain (ahem) Mark Kane recklessly risks the lives of his new crew each week in vain attempts to assuage his survivor guilt.

PLAY TILL YOU DROP!

Professional footballer Alec Shaw finds himself in the grip of a blackmailer, who has information that could ruin the sporting reputation of Alec's father. As the demands for money grow, Alec must play through injury to earn sponsorship monies with which to pay the blackmailer. Soon, Alec's teammates turn against him, believing his sponsorship deals are selfish and counter to the interests of the team.

BLACKJACK

'*When Blackjack hits you, you stay hit!*' This was the topline that introduced the tale of Jack Barron, a boxer, who discovers his dream of winning the world title is threatened by blindness. Barron could hang up his gloves and save his sight, but he continues for the sake of the neighbourhood kids that look up to him and see boxing as a way out of London's mean streets.

Features were not ignored in the new title and for the most part they had the distinction of being interactive. Again this was an example of *Action* setting the pace; it recognised that the traditional, passive relationship between 'reader' and 'paper' had to be re-engineered to fit the way readers were interacting with the other entertainment devices in their world, including the soon-to-arrive arcade games like *Pong* from Atari. The feature *Under a Quid* carried bargains spotted by the paper's 'best buy' expert, foreshadowing the 99p shops by a good twenty-five years. *So What?* ridiculed trivial facts that other titles might have pedalled with breathless enthusiasm. *Sports Stars of the Future* carried interviews with young stars of the future. One featured seventeen-year-old speedway rider Les Collins. Les informed *Action*'s readers that his dream was to ride in the World Championships Final, a dream he was to realise eight years later when he was a runner up in the 1982 World Championship at the Los Angeles Memorial Coliseum. Another feature invited readers to nominate cringeworthy celebrities as their *Twit of the Week*. Bamber Gascoigne was the first such 'Twit' and his smiling photograph was printed to prove it. Other features included a *Grumble and Groans* department, soccer coaching with *The Boss*, and a human brainbox called 'Knowall', who was on hand to answer even the most perplexing of questions. In a downgrading of the power of the popularity chart, the voting coupon restricted readers to 'liking' two aspects of the paper and 'disliking' one, rather than being asked directly which stories they liked best.

The most popular feature, though, had to be *Money Man*, the paper's 'Raving nutcase who just loves giving money away!' *Money Man* was played by my old *Valiant* editor Stewart and it was his task to visit a different town centre each weekend and award £5 to the first person carrying that week's copy of *Action* that challenged him. For the purposes of recognition, Stewart had to wear a black peaked cap and leather jacket. Out of interest I joined him on a trip to Brighton, where readers had been alerted that he would be in The Lanes area between 11 and 12 pm on Saturday 6 March. I couldn't help noticing the similarities between *Money Man*'s activities and those of the newspaperman in Graham Green's *Brighton Rock*, a certain Kolly Kibber, who travels to Brighton on a similar promotional activity and is murdered for his troubles. On arrival at the train station we disembarked and made our way to The Lanes, where we spent some time strolling about self-consciously, expecting to be challenged (or razored) at any moment. But, despite a swarm of kids carrying that week's copy of *Action* evidently looking for the Mad Money Man, not one of them appeared to recognise Stewart. Eventually, the penny dropped for one youth and he challenged Stewart successfully. The boy looked shellshocked when he was instantly handed a crisp £5 note and as we departed he remained rooted to the spot, staring blankly at the small fortune in his hands. Leaving The Lanes, we were then challenged several more times and the disappointment was palpable when we explained that the prize money had already been claimed. 'Was it Ratty Smith?' asked one disgruntled seeker, as if we knew the rodential credentials of every adolescent in Brighton. Resisting the urge to disclose 'Ratty's' last known position, for fear of provoking a riot, we slipped into the saloon bar of a pub and ordered refreshments on the justification that giving money away was harder work than it looked. As we waited, I pondered how Ratty had come by his nickname. Did he have a rat as a pet or was he the class sneak? Perhaps he was just easily maddened? My musings morphed into a reverie, for I am liable to such time slips whilst watching the stout settle, and soon I was in a very different Brighton, one populated by brooding comic characters lurking in The Lanes with blackmail and bloody Shakespearean violence on their minds. Flight was futile, for on the seafront prowled the ghost of a Great White shark, dressed in top hat and tails. My musings were interrupted by the sound of a woman laughing very loudly in the public bar, causing a man standing beside me to finish his drink hurriedly and leave. Or maybe that too was part of the dream, fed by the fevered imaginings of your average comics reader.

Despite his popularity, *Money Man* had a rival in the *Action* office and that person was *Action Man*, the paper's aforementioned stunt artist. In real life, I was *Action Man*. Again my 'booking agent' was Pat, who had suggested I take up the role on the basis that I was the only person in the building who possessed the rugged good looks of a stunt man. I think what he meant was that I have the kind of face that looks 'lived in', shall we say. Nonetheless, Pat's flattery worked and I agreed to become *Action Man*, not least because the £10 fee for each stunt made it an offer I could not refuse. Adding this payment to my scripting fees meant that, for a very brief period, I was earning a weekly wage similar to that enjoyed by a car worker. Having said yes, I immediately drew the line at the first stunt, which was to have involved being dropped into the North Sea, so that the Air Sea Rescue could then mount a daring retrieval operation. This proposal came from the company secretary, to whom my unspoken reply was, 'You look after the money and I'll look after the stunts.'

The selection process was that the readers would write in with challenges for me to undertake. The first of these was to 'get chummy' with a boa constrictor hanging out at Chessington Zoo. This involved the keeper bringing the snake out of its glass-fronted enclosure and wrapping its ten-foot body around me like a scarf while my photographer snapped away with a telephoto lens from a safe distance. 'Just grasp its neck firmly and you'll be fine,' called the keeper, somewhat cagily from behind the security of the camera. What was disquieting me, though, was the knowledge of an incident that had occurred as we had walked in mere minutes earlier. An explosion had shattered the prehistoric silence of the reptile house and a different keeper had come flying through the glass front of one of the enclosures, landing limply on a bed of shards at my feet. My first thought was that he had been attacked by one of his charges, perhaps even a boa. But while the glass was swept up assurances came thick and fast that the cage had been empty at the time of the keeper's sudden ejection, which had been merely the result of him tripping. Furthermore, there was no reptile on the loose, slithering about in the dark, waiting to coil itself around the next passing pair of legs, so the photo-shoot could continue. 'Well, they would say that, wouldn't they?' was the thought that preyed on my mind as I posed blithely with the boa. From their point of view the purpose of the photo-shoot was to encourage as many readers of *Action* and their families as possible to visit the zoo; the well-being of anyone foolish enough to pose with a boa constrictor in the first place was obviously of secondary importance.

The stunts came at speed after that, with a new one needed for each weekly issue. The most enjoyable one was to travel in a hot-air balloon, drifting serenely across the Hampshire countryside. I came down to earth with a bump, though, when next I was sent down the sewers of London, where there was a chance, slim but still a possibility, of catching Sewerman's Flu, a waterborne disease that results in two or three fatalities a year. Having survived that, I then found myself clinging to the top of a ladder, fully extended to one hundred feet high, dressed as a fireman. Such cosplay may have its attractions for some people, but as a fierce wind swayed me back and forth I couldn't think of any at the time. Other activities included completing an army assault course in full combat gear and executing a one hundred and eighty degree turn in a double-decker bus on the London Transport skid patch at Chiswick. I asked cheekily if they had ever overturned a bus and the speed with which the instructor shot a glance at his boss for guidance confirmed that they might have, but it would never be admitted.

My favourite assignment was to meet 'El Hakim' of Gerry Cottle's Circus and learn from him the closely guarded tricks of stilt-walking, lying on a bed of nails, and breathing fire. The circus was playing at Shepherd's Bush Green, so one cold, grey day Wilf the photographer and I drove there and parked outside in his battered Volkswagen Beetle. There's something forlorn about an empty Big Top at nine o'clock in the morning, but El Hakim greeted us with the traditional warmth of someone clearly born no farther afield than Yorkshire and without further ado he began to lash my legs to a lengthy pair of stilts. After standing me up and watching me fall, clutching gratefully each time to a safety wire, El Hakim then showed me how to eat fire. It's quite simple, really: take a swig of paraffin and exhale forcefully, sending the spray onto a burning stick held in your other hand. The trick is not to inhale or the flame will chased the combustible back down into your lungs. This I was able to do with great effect, despite being a heavy smoker. Imbued with the 'right stuff', I let El Hakim lead me to the bed of nails. I took off my shirt and accepted Hakim's assertion that provided I lay evenly I would feel nothing more than a sensation of pins and needles. He was absolutely correct: no punctures, no blood, not even a scratch. I learned later that 'El Hakim' was actually one Barry Wallis, a British circus performer of great repute with a career spanning three decades. I bet he never went down the sewers, though.

I enjoyed the buzz of being *Action Man* and undertook a dozen or so stunts in all. There is a minor confession to make: not possessing a driving licence, I was unable to drive the double-decker bus, nor indeed reach the ton on a racing motorbike. Kelvin Gosnell, who worked in the competitions department at the time and always carried with him a briefcase containing a cornucopia of sample prizes sent in by hopeful PR agencies, gladly undertook both these stunts on my behalf. Despite this deception my picture was being printed at the top of *Action*'s contents page, where I wrote a weekly introduction, making me the public face of what *The Sun* newspaper would soon come to call 'The Sevenpenny Nightmare'. However, in those early spring days of '76 it looked like Pat had created another winning title; one that was playing Clint Eastwood to *Battle*'s James Coburn, if you like. News of healthy sales figures, combined with the arrival of postbags bulging with reader feedback, soon filled the office. Apparently, *Action* was the talk of every classroom in the land, with readers agog at the limb and body count in *Hook Jaw*. I occasionally meet grown-up readers today who will retell, with stammering wonder and a faraway look, the explosive effect the title had on their youthful selves. By comparison *Bullet*, DC Thomson's rival publication, looked like a dud, making Fleetway appear to be top gun in the boys' market.

Back on *Battle* the preparatory work for breaking out of the bridgehead was complete. David had assembled an intriguing line-up of new strips for 1976. The first of these was *Iron Cross of Courage*, which told the stories of German servicemen who had been awarded the Iron Cross. I contributed a strip called *Hold Hill 109*, drawn by Jim Watson, which attempted to tell in real time a fictional six-day struggle by British troops to hold a strategic position in the North African desert. David's ace in the hole, however, was *Major Eazy*. He introduced this new character to the readers with the rather nervous coverline: 'Like him or hate him, you can't ignore Major Eazy.' A veteran of the Long Range Desert Group and the personification of über cool, Major Eazy drank, smoked and shot his way through the Italian campaign, upsetting both Axis and Allies powers alike. Major Eazy's laidback character traits were not unlike those of his writer/creator Alan Hebden, while artist/creator Carlos Ezquerra perfectly captured Eazy's languid approach to the irksome realities of war. Outrageous, funny and always one step ahead, *Major Eazy* quickly became one of *Battle*'s most popular strips.

Although *Battle*'s main competitor was *Warlord*, we knew that *Action* too would become a rival when it was launched. It was here that some pre-match tension began to bubble up between the two stablemates. Pat was always happy to discuss the concepts he was creating for the new title so we quickly learned the nature of the strips he planned for the first issue. Among the stories there was to be a war story featuring a German tank commander as the protagonist. This was a first in itself. Meanwhile, the cover to issue one was to feature artwork by Carlos Ezquerra depicting a footballer, a Great White shark and the German tank commander. The three pictures were eventually captioned: '*Striker! Killer! Invader!*' So far so good. However, for whatever reason David chose to commission Carlos to draw a cover featuring a shark for *Battle* and this duly appeared some weeks before *Action* was launched. Pat was not best pleased when he saw the issue and came up to the *Battle* office, where words were exchanged. I say words because as soon as I saw the thunderous look on Pat's face as he entered I knew there was going to be some kind of scene. Not wanting to be dragged into the showdown I pretended to drop my pen under my desk and quickly took cover as withering verbals pinged back and forth above like machine-gun fire. Not long after, Pat got wind that David was also planning a story with a German protagonist. This was true and appeared to be another case of 'claim-jumping', but David was able to placate Pat by not scheduling the story until *Action* had led with *Hellman* for a good six weeks beforehand. *Battle*'s German hero, when he appeared, was called *Fighter From the Sky*. Written by Gerry Finley-Day (who was also scripting *Hellman*) it went down a storm with the readers and completed the line-up of strips that were to see *Battle* through the summer sales period.

One office morning during this period I found myself subbing an episode of *Rat Pack*. The job was not urgent and I had time to work my way through a pack of Player's No.6 as I tweaked the dialogue in the script to suit the pictures. In due course I built up a small smokescreen around my desk and as I subbed, I began to feel I was actually there with the convict commandos, very much part of their latest mission. Things were not going well, however, and *Rat Pack* were having to fight their way out of a German army barracks. The picture I was looking at showed Ian 'Scarface' Rogan punching a couple of the Wehrmacht's finest to the floor. In the script the dialogue for this picture had Rogan saying, 'Gangway, Krauts!' This exclamation was standard issue for our boys, so to speak, but in the moment it seemed to me that Rogan should say something more in keeping with his background: Highland Infantry. Brilliant athlete. Court-martialled for desertion. Fifteen years. I decided upon, 'Just like Friday night in Glasgow, eh, Jerry!' as I had heard from my colleagues that brawls in that then fabled city were not unusual. Pleased with myself, I then contemplated changing 'Glasgow' to 'Glasgae,' for added authenticity but decided David would not approve on the basis that it was slang. We had already had words over a box I had written the day before which read, 'Sergeant Dawson burst in the room.' David declared this implied Dawson had wet himself in action, which was not my intention at all. I was well aware of the celebrated rule that one should never write 'FLICK' for fear of a drop of ink at the printers joining up the L and the I to make something considerably stronger, but I had not come across this particular interpretation of the word 'burst'. Amid my deliberations and the sound of knuckle on chin I became aware that David was speaking to me through the smokescreen. He was saying that John was looking for somewhere to live and that he might need a flatmate. Perhaps I would be interested? As it happened I was keen to move out of my present quarters, so I visited the *Valiant* offices to let John know.

Our search began the next day and eventually we found a top-floor flat to share in Camberwell New Road, South London. Across the road was a pub and next to it a fish-and-chip takeaway. The surrounding area was filled with high-rise council blocks and not much else. On weekdays we'd catch a bus for the short journey up the road to the office, John, now riding as the staff editor of *Valiant*, me still the sub-editor on *Battle* but now with a handy sideline in daredevil stunts. At weekends, when we weren't repelling burglars, we'd play chess, watch *Match of the Day*, read each other's scripts, contract food poisoning from the takeaway, and generally dread Sundays. When things got particularly dull we'd visit the pub to gawp at Robert Mitchum, star of numerous Hollywood films including my favourite, *Night of the Hunter*. Quite how 'Bob' came to be serving in a pub in South London I'll never know, but it was he all right. John and I would sit at the bar so as to observe the great man more closely. He'd changed his name, of course, he was 'Ron' now, not Bob, but we weren't fooled. He couldn't hide that famous cleft chin, and when he pulled a pint with his head cocked idly to the side, measuring the liquid through those hooded eyes, you could tell he was back in Tinsel Town, sharing a joke with Jimmy Stewart perhaps or maybe just batting the breeze with Bogie and Bacall on some zephyr-stroked backlot. In the character of 'Ron behind the bar', however, he was taciturn and barely paid us any mind, except to check that the British coins we gave him added up to the correct price for 'two pints of lager and ten Embassy'. I was itching to reveal myself as the famous English stunt artist known as *Action Man*. I wanted to tell him how, only the day before, I'd completed an army assault course and shouldn't we army buddies stick together because he'd been in a couple of war movies himself, right? Maybe we might even go 'Up West' one night and get into a fistfight, 'cause that's what movie folk did, right?

My thoughts were interrupted by a growl from my right. It was John. He had opened his first monthly payslip as a member of staff and was looking at it with disgust. 'That's awful,' he said, referring to the net take-home figure. I sympathised. Why be on staff when you could earn so much more as a freelance? Soon after, John left to do exactly that and, relieved of the need to live near the office, found a farmhouse to rent in Essex. I found a place to live on the Old Brompton Road, moving in with Olivia, my first proper girlfriend. She, John and I would go out for an evening whenever he was in town as we shared a mutual interest in trying out new restaurants. Before these epicurean excursions John would telephone me and teasingly ask how 'Miv' was, because that's what her short name of 'Liv' sounded like whenever I pronounced it. Later, Miv drew photo-referenced pictures of Hollywood film stars for *2000 AD* and some portraits of Tharg, before whispered claims of nepotism hastened her return to her career as a fine artist.

The last time I saw Ron, he was off duty, sitting at a table reading a daily newspaper, a pint of bitter by his side. But I knew, I just *knew* that the paper concealed a script from his agent in Hollywood, and that the 'warm beer' was just a prop and it would be iced tea, kept just out of sight, that would fortify him as he read through the ninety pages that might yet trigger his return Stateside.

Ever since my arrival at Farringdon Street a circular, thirty-storey tower block had been taking shape across the Thames. Once finished it dominated the skyline, but its Brutalist architecture promised nothing more than a decent view from the upper floors. However, the building was to be occupied by IPC Magazines, owned by Reed International. We were told our Juvenile Group would be joining them, dropping the name Fleetway and becoming known instead as the IPC Youth Group. The idea of working in a skyscraper was exciting. In addition, another good reason to relocate emerged when a pre-move briefing on the nearby amenities began with the fact that there were seventeen pubs in the locality. On moving in we found the Youth Group was to inhabit the nineteenth and twentieth floors, working in open-plan areas punctuated by the occasional managerial office, each one boasting a secretary sat outside and a drinks cabinet, liberally equipped with bottles of sherry, situated inside. The floor-to-ceiling glass frontage was sealed, apart from discreet entry points rather optimistically labelled 'Fireman's Access', which apparently could be opened in an emergency. In our *Battle* area we were fortunate to be facing the river and the view across London up to the hills of Hampstead and Highgate was indeed spectacular. Staff working on the other side had to make do with the rather less picturesque suburbs of South London, which stretched listlessly to the horizon, ending in the distant smudge of the Crystal Palace television transmitter. On the floor above us was *Country Life, a* magazine whose editorial philosophy seemed to be: 'If in doubt, put a wet dog on the front cover.' We shared a coffee machine with them by the lift but co-worker conversation was half-hearted at best, except on the occasions when we were all on strike, having 'deemed to have dismissed ourselves', during which times we were the best of mates. The floor below included pop titles like *New Musical Express* and *Melody Maker*, who were just coming to grips with the newly emerging forces of punk rock. One member of the *NME* staff, perhaps energised by this new wave, took exception to his lofty surroundings and initiated drastic action to get his magazine returned to earth by lobbing his typewriter through the fireman's window. It plummeted two hundred feet before narrowly missing an actor, who was hurrying to his performance as Hamlet at the nearby National Theatre. *NME* was subsequently banished to a Nissen hut across the street. As for the actor I heard later that he received a standing ovation that night for his unusually contemplative rendition of 'To be or not to be'.

Come September, I realised I had been in the job for three years. On joining I had been put on a percentage of the salary earned by a Grade 8 staffer, the lowest grade of all. This civil service-like pay structure ran from Grade 8 to Grade 1, the structure being agreed between the NUJ and a management negotiating team representing the board. I was now on one hundred per cent of the Grade 8 salary, but appeared to be stuck there. An editor was on Grade 3 and the grades in between existed for magazine roles such as senior sub, chief sub, assistant editor and deputy editor. But on a comic, where there were just two editorial staff, there was no ladder linking sub-editor and editor that one could climb. Elevation to Grade 3 would come about only on the demise of the incumbent editor or by being selected to edit a brand new title. However, grading was open to appeal, so I put in a claim to be put up to Grade 7 on the basis that while not a deputy editor, I was expected to run the title when the editor was sick, on holiday or otherwise engaged with duties outside the office. The union duly entered my appeal and I heard no more until one day the phone went and I answered it. It was a member of the appeals committee, who apparently were considering my application that very moment. They wanted me to come over and make my case in person, as my claim was the subject of some intense discussion. As it happened, David was away that day and I was able to say quite truthfully that I could not leave the office because I was deputising for him and we were very busy. This brilliant answer must have swayed any doubters on the committee because the next day I heard I had won the battle and got the upgrade to Grade 7. Nice.

On *Battle* itself things were getting better all the time. For his first freelance story since leaving, John had created the memorable *Darkie's Mob*. The story opened in the August issues with the following entry from the Battle-Log of one Private Richard Shortland:

This is the story of a madman. A hard, cruel son of Satan who led us into the very pit of Hell – and laughed about it. Then he began to turn us into animals, the most savage fighting force the Japs had ever known...

The 'madman' is the mysterious Captain Joe Darkie, who rescues a band of disheartened Tommies and sets about turning them into an unorthodox but deadly fighting unit. What followed was without doubt the darkest strip ever to appear in *Battle* or indeed any other 'children's' comic of the period. Set in the jungles of Burma, *Darkie's Mob* combined searing combat action with well-defined characters and a gripping plot told through the poignant diary entries of Private Shortland. Artist Mike Western delivered some of his best work on this strip, which ran until the summer of the following year and did as effective a job of reader retention each week as any serial by Dickens or Conan Doyle. About halfway through I suggested to John that the Mob needed refreshing and he came up with the idea of Flyboy Ferris, a Clark Gable clone whose film-star good looks jarred nicely with the other grime-ridden members of the unit. With *Darkie's Mob* now running alongside *Major Eazy* and *Fighter From the Sky*, *Battle* was pounding *Warlord* mercilessly every week at the newsagents.

Whilst things were going smoothly on *Battle*, however, news began to filter through that all was not well on *Action*, which was based on the floor below. By this time Pat had handed over the title to an editorial team, just as he and John had handed over *Battle* to David. I had stopped writing strips for *Action*, had retired as *Action Man*, and concluded writing the weekly introduction. However, my picture was still being used above the intros, now drafted by a ghost writer, who gleefully began to regale the readers with stories about 'me' getting drunk, involved in fights and other stupid activities. This recklessness seemed to spread to some of the strips, where well-plotted, fast-moving action scenes began to be replaced with random violence on the apparent premise that this was what the readers wanted. (Actually, young readers don't necessarily know what they want and even when they do they don't possess the emotional maturity to assess or regulate the potency of whatever's being beamed their way. As such, it is the editor's job to weigh the sensibilities of the readership and use this as a counter-balance to the writer's natural desire to shock. In short, give the reader what they want at your peril.) A groundswell of bad press began to build around *Action*, culminating in the publisher appearing on television to defend a scene in which kids had thrown a bottle onto a football pitch in one story and rioted on the streets in another. As it happened, far more graphic events were happening in *Darkie's Mob*, with its scenes of beheading, garrotting, amputation and near crucifixion, but the difference was each of these incidents was presented as part of the Burma campaign and in no way sensationalised. I watched in growing embarrassment as the interviewer tore the publisher to shreds. How could it ever have come to this? How could all the hard work and creativity that had been poured into *Action* end in this awful, teatime show trial, beamed live into every UK household?

In November, *Action* was withdrawn from publication, with promises that it would be returned once a few problems had been ironed out. Ironically, the job of cleaning up the title went to Sid, who was given a mere six weeks to restore order. *Action* returned, but mightily sanitised, just like one of the old-style comics it had tried so hard to replace. The title lumbered on for a year before being put out of its lobotomised misery by being merged into *Battle* in November 1977, to form the neatly titled *Battle-Action*.

The month before *Action*'s withdrawal had seen *Valiant* publish its last issue after fourteen years of weekly editions. As editor, John Wagner had introduced tremendous new stories like *One-Eyed Jack*, *The Lout That Ruled the Rovers* and *Soldier Sharp (Rat of the Rifles)*, but there seemed no real resolve within the company to back up his hard work with a sound publishing plan for the title. *Valiant* was merged into *Battle* in October 1976, the one positive being that its readers gave a significant boost to *Battle*'s circulation figures.

As 1976 drew to a close, it occurred to me that within the short span of my joining the company I had witnessed the merger of *Lion* into *Valiant*, and then the merger of *Valiant* into *Battle*. I had thought of *Valiant* and *Lion* as akin to the proud ocean-going liners of the 1950s and '60s, but now their sun-filled, colonial glory days were over, superseded by *Battle* and *Action*, whose editorial propellers were powered by the jet-fuelled imaginations of Messrs Mills, Wagner and Finley-Day. *Battle* had proved a worthy replacement, but *Action* had foundered. Which way was the industry going to go in 1977? I had no idea what the future held, there seemed nothing on the horizon, so I confined myself to the cabin-like area that was the *Battle* office and let the passage of time pass. What I did not know was that since handing over the reins on *Action*, Pat Mills had been hard at work on another new title. Just as with *Battle*, he had been working on the project in some secrecy, not only in case our publishing rivals got to learn of his plans, but also probably to avoid a repetition of his ideas being 'liberated' and appearing in other in-house titles before the launch. Either way, it was a title that was going to change the lives of everyone who was to become associated with it, not least my own.

1977: THE BEING FROM BETELGEUSE

1977 WAS A year of huge social and cultural change, so they tell me. The Queen's Silver Jubilee may have been celebrated with street parties up and down the land, but those who chose not to join in celebrated, instead, the arrival of punk culture. The Sex Pistols released 'Anarchy in the UK' and The Clash their eponymous debut album. Those who chose to celebrate neither of the above probably applauded the award of the Nobel Peace Prize that year to Amnesty International. In the USA, Apple shipped their first mass-market computer (the Apple II) and the revival of science fiction in the cinema was heralded by the release of *Close Encounters of the Third Kind* and *Star Wars*. Elvis may have left the planet but Sarah Michelle Gellar, among other future stars, was born. There was another ingredient added to the year's bubbling cauldron of change and reinvention: the launch of Pat Mills' secret project, *2000 AD*.

As the new year dawned the Youth Group had organised itself along the following lines: humour department, adventure department, and a nascent teen department that was soon to be churning out photo-romance titles such as *Oh Boy!, Photo Secret Love* and *My Guy*. In the adventure department, *Tiger* had re-positioned itself very much as a sports-based title, with lead character *Roy of the Rovers* reflecting the emergence of football as a national passion once more following its decline at the start of the decade. *Battle* and *Action* comprised the other two titles with *Battle* thriving but, as we have seen, *Action* merely a shadow of its former cocksure self. Meanwhile, the humour comics were making a spirited job of providing a joke-filled response to the weekly bombardment from *The Beano* and *The Dandy*, both owned by DC Thomson, even if the response was more about quantity than quality. *Buster, Monster Fun, Cheeky Weekly, Cor!, Shiver and Shake, Jackpot, Whizzer and Chips* and *Knockout* were all titles in the humour stable. (The mere mention of these names during meetings of the company's NUJ Chapel used to make the refined ladies from the knitting section of *Woman's Own* titter uncontrollably.) It was into this market, like a World War II Mills bomb, that *2000 AD* was hurled.

The title was launched in February '77. Promising 'Tomorrow's Thrills Today' it was hosted by Tharg the Mighty, a green-skinned being from Betelgeuse, who proclaimed to his new Terran readers that he had journeyed to Earth to deliver the benefits of 'Thrill-power' in the shape of *2000 AD*.

The background to *2000 AD*'s development and launch was slightly less exotic. Staffer Kelvin Gosnell had read about the forthcoming cinematic wave of family films to be based on the SF genre, notably the one to be called *Star Wars*. To most people at the time science fiction was a form of entertainment that had had its day in the 1950s and good riddance. But, as he later described it to me, what Gosnell saw in *Star Wars* was not science fiction but what he called 'space opera'. A management team, still smarting from the debacle of *Action*, reacted favourably to his suggestion that the company publish a title to cash in on what was sure to be the next trend in children's entertainment. The project was passed to Pat, giving him a hat-trick of launches to his name.

My first real sight of *2000 AD* was the printed first issue. Unlike *Action*, where I had been involved in the development of the title, *2000 AD* was engineered quite discreetly. Pat found himself an office a few floors above the Youth Group so there was no chance of anyone from the adventure department glimpsing a script or a page of artwork. As it happened, I did find myself up there once. The floors of King's Reach Tower were circular and open plan, meaning you could walk right round whatever floor you were on and catch sight of whatever editorial matter the staff on that particular floor were working on. I think I was looking for the production department when, to my surprise, I came across Pat and Doug Church working together at an isolated desk. Before them was a script and Doug was clearly laying out the first page for an artist to follow. Doug's layout appeared to show a cowboy being bitten in half by a huge dinosaur. This puzzled me, as the little I knew about the new title was that it was supposed to be based in the future. Pat looked at me suspiciously, as though I was on a deliberate spying mission, and that the front cover of the next issue of *Battle* would now feature a snarling Tyrannosaurus Rex, perhaps clutching Churchill in one terrible claw while a grinning Adolf Hitler looked on, snarling, 'Mein Rex is dying to meet your Queen, Mr Churchill!' I realised that my presence was perhaps not entirely welcome and (ever the diplomat, as Pat used to say) carried on walking.

Eventually, though, Pat had to staff the paper and a larger

office was found on the floor above *Battle*. Meeting Pat in the pub one lunchtime, and sharing a couple of gins, he invited me to pay a visit to his new office. I did the next day and my first sight of *2000 AD* was Kevin O'Neill, working as art assistant, surrounded by pages and pages of artwork that had been drawn by Spanish or South American artists. I gathered that their renditions of the scene descriptions in the scripts were too visceral by half and Kev had been tasked with toning down their imagery by using white paint to remove as much of the gore as he could. Janet Shepheard, my old friend and supporter from *Valiant*, was sat at another desk, installed, it appeared, in the role of art editor. Pat was there too and he seemed pleased with how it was all going. He had a streaming cold but had obviously dragged himself in from Colchester to meet the first looming deadline of a weekly production schedule. Taped to a filing cabinet was a page of script from a nameless freelance writer. Eighty per cent of its text had been crossed out and all that was left was a single picture description and its accompanying dialogue. I guessed there was a new Hack Pack in town and Pat was once more having to bring their scripts up to scratch. It appeared Pat was on his own editorially, but that was soon solved when he arranged for Kelvin to leave the competitions department and join him. (The two made an awesome team, that's for sure.) But, as I stood in the office and looked around, it all seemed like chaos to my eyes, not to mention I had espied a character design for a man who looked like a pirate, which added to my concern: dinosaurs, cowboys and now a pirate? This was more like the line-up of an adventure title than one based in the future. Had Pat lost the plot? Was *2000 AD* going to be a flop, its demise foretelling the creeping death of all the comics in the Youth Group? The answer was provided

a few weeks later when I read Programme 1 (the first issue).
As the front page of *The Guardian* newspaper put it, *2000
AD* had landed with the impact of a 'thermo-nuclear bomb'
and I was left in no doubt that Pat had produced another
winning title. It was also, as it turned out, one that would
become the jewel in the crown of British comics.

There were three unique selling points that distinguished
Prog 1 of *2000 AD* from its rivals in the market place and
all three were visual. Firstly, instead of the standard line-
up of eight stories, there were just five. Learning from his
work on *Battle* and *Action*, Pat had obviously come to the
conclusion that in an eight-story matrix there were always
going to be two unpopular tales, however often they were
replaced, so why not change the formula instead and go for
fewer stories? The immediate benefit of this was each story
could run over five or six pages instead of being crammed
into three. Each story still had the usual number of pictures,
but the extra pages allowed the pictures to be drawn larger,
extracting the full drama from their relevant descriptions.
Secondly, the first page of each story was designed as if it
was a cinema poster, hyping the excitement and thrills to
come in the forthcoming pages. Thirdly, machine-generated
lettering for the word balloons was retired in favour of the
more expressive hand-lettering. This alone made *Battle* and
Action look dull and they quickly copied *2000 AD*'s lead.
Doug's flamboyant design fingerprints were all over the
title, from the *2000 AD* logo to the layouts of the opening
pages and the whole issue was a visual treat. To the potential
reader, though, perhaps the most engaging aspect of the title
was its name: *2000 AD* conjured up exciting visions of what
seemed a distant future, a world away from the boring daily
grind of home, school, homework. It promised a weekly

trip to experience the thrills of tomorrow and all for just 8p (Earth Money).

To my mind *2000 AD* was not a science-fiction comic, it was a comic that took traditional adventure stereotypes and recast them in the future. The title *2000 AD* communicated exactly what the paper contained. Speculative fiction, future fiction, call it what you will, but it wasn't science fiction. For example, early issues featured Future Cops, Future Sportsmen, Future Warriors. Yes, the comic explored time-travel and featured robots and cyborgs, but the thrills came from the heroes and the situations they found themselves in, not from the dull thud of hard science. Yes, the title brought Dan Dare, pilot of the future, and onetime hero of *Eagle* comic, back from retirement, making him the lead character, luxuriating in glorious colour in the centre pages, but only as a sales gimmick. What follows is a review of the stories in Prog 1:

INVASION!

What better way to start off a new comic in 1977 than have a British Prime Minister shot on the steps of St Paul's? That was the talking point in the story *Invasion!*, set twenty-two years in the future, in which the Russians (sorry, Volgs) invade Britain having first dropped a nuke on Birmingham. You can imagine the team laughing as they pondered which British city should be the unfortunate recipient of four megatons of honest Soviet plutonium. A resistance movement to repel the invaders soon emerges, among the cadre one Bill Savage. This Stanley Baker lookalike has plenty of Cockney chutzpah and is soon introducing the Volgs to the business end of his shotgun. In short, *Invasion!* was a thrilling case of lock, stock and double-barrelled bile.

M.A.C.H. 1

This 'Man Activated by Compu-Puncture Hyper Power' strip was a tacit bow in the direction of television's popular series *The Six Million Dollar Man*. In *2000 AD*'s version, secret agent John Probe has his physique hugely enhanced by a form of electro-acupuncture. Such power requires a computer to control it so Probe's brain is implanted with sentient computer circuits. In episodes one and two terrorists hijack a Vulcan bomber and Probe has to save London. It was adventures like this that made *M.A.C.H. 1* the most popular strip in *2000 AD* during the early issues.

FLESH

Time-travelling cowboys hunt dinosaurs and beam their flesh back to the future, there to feed a starving world population. The opening page was the one I had espied Doug laying out for Pat, so that solved the mystery of the cowboy and the dinosaur. *Hook Jaw* had been hugely popular in *Action* so it was no surprise to find another carnivorous monster stalking the pages of *2000 AD*. Shark or dinosaur, the end result was the same – lots of gore and plenty of 'Aaaarghs!'.

DAN DARE

Actually, this was the 'new' *Dan Dare*, complete with '70s 'glam' styling and modern plots. I know a huge amount of effort was put into reviving this '50s icon, but Dare and his adventures just didn't seem to fit in the dystopian futures that were on the menu in *2000 AD*. Dare simply couldn't live with the gritty realism of the other strips in issue one, despite a very fancy spaceship and some wonderful artwork by Italian maestro Massimo Belardinelli.

HARLEM HEROES

It must have been frustrating trying to find artists to draw the scripts for *2000 AD*. All the best British artists were working for *Battle* and *Action*, where their respective editors guarded them jealously. Foreign artists (to use the argot of the day) were brilliant at drawing for the girls' titles but sometimes not so good at drawing for a boys' title. And of all things, they were useless at stories set in the future: their artwork looked terribly dated, redolent of the 1950s not the twenty-first century. Renowned Spanish artist Ramon Sola was an obvious exception; his work on *Flesh* was outstanding. *Harlem Heroes* was a future sports story featuring aeroball, an aerial version of American football. Having read it I wanted more, especially when the final page showed the team's manager was a pulsating human brain barking orders from a glass bell jar. I learnt the first four pages of art were the work of a British artist and one that I had never heard of before. His name was Dave Gibbons and I instantly liked his style and storytelling. It felt fresh and modern by comparison to the foreign art. Little did I know that there were several other young British artists on *2000 AD*'s roster and soon they and their work would coalesce to form the artistic heart of the title. In time, their work would inspire the next generation of comics-loving kids to follow in their brushstrokes. Eventually, these pioneers would become well known across the Atlantic, where they would be headhunted by one of the big American comics-publishing companies such as DC or Marvel Comics, but, for the moment, they were artists in residence at *2000 AD* and it was incredible to see their style develop with every issue, until each had found his own, authentic, artistic 'voice'.

The advert for the next issue at the back of the comic

alerted readers to a new character starting in issue two: he was a future cop called Judge Dredd, and the image solved the mystery of the 'pirate' sketch I had seen. It was obviously an early design for the Judge's uniform, which had since been changed quite a bit. The Judge rode a 'Lawmaster' motorbike and I couldn't wait to see him in action combining the duties of judge, jury and executioner in a city of eight hundred million people, each one a potential criminal. A week may be a long time in politics but it's an even longer time when you're waiting for the next issue of your favourite comic. And when it did appear, Prog 2 was even better than Prog 1.

As its free gift for Prog 1, *2000 AD* got handed a piece of red plastic in the shape of a modern day no-entry sign. In response to uncomprehending stares, the free-gift department airily described it as a flying disc. An ebullient man with a handlebar moustache, who I assumed had been a fighter pilot in the war, ran the department. Fair enough, but it was a source of some ire among the young dudes in editorial that his free-gift cupboard contained samples from a bygone age; old-fashioned gadgets that had no chance whatsoever of appealing to the more discerning youth of the '70s. I remember looking in the cupboard once and asking (rather like Oliver Twist) 'Have you got anything else?' This was not well received and for a moment I thought I was going to be locked in the cupboard for the crime of 'being cheeky'. Oh yes, one could still be collared in those days for being cheeky. Indeed, an old-school editorial manager, who shall remain nameless, once slapped me round the head for a supposed similar offence. I sprung to my feet in anger, which alarmed him somewhat. Kevin O'Neill caught my eye as if to say, 'Be cool', but my blood was boiling. My indignation seemed to perplex the manager, who suggested that I was over-reacting, as if such treatment was part and parcel of office life. I let him know that this was not the case as far as I was concerned, and if he hit me again I would inform my union rep who, undoubtedly, would call an immediate strike. (To the probable fury of the knitters from *Woman's Own* but, hey, we've all got to drop a stitch sometime.) Anyhow, forced to take the flying disc, the *2000 AD* team put their heads together and rebranded it as a 'Space Spinner', thus launching UFO sightings in playgrounds across the UK and raising *2000 AD*'s profile at launch no end. The gift is still remembered fondly today by grown-up readers. Moral: 'What's in a name? Everything.'

The 'Biotronic Stickers' presented with Prog 2 looked great but they had one unseen drawback: they didn't come off. Phone call after phone call was received from maddened mums who could not remove the stickers from little Johnny at bath time. 'How can he go to school looking like a blooming robot?' was the oft-heard refrain down the telephone wires from the Orkney Isles to Land's End.

The *2000 AD* launch went well. A bulging postbag showed that the readers (Earthlets) were keen to enter into the spirit of the title and were corresponding enthusiastically with The Mighty Tharg. They had been energised by the hype around *Star Wars* and were fascinated by anything to do with the future. Feedback from the voting coupons received showed *M.A.C.H. 1* and *Flesh* to be the most popular, with *Invasion* and *Dare* and *Harlem Heroes* close behind. This line-up remained the same for the rest of 1977, save for the introduction of a series of one-offs known as *Tharg's Future Shocks* in May of that year, and the debut of *The Visible Man* in October and the replacement of *Flesh* by *Shako* (the Eskimo name for a killer polar bear). Judge Dredd made his debut in Prog 2 but it took a while for him to become the paper's most popular character. He caught my imagination totally with the introduction of the *Robot Wars* story, which began in Prog 9 and concluded eight issues later. It was Dredd's first long storyline and was soon followed by other epics such as *The Cursed Earth*, *The Day the Law Died*, *Block Mania*, *The Apocalypse War* and *The Judge Child Quest*. *Robot Wars* was scripted by Dredd's writer/co-creator John Wagner and deftly visualised by Carlos Ezquerra, Mike McMahon and Ian Gibson. Suddenly the boys' department was humming once again: *Battle*, *Action*, *2000 AD*: here were three new-wave comics covering the past, present and future with a combined weekly sale of 300,000 copies.

Although I was not involved in the creation of *2000 AD* I did contribute scripts for *M.A.C.H. 1*. This strip was similar to *Rat Pack* in *Battle* in that it needed a stable of writers and artists to create the content required to feed the weekly publishing schedule. Six different writers had supplied scripts for the first thirteen episodes. As such I was very pleased when Pat asked me if I would like to write a couple of episodes for him. We worked as we had on *Action*; Pat always had the initial concept and would send me off to flesh it out. When I returned with a rough draft we would go through it in the *2000 AD* office. 'Going through it' included Pat acting out the action scenes in my scripts to get a better idea of what the pictures would look like. As John Wagner said to me at the time, 'Pat's great strength is he always gets his pictures in.' Thus the sight of Pat hanging from the ceiling or perhaps somersaulting down the corridor as he imitated *M.A.C.H. 1* in action would often confront the casual passer-by. It was hilarious and these pop-up script conferences only seemed to confirm the suspicion of the staffers on the grown-up magazines situated nearby that we comics people really were childish – but we didn't think it too silly.

Our first collaboration was a story called *The Chinese Formula*, in which John Probe is sent to Red China (as it was known then) and ends up pitting his Compu-Puncture Hyper Power against a man powered by another ancient Chinese force, the power of Ch'i. We followed this with an episode set in Tokyo as we considered that city an exotic place at the time. On one occasion Pat called me and said excitedly, 'We need to write about "the balls of the gods"!' We both liked the aliens-on-earth theories of Erich Von Daniken and this became the starting point for a story called *The Death Trumpet*. In this, an Inca temple turns out to have been an alien spaceship that had crashlanded eons in the past. Reactivated, the ship's cyber-crew prepares to take off, with Probe still on board. He bails out at 80,000 feet, thus breaking the world record for the longest drop without a parachute. During this period Pat told me about the idea of there having been a series of prototype M.A.C.H. agents, initial experiments in Compu-Puncture Hyper Power, who had been unable to control the huge energy created by the process. The final prototype (M.A.C.H. Zero) would be still alive, but confined in a secret government underground facility. My brief was to have M.A.C.H. Zero escape, go on the run and then be recaptured. I was watching *The Muppet Show* on Sunday evenings at the time and I thought it would be great if M.A.C.H. Zero were also a fan of the show. Perhaps a looped tape of the series would be played constantly in his cell to soothe his tortured psyche. For good measure I gave him a frog t-shirt to wear, a visual trinket that communicated the pathos of the story. *M.A.C.H. Zero* ran to four episodes and it seemed to strike a chord with the readers, not least because of the story's superb artwork from Ramon Sola. Now, I am not a natural comics writer, but my dialogue isn't bad, and if your pictures are good and you can supply some choice dialogue, you can get by without too many people noticing your drawbacks. The next thing I wrote, *The Dolphin Tapes*, was based on the rumour that the US Navy was secretly training dolphins for military purposes. I had Probe travel to Miami to get involved but it was very dull and the pictures were incredibly pedestrian. By this time Pat had handed over the editorial reins to Kelvin and had returned to freelance writing. My scripts sorely lacked his creative input and what I submitted was heavily edited to suit the tastes of the sub-editors working under Kelvin. Consequently, and not long afterwards, I decided to stop writing for a while and devote my creative energies solely to the role of being the sub-editor on *Battle*. After all, that's what I was being paid for.

Back on *Battle* we had watched the arrival of *2000 AD* with mixed feelings. It was great to have a new paper in the comics stable, but would its arrival cannibalise our sales? As it happened, four weeks before the launch of *2000 AD* we had celebrated our hundredth issue, dated 29 January. David had assembled a really strong line-up of new stories and old favourites for this landmark event. Indeed, if *Battle* had a golden era during its thirteen years of publishing, I would suggest 1977 marked the start of it. *2000 AD* may have dazzled an unsuspecting market with the brilliance of strips like *Judge Dredd*, but *Battle* was able to reply with its own stellar creations, not least the strip called *Johnny Red*.

Unjustly discharged from the RAF, nineteen-year-old Johnny 'Red' Redburn joins the merchant navy where, in the heat of a battle in the Barents Sea, he finds himself at the controls of a 'Hurricat' fighter. After helping defend the convoy from aerial attack, he chooses to save his precious plane rather than ditch it and flies it towards one of the big Russian airfields around Murmansk. Losing his bearings he lands instead at the base of a dejected Russian frontline fighter-bomber squadron known as the Falcons. Johnny undertakes to fight and fly with the Falcons, so beginning a ten-year odyssey that would see the strip become the longest-running serial ever to appear in *Battle Picture Weekly*. Ask any former reader of *Battle* to name their top three strips and without doubt one of those cited will be *Johnny Red*. Writer Tom Tully excelled himself on the strip and artist Joe Colquhoun's powerful depiction of the hell of the Russian Front provided a foretaste of his work to come drawing Pat Mills' acclaimed First World War story *Charley's War*.

Also appearing for the first time in issue 100 was the previously mentioned strip *Joe 2 Beans*. Written by John Wagner, this was set in the Pacific theatre of World War II, and told from an American viewpoint. There were new adventures for old favourites like *The Bootneck Boy*, *Darkie's Mob*, *Secret Agent Mike Nelson*, *Major Eazy* (forming an unlikely alliance with *Rat Pack*, but worth the experiment) and a survivor from the merger with *Valiant*, called *One-Eyed Jack*, a stylish, Magnum-wielding New York detective and in many ways the comics antecedent of Judge Dredd. Last but not least, and only recently introduced to the readers, was probably my favourite ever *Battle* strip, *Panzer G-Man*. Written by Gerry Finley-Day and drawn with consummate skill by Geoff Campion, the strip tells of the abrupt fall from grace of Kurt Slinger, a tank gunner in the Panzers during Operation Barbarossa, Hitler's ill-fated attack on Russia. Wrongly accused of cowardice, Kurt is demoted to being a Panzer Grenadier, one of the infantry soldiers running alongside the Panzers and known as 'dog soldiers' by their sneering superiors. Quite why the British have an obsession with underdogs I don't know, but we readers watched in fascination as Kurt endured the frozen horrors of the Russian Front and then the fearful carnage of Monte Cassino in the Italian campaign. The strip ended in the rubble of Berlin, where the last picture shows Kurt defiantly discharging his Maschinenpistole 40 at the advancing Russian troops.

Despite the pitfalls of using an eight-story matrix David had managed to assemble eight stories of equal strength. There was not a dud amongst them, although the notion of *Major Eazy* teaming up with *Rat Pack* was a little far-fetched and *One-Eyed Jack*'s urban war was set in the 1970s, not the 1940s. More new characters appeared during the course of the year. Among them was *The Sarge*, a pipe-smoking veteran of World War I, who proved an exception to the rule about, er, pipe-smoking heroes. Through the seventy-odd episodes in the first series, Sergeant Jim Masters coolly shepherds a unit of much younger recruits through nearly five years of action in World War II, from the beaches of Dunkirk to the beachhead at Anzio. At first glance, this story about an old-timer would appear to have had no chance against the other stories in the *Battle* stable, with their flashy, cigar-chewing protagonists and characters with a dark past and even darker thoughts. But, in fact, after two years of publishing the audience had matured alongside the title and was ready to appreciate the bald subject matter of warfare itself (with all the everyday, mundane and occasional murderous events that entails) just as much as the entertainment-led strips. In the summer, and in a nod to the appeal of the novel *Das Boot*, readers were introduced to the captain and crew of U159, a German type-VII U-boat. The strip was called *Sea Wolf*. At the same time David accepted a proposal from Carlos Ezquerra and Alan Hebden for a story war featuring a former slave-come-bounty hunter playing both sides in the American Civil War. The strip was called *El Mestizo*, which is an old Spanish term to denote a person of mixed race. As mentioned, the artists drawing for *Battle* in 1978 were the pick of the old Fleetway stable. Eric Bradbury, Mike Western, Geoff Campion, Joe Colquhoun – all had responded magnificently to the task of adapting their comicky styles to reflect the grit of the 1970s. Alongside them were Pat Wright, whose photographic style had helped introduce Mike Nelson two years earlier, and a new recruit named John Cooper, whose lean, urban art suited *Battle* perfectly.

The year ended with the conclusion of *The Bootneck Boy* and the merger with *Action* in November. That union brought the aforementioned war strip *Hellman of Hammer Force* into *Battle*, but also the not so welcome sports strip *Spinball*. *Dredger*'s gritty adventures were appreciated but diluted the blend of stories David had worked so hard to put together.

Nonetheless, *Battle* was producing hit after hit in well-ordered salvoes. By contrast, to my mind at least, *2000 AD* was beginning to look weary after its stellar start. Both *Invasion* and *M.A.C.H. 1* were suffering from a surfeit of insipid artwork and the self-contained episodes of *M.A.C.H. 1* allowed no room for story development. *Shako* was a poor replacement for *Flesh*, while *Dan Dare* was struggling to fulfill his early promise. David Bowie may have made a success of the androgynous persona that was Ziggy Stardust, but Dare's semi-glam spacer look never really connected with the readers. *Harlem Heroes* was serving up good thrills each week, thanks to some crafted debut artwork from Dave Gibbons, but on the whole *2000 AD* appeared to be adrift. As an outsider, it seemed that only the adventures of *Judge Dredd* were keeping the title afloat. Comparing the two, I felt *Battle* was in a much stronger position and I had no thought of leaving. However, this comfortable status quo was about to be disrupted by events. Not only was I to leave *Battle*, but within six months I would find myself working as chief sub-editor on *2000 AD*, blessed with the opportunity to help the title rediscover its mojo. But there was to be a small detour along the way, and that detour's name was a new launch entitled *Starlord*.

1978: FAIL, STAR TROOPERS

'THE KING IS dead, long live the King!' These words, uttered on a flying visit by a member of management, proclaimed the premature demise of *Starlord*. I and the three other members of its staff listened in stunned silence. After just twenty-two issues *Starlord* was to cease publication as a standalone magazine and be merged into *2000 AD*. I had been the beneficiary of two previous mergers – now it appeared I was to be on the losing end. What had gone wrong?

Starlord had been the creation of Kelvin Gosnell. His initial concept was a monthly science-fiction title that would sit comfortably alongside magazines such as *Omni* and *Metal Hurlant*. Both these titles were printed on glossy magazine paper and were aimed at fans of science-fiction stories and comic strips. To peruse a copy of *Metal Hurlant*, with its gorgeous colour artwork by Europe's top artists, was a salutary experience for anyone working in British comics at the time. *Omni*, published in America by the owner of *Penthouse* magazine, was equally rewarding in terms of whetting one's appetite for what the future might hold for humankind. I savoured both titles at the time, not just because of their production values and editorial content, but also because they seemed to be speaking my language. The sensation was the same as discovering my first issue of *Rolling Stone* magazine at the age of thirteen. This had a page entitled *Ransom Notes* (a pun, I guessed, on 'random notes') and just that whiff of West Coast counterculture had me cancelling my subscription to *Valiant* comic there and then.

Kelvin's vision for *Starlord* embraced all that was good about *Omni* and *Metal Hurlant*: vibrant science-fiction and science-fantasy comic strips would feature alongside features relevant to the genre. In short, an aspirational read for the younger reader and a more grown-up read for the older reader (who otherwise might have been thinking of giving up his weekly comic and saving up for a motorbike instead).

It was with this new publishing model that Kelvin had pitched me when he asked if I would like to work under him as the sub-editor on the title. I didn't have to think it over for very long, despite my disquiet at the thought of breaking my partnership with David. The fact was I had been on *Battle* for three years, not quite the length of World War II but a good chunk of it, and I was ready to move on. The thought of progressing to a more mature title was attractive. At the time, IPC published dozens and dozens of consumer magazines – respectable monthlies and weeklies with such names as *Horse & Hound*, *Country Life*, *Anglers Mail*, *Yachting Monthly*, *Airplane Monthly* and *Superbike* to list but a few. Who knew, perhaps *Starlord* would come to be considered a magazine too, and I could then hold up my head in the queue for lunch in the staff canteen and nonchalantly discuss the minutiae of the consumer magazine market with all the other 'proper' journos. Heck, I might even get an invite to spend the weekend at the estate of the editor of *Sporting Gun*, where I would airily discuss the finer points of the twelve-bore shotgun. Or, and here my heart began to beat really fast, or I might find myself chatting drolly to one of the smart staffers that graced the girls' photo-romance titles. Previous attempts to engage these ever-busy women in a bit of a natter had always produced the kind of sorrowful look one imagines Noah casting at late arrivals unable to board the Ark. My mind was made up. A date was set for my demobilisation and I began to tick the days off on my handy *Battle Calendar*. To paraphrase Nina Simone, it was to be 'a new dawn, a new day, a new life' for me. In due course, the leaving day arrived and I departed *Battle* with David's best wishes for the future ringing in my ears.

However, when I joined *Starlord* I discovered that the carefully laid plans for the title's launch were in disarray. Out of the blue, management had decreed that the frequency should be weekly, not monthly. This single change more or less ruined the title's chances of establishing itself as a serious science-fiction magazine. The editorial content had to be restructured to meet the demands of a weekly publishing schedule and the changes left *Starlord* looking more like a stablemate of *2000 AD* rather than something that title's readers could move on to as they grew older.

Whatever the rights or wrongs of the decision, the fact was that an on-sale date had been set for early May and additional editorial matter had to be scripted, drawn, coloured and lettered to meet the new production schedule. My first duty was to write the introductory letter from Starlord, the title's fictional editor. I was disappointed to learn that his *raison d'etre* was to warn the people of Earth about a 'forthcoming cataclysmic calamity'. Only by following *Starlord*'s weekly Stellar Strategies could the readers become Star Troopers and so train to avert the danger that was too terrible to mention. Visually, *Starlord* looked a little too well-groomed for my liking and I found him and his cosmic mission a tad juvenile. This was not the mature magazine I had thought I was joining and I struggled to put *Starlord*'s planet-saving mission into words. The author Chris Lowder, who was helping out in the *Starlord* office and scripting *Timequake*, rescued me by rewriting my text and turning it into the punchy call to arms it was meant to be. Matters improved when I began to see the strips that had already been commissioned for the launch. My favourite was called *Strontium Dog*, with script by writer/creator John Wagner and art by artist/creator Carlos Ezquerra. This was more like it: a troubled, offbeat protagonist named Johnny Alpha working as a mutant bounty hunter in the twenty-second century. His sidekick was a bearded Scandinavian named Wulf Sternhammer, although initially I heard there was talk of this character being modelled on a wisecracking Manhattan taxi driver, as featured in *Taxi*, a popular television show at the time. Either way, with colour art to rival any of that in *Omni* or *Metal Hurlant*, *Strontium Dog* was absolutely what I had envisaged *Starlord* would contain. The next strip I read, *Ro-Busters*, spoke with the same novel voice. Imagine *Thunderbirds* with robots instead of puppets, crossed with any comedy double act you care to name. With script by writer/creator Pat Mills and art by Carlos Pino, based on designs by Kevin O'Neill, it was quirky, knowing, funny and immediately likeable. The next strip I saw was Lowder's *Timequake* and as a fan of all things to do with time travel I was prepared to give its unappealing artwork the benefit of the doubt. Unfortunately, the constraints of the schedule meant a poor relation to these stories had to be included in the first issue. It was called *Planet of the Damned* and featured a commercial airliner warping through the Bermuda Triangle before dumping its bewildered passengers on a world very different to the one they had taken off from. The group's trials and tribulations on this ab-world could be said to predate the plot of *Lost*, but that's about the only compliment one can pay the strip. All in all, though, and puerile fictional editor aside, *Starlord* looked a good bet to succeed, especially with its painted colour artwork, which could not be reproduced by the letterpress printing process employed on the other weekly comics at the time. Cover dated 13 May, the title launched at 12p, being 3p more than *2000 AD*, and made a handsome addition to the newsagents' shelves. Unfortunately, the issue dated 7 October of the same year was its last issue, with *Starlord* himself seemingly set to return meekly from whence he came. No reason that I can recall was given for the closure of *Starlord* and I didn't question the decision. Launches, mergers, closures: these were part of the company's publishing cycle. As for *Starlord* being merged into *2000 AD*, well, it made sense to me on the basis that there was nothing else to merge it with. Also, *Starlord* was still a relatively unknown quantity to the five thousand odd newsagents who stocked comics and magazines at the time, whereas they'd had a year to grow accustomed to *2000 AD*. If familiarity is akin to liking then that fact alone must have made sense of merging *Starlord* into *2000 AD*.

Such musings meant nothing to me, anyway. I was well aware of the accepted custom that staffers on the title being closed were in a precarious position. As I stared out of the twenty-third floor window in the *Starlord* office, my hand toying with the handle that would open the fireman's window, I ruefully recalled my fantasies about country-life capers and passionate urban encounters. Not this time, brother. The fact was I was teetering on a career precipice, seized by vertigo.

The staff of *2000 AD* must have been rubbing their hands with glee at the prospect of the merger with *Starlord*. They would be the recipients of the title's top two stories, namely *Strontium Dog* and *Ro-Busters*. This injection of creative talent can be likened to a team in the Premiership acquiring two world-class players for free. But there was a sting in the tail and it made for an uncomfortable start to the proceedings for all concerned. Management had decided that I should be part of the merger. I was to take up the chief sub-editor's role on *2000 AD* with the unlucky incumbent being summarily moved to *Battle*. I can't say I felt good about the decision, but I wasn't going to object either. I had been spared the fireman's exit.

My opposite number on *2000 AD* was a relative newcomer to the company and someone I had not really got to know at all. Starting on *Action* he had moved to *2000 AD* early on in the title's first year. His name was Nick Landau and effectively his role as chief sub-editor had meant he was in charge of the day-to-day running of the title because Kelvin Gosnell was busy creating *Starlord* at management's behest. News of my imminent introduction must have been a bitter pill indeed, especially as Nick and his team had proposals to rescue *2000 AD* from its creative torpor. Alas, events had overtaken them. Although *Starlord* carried on until the October, I was told to join *2000 AD* straight away and so it was one August morning that I gathered up the tools of my trade in a box (scalpel, ruler, pencil, em rule, dictionary, eraser and other scholarly gear) and walked down the stairs to the *2000 AD* office on the floor below. I entered the open plan office, holding my box in my hands, and then realised I had absolutely no idea what to do next. Four desks lay before me, each occupied, but with no one talking. Heads were buried in work and an awkward silence settled around us with all the chill of a sudden San Francisco fog. Time passed. Telephones rang softly in the distance. At least someone somewhere was talking. I realised that I should have smoothed my arrival with a phone call of my own, one that offered commiserations and spoke of life's rich pageant, perhaps followed by a coffee in the canteen, sipped bitterly on the one side and nervously on the other. Even a briefing on the benefits of working for *Battle* would have shown willing, but I had done none of these things. I stood in the middle of the room feeling like a dud avocado, severe embarrassment being the price of my failings. In the end all I could do was turn around and return quietly upstairs.

The matter sorted itself out within an hour and then I was back in the *2000 AD* office, this time being briefed by Nick on what scripts had been commissioned for the next few issues. He looked at me keenly at the end of each sentence, perhaps still baffled as to why he should be making way for me. We knew he was the victim of a management decision to remove him from the title, but no one was providing a valid reason why. I absorbed as much as I could, nodding my head earnestly, while scanning the title's make-up book, which charted the status of the content for the next few issues.

With the handover complete, Nick departed for his new duties on *Battle* and I sat down at his desk. A week or so later I popped up to see him and enquire how he was getting on. He replied rather acidly that he had just had finished subbing one of the title's scripts and everything was fine. I could tell it was not and some time afterwards he left to open a bookshop in London's Denmark Street. A couple of years later, though, I was able to do him a good turn which I hoped made up for the events just described.

For myself it was a different story. I had now risen to the role of chief sub-editor and as such was eligible for an increase in salary concomitant with Grade Five on the pay scale. However, such a rise would have to be approved by the same review body that had promoted me from Grade Eight to Grade Seven. An appeal would have to be lodged to trigger the review process, which is what I did. I then left those civil service-like wheels to turn in their own time and focused my attention on the editorial duties associated with my new role. Chief among these was getting to know the other members of the editorial team, who were probably feeling just a little sore at the way events had unfolded.

Kevin O'Neill was now art editor, and with him on the art side was Colin Wyatt. On the editorial side, the sub-editor was a jovial man named Roy Preston, who had recently joined from the competitions department. Nowadays, employees are coached endlessly in how to perform effectively as a team. For example, ex-members of the SAS have spent days in darkened rooms explaining to me (and others) how teams 'form, storm and reform', suggesting that you can't 'manage people as if they were parcels', rather that 'leadership' is what best motivates a team. We were to 'grip the task through the team, as if the team were a glove', and so on. All good stuff, but back in 1978 we knew none of this. So we did what every new team did then: we went to the Dogget's pub at lunchtimes and drank gin and tonic until it came out of our ears.

These frequent bonding sessions meant that before long, socially at least, we all got on. I liked Roy's stories about the pigmen of Norfolk from where he hailed. Kevin, meanwhile, had a passion for the cinema, especially science-fiction films, and held up the closing soliloquy of *The Incredible Shrinking Man* as one of the genre's greatest moments. The first two *Superman* films were being shot at Pinewood at the time and he interviewed Derek Meddings, the creator and director of model effects on the set. Kevin later wrote the interview up as a two-page feature and we published it in *2000 AD* Prog 99. At the end of the feature I wrote a short panel, which read: 'Until recently, Kevin O'Neill was the art editor of *2000 AD*. Publisher of *Just Imagine*, the intermittent magazine on movie and TV special effects, he is currently drawing a new *Ro-Busters* story which begins in Prog 102.' When I presented the spread for approval (to the same editorial manager who had clipped me round the head) the feature drew a snort of disapproval. Shaking it with both hands, he berated me for the text, complaining irritably, 'Why have you given him such a puff?' I muttered something about how Kevin had championed creator credits in *2000 AD*, so it seemed only fair to give him a writing credit, and this answer seemed to thwart any further objections.

Professionally, of course, the team may still have had reservations about my ability to do the job but, fortunately, the merger meant that we were to be handed prime content that would camouflage any creative failings on my part for quite a while. In terms of planning for the merger, we knew we were going to get *Strontium Dog* and *Ro-Busters*, so we were able to bring a so-so strip called *Ant Wars* to a close in the previous issue and give *Dan Dare* a rest. At the time Judge Dredd's adventures in the Cursed Earth were carrying *2000 AD*. This twenty-five-episode epic was where the new young British artists Mike McMahon and Brian Bolland had coalesced, their artwork galvanised by Pat Mills' fever-pitch scripts (with contributions along the way from Chris Lowder and John Wagner). Wisely, the editorial team had chosen to feature *The Cursed Earth* on the front cover as often as they could, resulting in eleven appearances for the Judge, nine drawn by McMahon and two by Bolland. These covers had a raw excitement that really caught the eye and set the imagination racing. Given the choice between buying a copy of *Starlord* or *2000 AD*, I'm sure potential new readers at the time would have chosen the latter, despite *Starlord* having the better quality paper and painted art. The fact was, *The Cursed Earth* covers buzzed with the promise of outlandish new experiences, whereas the *Starlord* covers, although more sophisticated, seemed to hark back to a different, more sedate world whose appeal had clearly faded.

'TWO SCI-FI GIANTS UNITE IN A GIANT LEAP FOR MANKIND!' screamed the topline above the *2000 AD* and *Starlord* logos. This was Prog 86, dated 14 October 1978, the merge issue. A powerful composite picture of the new story line-up, drawn by Dave Gibbons, carried a further caption reading '*Judge Dredd*, *Strontium Dog*, *Ro-Busters* and *Flesh*. Join them in a double-barrelled blast of sci-fi comic hyper power!' It was an unbeatable line-up that was set to run unchanged for the next twelve issues. Who could resist?

1979: YOU CAN CALL ME ED (PART ONE)

RETURNING TO WORK on 2 January after the Christmas break, I took the lift to the twentieth floor, sat down at my desk, lit my morning Malboro and gazed out of the window, glad to see aliens had not extracted all the hydrogen from the Thames with which to power their passing spaceships. Yes, we lived to edit another day, and life was sweet. The response to the merger issue and the ones following had been extremely favourable and I was looking forward to the new year. No January blues for this boy. As I sat there, the rest of the team began to arrive one by one: Kevin travelling in from South London, Roy from Norfolk, and Colin from Canvey Island. We set about our usual tasks and slowly the weekly publishing routine had us in its vice-like grip once more. By the end of the month, however, the team had changed dramatically. Kevin had departed to go freelance working, among other things, as one of the artists on *Ro-Busters*. (Before leaving he checked, jokingly, that *2000 AD would* buy his artwork and I reassured him. Anyway, I liked his unique style and thought it would be a great addition to the title.) Roy, too, was on his travels, this time to work with Kelvin on a new anthology title for boys, due to launch in March.

I was surprised when I heard that management wanted to

publish such a title. Hadn't we seen that anthology comics were a thing of the past? Didn't they get it that genre-specific, niche titles were where the market was going? Despite this handicap, Kelvin set about the assignment with his customary gusto, using the old *Starlord* office as his base. Downstairs we soon learned that the new title was to be called *Heroes*, this being the hook the stories would hang on. Past, present, future; the strips would share a heroic theme. I thought this was rather clever and my doubts began to ease. Sadly, the single-page advert announcing the new title was a massive damp squib. The advert appeared in every title in the adventure and humour departments, but the wording was abysmal (although I was thrilled to learn that the spud gun had been brought out of retirement and would be the free gift accompanying issue three). The lacklustre text of the advert is repeated below as evidence of the advert's failure. For enlightenment I have added a translation for each unintelligible caption (in brackets underneath).

VICTOR DRAGO
'From out of the eerie shifting wall of fog his first encounter with the Terror of Troll Island.'
(No shit, kids, it's a Sherlock Holmes tribute strip.)

THE ANGRY PLANET
'Space settlers carving out a new life on the red planet do battle with the powerful Mars Incorporated.'
(Ouch! First generation Martians get hassled by the mad men of Mars, Inc.)

BENKEI
'His favourite sport was the challenge until he met his match in Yoshitsune.'

(Meet the warrior monk with attitude, his tasty tales torn from Japanese folklore!)

E.S.P. SMITH
'His teachers refuse to believe his mind has the energy of a miniature cyclone.'
(This kid's mind is lethal. Watch what happens when he gets 'Carrie-d' away!)

WAGNER'S WALK
'Between slavery and freedom lie 2,500 miles of frozen wastes and burning deserts.'
(P.O.W! Three German dudes sag off from their Siberian gulag and stroll to freedom.)

CAPTAIN KLEP
'Up, up, oops and away... this super-nit superhero is unleashed on an unsuspecting universe.'
(Now you've got it.)

The advert also called the new title *Tornado* as in 'Storm Warning! *Tornado* strikes today!' Sitting on the twentieth floor we could only imagine the anguish that was going on upstairs. *Heroes* had made sense, but something very recent had clearly made the team ditch the title and that can only have been a last-minute management dictat.

Meanwhile, in the *2000 AD* office, Colin and I had been getting to know the new members of our team. Kelvin had recruited a friend of John Wagner's named Alan Grant as sub-editor and had hired a college graduate named Robin Smith as art assistant, taking over Colin's job because Colin had been promoted to art editor. This would be the team that ran *2000 AD* for the next sixteen months or so. Looking ahead for an issue to make our mark on, I chose Prog 100 and we set about programming its Thrill-power output to maximum. The line-up was as follows:

JUDGE DREDD in *The Day the Law Died*

This was Dredd's next epic after *The Cursed Earth*, amounting to twenty episodes of Mega-City One being terrorised by the insane Chief Judge Cal. Only one man can save the city: the outlaw Judge Joseph Dredd!

DAN DARE in *Servant of Evil*

Written by Tom Tully and drawn by Dave Gibbons, this *Dare* strip was another epic, running for twenty-six episodes. The story saw the return of Dare's great adversary, The Mekon, who tricks Dare into searching for the crystal of life, which will grant the alien slaphead immortality (so that's two stories featuring megalomaniacs, then).

RO-BUSTERS in *The Terra Meks*

Actually part three of a four-parter, this gem from Pat Mills and Dave Gibbons was perfectly realised. With his art on *Dan Dare* in the same issue, Dave Gibbons found himself occupying fourteen pages out of the thirty-two available. When he drew the cover for Prog 101 this figure increased to fifteen pages, very nearly half the comic's content.

ROBO-HUNTER

This strip by John Wagner and Ian Gibson had actually started in Prog 76, but had been interrupted by the merger with *Starlord*. The star of the strip was Sam Slade, a detective hunting delinquent droids for creds in a sharply observed, beautifully drawn satire that would become one of *2000 AD's* most popular strips.

Three weeks later, in Prog 104, these strips would be joined by the return of *Strontium Dog*, giving *2000 AD* a five-story line-up. In terms of writers, three of the strips were written by Wagner, one by Mills and one by Tully. The art roster, meanwhile, featured the soon-to-be famous line-up of British talent comprising McMahon, Bolland, Gibbons, O'Neill and Gibson. Later in the month would see debut art from Brett Ewins and later in the year the stable would welcome Ron Smith and Cam Kennedy. The new wave had arrived – all backed up by Carlos Ezquerra, whom I thought of as an honorary Brit anyway.

It was during this period that the phone rang one afternoon and I answered it to a member of the review panel who had good news for me. Apparently, my appeal to be put up to Grade Five had been successful. 'Congratulations!' said the voice at the end of the line. 'You are now Grade Five and your next pay packet will reflect the appropriate increase in salary.' I replaced the receiver and just sat there, motionless, letting this fantastic news sink in. Publishing is not the best-paid job in the world so any increase in salary was much appreciated. Maybe I wouldn't have to give up smoking and going to the pub after all. Maybe I could afford to start going to the footie once more, although the real reason I had stopped was the fear of getting caught up in the maelstrom of hooliganism that blighted the game during the 1970s. I did accompany Mike McMahon to one match at the Arsenal, but being a Spurs fan I felt a bit of a traitor.

Whilst I was revelling in my newfound financial status the most bizarre thing happened. Kelvin strode into the office in a state of high anxiety. I thought I would share my good news with him on the grounds that it might dispel whatever cloud of gloom had callously decided to envelop him, but before I could speak he announced that he was resigning as editor of *Tornado* and of *2000 AD*. This was to happen immediately. He ended his address by pointing at me and declaring, 'You are now the editor of *2000 AD*.' With that he turned on his heel and disappeared. We knew there had been other irritants for Kelvin in addition to the change in his title's name, but we didn't realise just how bad things had got for him. Something had obviously occurred upstairs that was the last straw. Thinking of camels collapsing made my own legs unsteady and I tottered weakly back to my chair. The office spun round and round. In the space of thirty minutes I had gone from Grade Seven to Grade Three. Not only that, I was now an editor. And not only that, I was now the editor of *2000 AD*, the Galaxy's Greatest Comic. Suddenly I was responsible for a staff of three, a stable of thirty freelancers, and I had the task of entertaining 100,000 kids – every seven days. '*Quaequam Blag!*'

1979: YOU CAN CALL ME ED (PART TWO)

'DO YOU DRAW the bubbles?' This was a common question at parties when I said I worked in comics. There was no reason to expect that someone from outside the industry would know how a comic was put together but the half-stifled titter that often accompanied the question was always aggravating. In the end I found it easier to refer vaguely to a role in publishing rather than attempting to explain the job itself. I had tried once or twice, bravely describing how the process involved first a script from a writer, which was then sent to an artist, whose artwork was then returned and handed to a letterer, who would letter the script's dialogue onto the artwork and then draw the aforementioned bubble around the speech, adding a neat tail to the character speaking. And how this process was initiated and then trafficked by yours truly, the editor, with help from a sub-editor, whose input could rescue or ruin a strip, depending on their mood that day. And how a senior manager could then request changes on deadline day, creating the desire to throw either oneself or them or both parties out of the fireman's window, without bothering to open it first, of course. But on these occasions I always found the tone of my voice becoming more and more serious, my gestures more animated as a glazed look began to cross the face of my fellow partygoer. In the end they would be none the wiser, except to know that comics weren't the jolly jape they had supposed they were, and how come they'd got stuck talking to me anyway, when there was a handsome musician standing in the kitchen telling hilarious jokes involving buns, bums and the Elephant Man?

At its most basic, the function of the comic editor was to prepare and send an issue of his title to the printer each week in accordance with the production schedule. The schedule allotted six weeks to the development process, so the scripts would be commissioned six weeks before the on-sale date. In other words, comics followed a magazine development process rather than that of a newspaper, whose front page can be updated right up to the day of publication.

An issue of a comic was thirty-two pages, with twenty-eight pages being strip, and three being features (letters page, intro page, back cover), and of course there was the front cover. The content was commissioned from freelance writers, artists, letterers and colourists, and their efforts assembled in-house by the editorial team. The content had to be legal and above all contain nothing that could be copied by the audience. The greatest mistake made in British comics was the strip that showed a child climbing into an abandoned fridge to hide and then closing the door. This was in the days when fridge doors could only be opened using the handle on the outside. Almost as important was the tenet that an issue should not contain one single spelling mistake or, God forbid, a grammatical error that could be seized upon by a parent. Since comics had a trashy reputation (spawn of the penny dreadfuls), parents at the time seemed to spend their waking hours watching like hawks for the slightest printed error so they could write to the publisher declaring the end of Western civilisation and demanding the editor's immediate sacking. One such victim of this was the editor who ran a headline saying, 'We should be hung if we don't qualify for the World Cup.' This drew a sharp rebuke from management, who stated that the correct tense used should have been 'hanged'. 'But I checked with a teacher,' the unhappy editor wailed to me later in the pub.

Financially there was a strict budget for each issue and any over-spend would generate a mocking telephone call from the finance department, drawing attention to your profligacy and dryly wondering whether you had considered an alternative form of employment, such as gravedigging. This fiscal regulation meant the commissioning process was almost Toyota-like in its adherence to just-in-time (or last-minute) ordering. The artists in particular were under huge pressure to meet their weekly deadlines; there was no slack in the schedule and no stockpile of completed episodes to act as a safeguard. As such, no one was ever ill – they could not afford to be. One writer who was injured in a car crash had his scripting duties taken over by a kindly fellow scribe, who wrote the necessary episodes required by the schedule for free until the writer had recovered sufficiently to take the cover of his own typewriter once more.

Socially, the editor was expected to attend the editors' Christmas lunch, usually held above a pub in Fleet Street. At these occasions you were not to snigger if a more senior manager announced (to no one in particular), 'I've been working my arse off in Manhattan all month.' You were certainly expected to hold your beer, be passionate about a football team (the lower the division the more passionate you were deemed to be), and to watch Bruce Forsyth and the *Generation Game* every Saturday evening. *Match of the Day* rounded off the night's viewing and this was to be followed by the weekly bout of marital nookie. Sundays were spent in the company of *The Big Match* (expertly presented by Brian Moore) and *Kung Fu* (David Carradine's Shaolin monk kicks cowboy butt). Both shows were compulsive viewing.

Not least, an editor was expected to possess a burning love of comics and be able to tell good artwork from poor artwork. Briefing writers was a skill learnt by listening to editors converse with their writers over the phone. How to sub a writer's script was a skill previously learned by looking at scripts that had first been through the editor's hands.

This, then, was the editor's role and the whole production process was repeated year in, year out until their title was either merged or closed. For editors of popular titles, that had meant years of happy editing, cocooned in a world of postwar prosperity that stretched right up to the last days of the 1960s.

It was into the new role of editor that I was now flung, with all its attendant pitfalls and pratfalls. Before I could send anything to the printer, though, each issue had to be approved by the same editorial manager who had objected to my bigging up of Kevin O'Neill in his *Superman* article. Very early on in my editorship, the manager took particular dislike to an episode of *Ro-Busters* that Kevin had drawn. In it, a futuristic vehicle (the Satan Dart) is chased at dizzying speed along an expressway shaped like an underground tunnel. The driver, in an effort to shake off his pursuers, steers the car up the side of the tunnel and along the roof, so the car is now travelling upside down. This completely threw the manager, who kept rotating the artwork to orientate himself. I tried to explain that the idea was that he (and the reader) should actually feel disorientated, giddy even, so that their experience of the strip was enhanced, but my entreaty was met with disdain. The manager decided he wanted several of the pictures redrawn and it was a long walk for me back to the office to return the artwork to Kevin with a mournful account of the changes required. This was no fun. I didn't recall David having to show issues of *Battle* to anyone before they went to press and it felt like *2000 AD* was being picked on. In fact, for much of its early life in the Youth Group, *2000 AD* was regarded as the odd one out, the different drummer marching to its own beat. In due course the title's stellar sales and impressive revenues (not to mention growing cult status) made everyone want to be best pals with us, join the team even, but in 1977 such approbation seemed a world away.

The rich vein of Thrill-power mined by Prog 100 was tainted in Prog 113 by a six-part story I had inherited called *Rick Random Space Detective*. Apparently, the strip was a revival of a hugely popular 1950s strip of the same name. I detested it. I loathed the concept and the artwork set my teeth on edge, but I had no choice except to run it. The women's magazines would often commission several features on an exact same topic, only to discard all but one of them (writing off the cost of the others at the end of the financial year) but such fiscal extravagance was absolutely forbidden in the Youth Group. I learnt that the artist, Ron Turner, was considered to be the definitive *Rick Random* artist and that his style was much admired. He may have been venerated in his time but to my mind he was never suited to *2000 AD*. To make matters worse, we already had two space adventures running, with *Dan Dare* and *Strontium Dog* trading cosmic thrills from opposite ends of the paper. I gritted my teeth in the knowledge that the strip's six-week run would soon pass, which it did, but the ghost of Turner was to haunt the office for many a month afterwards. The ghost even had physical form. It was Turner's agent, who was called Mr Hall. This secretive gentleman in his late fifties would deliver Turner's artwork in person, but from behind blue sunglasses, which he never removed. We began to wonder if he wasn't Turner himself, as we were never allowed to speak to or meet the artist. Any enquiry after Turner's health or whereabouts was batted away with an agent's practised ease. (After all, it's their job to keep you from their artists in case you suggest to the artist they work directly for you and cut out the agent's fee.) The haunting itself was carried out down the phone line, in the style of *Play Misty For Me*. After lunch about once a month the office phone would ring and it would be Mr Hall, who would commence a slurred, lengthy lecture about some obscure subject or other. These calls were interminable so I used to put the receiver in my metal wastepaper bin, which would amplify his droning tones just enough for me to know when to pick it back up and offer an encouraging 'Is that so?' or a gasped 'Really?' before replacing it in the bin. These mid-afternoon calls went on for a couple of years, and then, one day, we realised they had stopped. Had Mr Hall joined Flo, the tea lady, in cartoon limbo – that sorry, sombre place populated by the frustrated spirits of former comic characters, their creators and associated industry workers? We were never to find out.

What we did know was that the *Strontium Dog* adventure *Journey into Hell* was turning into a gripping thriller, with compelling cliffhangers at the end of each episode. *Ro-Busters*, too, had blossomed and the thirteen-part adventure

The Fall and Rise of Ro-Jaws and Hammerstein certainly kept the readers returning for more 'good droid action' each week. At the time, Pat would phone up and describe his plans for the story, giving a brief synopsis of how the episodes would pan out. You can tell if a writer is on to something good from the way they describe to you what they going to write. If they get a faraway look in their eye, then laugh at the story, as if they were hearing it from someone else, you know they've struck gold. I could not see Pat, but the way he was laughing down the phone was enough to suggest that *The Fall and Rise of Ro-Jaws and Hammerstein* was going to be a great success, and so it was. The plot concerned a sanctuary for abused robots, located on Saturn Six. Ro-Jaws and Hammerstein find themselves organising a secret exodus of Earth's downtrodden droids to this offworld haven, all the while being hunted by Gestapo-like security forces named P.D. Troopers. At the time a TV show called *Secret Army* had begun on BBC 1 and had popularised the notion of 'sending agents down the line'. Pat satirised this in the story and the readers got the joke immediately, revelling in the knowing humour. Joining artists O'Neill and McMahon on the strip was another young British illustrator called Mike Dorey, who always arrived at the office wearing a World War II flying jacket. I couldn't think of him as part of the new wave, though, as he preferred to keep his options open and divide his workload between IPC's comics and those published by DC Thomson. But his art on *Invasion*, *Hellman* and indeed *Ro-Busters* (not to mention *M.A.C.H. Zero*) was always completed with great individual style and I often felt he could have gone a lot further in comics than he did. His pseudonym, when he wasn't happy with his art, was 'J. Clough', which was a pun on the famous J-Cloth cleaning product. Why? Because he said when his art was rushed it looked like it had been drawn with one.

Despite the blight of *Rick Random* (and another short-lived turkey called *Angel*) it seemed to me that *2000 AD* was developing nicely. It was at this juncture, around May, that I got a call to report to the publisher's office on the floor below. In fact, the publisher had now risen to become managing director and while waiting outside I chatted idly to his secretary, who only the night before had engaged in a speed-typing contest with Alan. There was some doubt as to who had won but I think we agreed that hanging around the office at seven in the evening, when the Stamford Arms had been open since five-thirty, was not the best use of our time. I was about to suggest that she and I go to the pub that evening, where we would try out the newly installed *Space Invaders* machine. She would hold a white wine spritzer and I would brandish a pint of lager. Dotted around us would be our fellow workers, enveloped in a haze of blue tobacco smoke. As Blondie's 'Sunday Girl' blasted from the jukebox, the libidinous staff of the photo-romance titles would pair up, break up and then make up with baffling speed. Alongside them, the sober editors of titles such as *Practical Woodworker* and *Practical Hi-Fi* would nurse pints of bitter as they contemplated the speed-walk to Waterloo, there to catch the slam-door trains that would rattle them home to their various 'Good Life' abodes. At the bar, sinewy stagehands from the National Theatre would gather around the platinum blonde, whose silver-tongued motto was 'Up and at 'Em'. And into this social tumult each evening would stroll the posse from the postroom, nonchalantly sporting red LED digital watches and basking in continuing rumours of first-class hanky-panky among the second-class mailbags.

Yes, a trip to the Stamford Arms was what I intended to propose, but my invitation was interrupted by a barked summons from within the MD's office.

Once inside I was glad to see that he was not wearing his trademark telling-off sunglasses, but what he had to say was still a bit of a shock. He told me that he wanted *2000 AD* to become adventure-led. I got the impression that he wanted me to steer the title away from its science-fiction roots and turn it into just another adventure title. At the time I did not twig his motive, but I realised later that *Tornado* must have been in trouble and he was lining up a merger between it and *2000 AD* for later in the year, with the end result being a new adventure paper for the 1980s. What he failed to appreciate was that I didn't see *2000 AD* as a science-fiction paper in the first place. As previously mentioned, I saw it as a comic that took traditional adventure stereotypes and recast them in the future. So, if he thought our conversation meant I was going to ditch characters like Joe Dredd (Cop), Sam Slade (Detective) and Johnny Alpha (Bounty Hunter) then he was mistaken. But I didn't say that. I just concurred politely and left. Nonetheless, this was no fun. Another person might have had a flaming argument and ended up resigning on the spot, or getting the sack even, but I chose to buy myself time in the hope of finessing my superior's instructions. However, when I explained the gist of the conversation to the guys back in the office it caused some disquiet and I got the feeling they felt I should have stood my ground. I decided to let events be my judge and hurried off to consult Kelvin.

Following his dramatic double resignation Kelvin had not actually left the company. In fact he had been asked to stay on, assuming the role of special projects supremo or some such. In publishing speak, anyone assigned to special projects is understood to be waiting for the chop, but in Kelvin's case it was clear that management really did want to keep him and his avowed passion for publishing. I told Kelvin what had happened and he suggested bringing in a couple of strips that would carry out the MD's wishes without destroying the essence of *2000 AD*.

The first strip was called *Disaster 1990*. At the cinema, disaster movies were all the rage. We'd been treated to *Airport* (1970), *The Poseidon Adventure* (1972), *Earthquake* (1974) and *The Towering Inferno* (1974), so the notion of a disaster strip set 'the day after tomorrow' seemed to satisfy everyone. The story was that a nuclear explosion at the North Pole had melted the icecaps, flooding much of Britain in the process. Scattered survivors roamed the rooftops, among them a young Bill Savage, who ten years later would star in the story *Invasion 1999*. In retrospect, *Disaster 1990* couldn't emulate the thrills being generated by the other strips of the time. It wasn't a disaster, but once you've seen one picture of London flooded you've seen them all. I realised I had read a similar story in *Eagle* as a child, and its pictures of St Paul's and other London landmarks reduced to mere islands may have seemed wondrous at the time, but foisting what you once liked in your youth on a contemporary audience is always a mistake.

The second strip was *Project Overkill*, a present-day mystery in which the protagonist battles shadowy forces protecting a top-secret project that not even the US President knows about. We picked Prog 119 as the issue to launch these strips and put a picture of Roger Moore on the cover in his role as James Bond in *Moonraker*. With *Dan Dare* and *Judge Dredd* untouchable we could creditably claim to have steered the rest of the title towards the adventure genre. And so it seemed on a cursory inspection. But a third strip was starting that issue and it was our secret weapon in the war to retain *2000 AD*'s essence. That strip was the *ABC Warriors*.

Like *Judge Dredd*, *ABC Warriors* is regarded as one of *2000 AD*'s finest strips. At first glance all that had happened was that *Ro-Busters* had morphed into a war strip, losing Ro-Jaws along the way, with Pat's scripts swapping music-hall humour for black humour. But the strip became much more than that, with six new robo-characters being recruited under the command of Hammerstein. The warriors were: Joe Pineapples, Happy Shrapnel, Mongrol, Blackblood, Deadlock and Steelhorn. The initials ABC stood for atomic, bacterial and chemical, meaning that the droids were resistant to such methods of attack. Very soon, the strip was challenging *Judge Dredd* for top spot in the popularity poll. All in all, it felt like we had done a good job deflecting the call to follow an adventure-led route and with that battle seemingly won, I went on holiday for three weeks, leaving the title's editorial duties in Alan's hands.

I was in for a surprise when I returned. In my absence, management had taken the decision to merge *Tornado* into *2000 AD*. They had waited until I was away, probably under the assumption that I would have fought such a move, and in such circumstances there's nothing like a *fait accompli* to forestall any possible resistance. It turned out we were going to have to accommodate three strips from *Tornado*: the aforementioned *Wolfie [E.S.P] Smith* and *Captain Klep*, and a third, newer strip entitled *Blackhawk* (Roman gladiator finds himself fighting in a savage alien arena). Alan had been press-ganged into putting the merger together, under the threat that if he didn't someone else would, which left him little choice really. Nonetheless, I was livid. This was no fun.

Then I began to suspect that the whole thing had been an act of provocation, designed to get back at me for sabotaging the command to convert *2000 AD* into an adventure title. With that suspicion in mind I decided to play it cool. You have to pick your battles and this potential skirmish was clearly a trap. Besides, it had become abundantly clear that it was *ABC Warriors* and *Judge Dredd* that were the main attractions for readers anyway, so I consoled myself with the thought that as long as they were running it didn't matter what else was in the paper. The merger took place with Prog 127, cover-dated 25 August, and the new line-up of strips continued through to Prog 139. As those strips ran, more or less taking care of themselves, an additional editing task came up for grabs and I made sure to use my authority as editor to secure it for myself. The job was a peach: to produce the first ever *Judge Dredd Annual*. It would go on sale in the autumn of 1980, but would be dated 1981, as was the custom. Work needed to begin immediately as annuals obeyed the lengthier production schedules used by book publishers.

In times past the comic annual was one of the staple presents bought for a child at Christmas. It was an irrefutable truth that if little Jimmy was a regular reader of *Battle Picture Weekly*, then he would be overjoyed to be given that title's annual. If he were from a poor family, little Jimmy would get the annual as his main present. If his family circumstances were slightly more comfortable, then that clever Santa would tuck the annual into his stocking. Either way, the gift was the same: 256 pages of non-stop action, featuring all his favourite characters, many in glorious colour, and all bound up inside shiny, hardback covers. What better gift could Granddad Mark or Dad Vinnie choose? Everyone was a winner: receiver, giver, and publisher. In particular the publisher, who, behind the scenes, was rubbing his hands with glee. Annuals were a huge source of revenue, clocking up sales that matched or surpassed those of the host title. Indeed it was for this fiscal reason that some annuals continued to be published long after the demise of their host title. Regrettably, as the years passed and circulations declined, the annual came under increasing pressure to replenish a title's declining profit contribution. Editorial budgets for annuals began to be cut. Formats themselves began to shrink. Where 256 pages had once been the norm, suddenly it was 128 pages, and then just ninety-six. One item that never decreased was the price. That just kept going up and up. After all, who could accurately recall last year's price of milk, let alone the cost of an annual? And, as it was a present anyway, there was little purchaser resistance. By the time the *2000 AD Annual* dated 1979 came to be put together, its producers faced an almost impossible task. The first annual (1978) had at least contained some material relevant to the brand. These were strips that had been commissioned for the early issues of the weekly, then put aside as 'annual fodder'. But for the 1979 annual there was no such stockpile. And with editorial budgets by now paltry, only a few pages of new material could be commissioned. The producers did the best they could, but even so that second annual must have been a bitter disappointment to the *2000 AD* reader on Christmas morning. Of its 128 pages many were generic science-fiction strips dredged up from the art library and passed off as *2000 AD* content. It was an embarrassment for all concerned.

As such, I was determined the first *Judge Dredd Annual* would be a thing of beauty, a ninety-six-page Thrill-fest featuring Dredd, the whole Dredd and nothing but Dredd.

Now here was a battle worth fighting. I lobbied for and was given a decent editorial budget. Working with Colin as art editor, I commissioned three *Judge Dredd* stories to be written by John Wagner and drawn in full colour by Mike McMahon. Ah, the luxury of full-colour art. We then commissioned a front cover from Brian Bolland and an inside front cover cityscape by Ron Smith. That was thirty-two pages accounted for, but with them went most of the budget. There was just enough left to commission a strip called *Max Normal, The Pinstripe Freak* (he's Dredd's informer) and a strip about *Walter the Wobot* (Dredd's one-time robo-servant). After that, I would have to fill the remaining pages without paying anyone and without resorting to non-*Dredd* filler. I got lucky when I pulled open the plans chest we used to store artwork and came across all sorts of early sketches of *Judge Dredd* by Carlos Ezquerra. There was even a five-page episode drawn by Carlos featuring Dredd in action, thwarting a futuristic bank heist. I discovered that although Mike McMahon's Dredd had been the first published version, it was actually Carlos who had visualised the character and drawn the first episode. This discovery led me to decide to research and write the factual story of *Judge Dredd*'s creation and feature it in the annual (I felt our audience would be genuinely interested in the true-life genesis of the Judge). We included the bank-heist strip, explaining that it was the previously unpublished first *Dredd* story. The annual's content was developing nicely, but there were still a goodly few blank pages left to fill so I decided to write them myself. For the tech-heads we designed features on Dredd's Lawgiver gun and his Lawmaster bike. To flesh out Dredd's twenty-second century world in post-apocalyptic North America we put together a map showing his route across the Cursed Earth and the location of the surviving Mega-Cities. For fun we devised a Judge Dredd quiz. Lastly I wrote a time-travel guide to Mega-City One as though the visitor was from the 1980s. With only five pages left to go, I was really pleased with what we had assembled. Here was a debut annual everyone could be proud of: writers, artists, letterers and, of course, the editorial team. Not to mention the publisher, who had fixed the cover price at £1.80, making it twelve times more expensive than *2000 AD*.

It was during the course of putting the annual together that my phone rang. It was Kevin O'Neill. He didn't sound too happy. 'What's up?' I asked. 'It's Pat,' came his somewhat exasperated reply. Apparently the two had had a falling out and would not be collaborating with each other for the foreseeable future. Kevin sighed down the phone that he was therefore available for work and would even draw a *Future Shock* if need be. I said there weren't any scripts going at that time but that I would let him know as soon as something came up. Shortly afterwards he appeared in the office (or Command Module as we had begun to call it) with some rough pages for a potential one-off strip called *Shok!* Kevin took me through the story, explaining each picture as we went along. It was about a strato-bat pilot who brings home the remains of a war droid, dug up from the Cursed Earth. Kevin asked if I would like to dialogue the story and we could publish it in *2000 AD*. I rapidly agreed and even suggested a scene where the victim outwits the droid, which has cunningly reactivated itself. Together we finished the strip, Kevin pencilling and inking, me writing the dialogue. At the end it struck me that the strip was set in Dredd's world and was five pages long, just the number I needed to finish my editing task. I switched it to the annual and the ninety-six pages were complete.

Back on *2000 AD*, the new guys seemed to be settling in well. Colin was doing a great job tutoring Robin in the duties of an art assistant. Both of them also contributed pin-ups and front covers to *2000 AD*: Colin a Tharg cover and a pin-up of Blackhawk, Robin a Captain Klep pin-up, and later on he drew the strip itself. Alan had taken over writing the Tharg stories, first introduced in Prog 24. He had a real knack for spinning tales around the Mighty One and his scripts were always very funny and topical. These behind-the-scenes glimpses at the production of *2000 AD*, where Tharg's robots supposedly created the scripts and artwork, were a marvellous piece of fun with brilliant staff and creator caricatures by Carlos Ezquerra. It must have been a comfort to some of the more nervous parents to know that there was a sense of humour behind this comic that was otherwise so full of grim anti-heroes. Alan got on famously with Kelvin and the others, but our relationship was always hindered by some unspoken conversation that we never seemed to have. It didn't matter; the main thing was we were getting the paper to the printers on time each week and we all had the readers' best interests at heart. Magazines aren't a social club: the point of working on one is to entertain the readers, plain and simple.

We must have been doing something right because the next thing I knew I was being told that *2000 AD* had won an Eagle Award for favourite British comic, with Judge Dredd winning the category for favourite British comics character. 'What the heck are the Eagle Awards?' I asked. I discovered that one of the founders, Richard Burton, had recently joined the company and was working as the sub-editor on *Tiger*. It transpired that the awards were a newly established event organised by British fans of American comics. The idea was to honour professionals in the American industry with fans casting votes for their favourite writer, artist and, indeed, comics character. The arrival of *2000 AD* had encouraged the creation of a category featuring UK creators and comic titles. Fortunately, *2000 AD* now credited its contributors, something Kevin O'Neill had successfully championed, although the use of pseudonyms occasionally meant the true identity of the winner remained a secret. For example, T.B. Grover, who won favourite comic-book writer in the UK category, was none other than John Wagner. He told me he had chosen the name after listening to a radio play in which a distraught youngster announced to his mam that he had just been duffed up by 'Tubby Grover'. Such was the fervour of these comics fans that they organised conventions to celebrate their passion, even inviting a favoured writer or artist over from America to attend and speak on a panel. Feeding this passion were specialist importers of American comics. These youthful entrepreneurs would organise comics marts, where British fans, keen to fill gaps in their collections, would gather *en masse* to scour stalls laden with back issues of such titles as *The Flash*, *Green Lantern*, *Batman* and, of course, *Superman*.

It was a whole new world to me and I was struck by its cultish customs and practices. Comics marts in London were often held at the Central Hall in Westminster. These gatherings also provided an informal meeting place for UK professionals and it was not unusual to see the cream of British talent scoffing tea and iced buns in the café on a wet Saturday afternoon, most of them in a breakout session from an intense period of autograph-signing in the main hall. Nearby stood the Houses of Parliament, but I often thought it was the writers and artists, not the politicians, who were shaping the views of the savvy young collectors who thronged the Hall's cavernous rooms.

Despite this introduction to the world of comics conventions, marts and fans, I remained convinced that the majority of *2000 AD*'s readers were everyday schoolkids. Sure, some of them would develop a passion for *2000 AD*, but not one I suspected that would make them paid-up members of the larger world of 'Fandom'. Either way, we chose to celebrate the awards by announcing them on the front cover of Prog 134. For the cover image, Brian Bolland drew Judge Dredd superimposed on a picture of the awards logo, taken from the *Eagle* comic logo. It was a sweet rejoinder to our internal critics who still regarded *2000 AD* as a space oddity: to be tolerated, but only from behind raised eyebrows. No one dared challenge the credibility of the awards, however, for to do so would be to sully the legacy of the *Eagle* itself, and that was a cherished part of the company's history.

The boom in science-fiction films aimed at a wider family audience had continued into 1979, with space being the primary theme. Disney released *The Black Hole*, which was followed by *Buck Rogers in the 25th Century*, albeit a made-for-TV movie. Former James Bond Sean Connery popped up later in the year in the disaster movie *Meteor*. Adult fans got *Alien* (rated 15 by the British Board of Film Censors) and *Mad Max* (rated 18) among other, more offbeat releases. However, the big, big film due for release at Christmas was the hugely anticipated *Star Trek: The Motion Picture*.

Fortunately, two unrelated projects had recently come into *2000 AD*'s orbit that allowed us to surf this wave of space movies and trade on its popularity. The first project was a strip that had been scripted for *Starlord* but which not been drawn. The second was from a much more unusual source: it was a comic-strip adaptation of a novel starring Slippery Jim DiGriz, otherwise know as *The Stainless Steel Rat*.

The person behind the idea to seek permission for a comic-strip adaptation of *The Stainless Steel Rat* was Kelvin Gosnell. The book's author was Harry Harrison, famed figure in science-fiction circles, itinerant writer and prolific author. At their first meeting, Gosnell and Harrison got on like a house on fire and when Carlos Ezquerra came aboard as artist the project had 'winner' written all over it. In an introduction written specially for *2000 AD*, Harrison described his cosmic crook as 'a super dropout. The antihero who does all the things we wish we could do ourselves and gets away with it'. Unfortunately, an error on my part led to the intro appearing after the story (rather than before) generating a humorously scolding letter from Harry, which we printed, thereby gaining him a £3 postal order prize, and my lasting appreciation for being so understanding. Happily, the strip was a big success with the readers. Internally it gave us a measure of prestige, too, completely wrong-footing the raised-eyebrow brigade. Two more keenly scripted adaptations were to follow from Kelvin, but in 1988 a suggestion to adapt a fourth book was received coolly by the editorial team at the time, and *The Stainless Steel Rat* has remained under the comics floorboards ever since.

The strip that had been scripted for *Starlord* was by Gerry Finley-Day. It was called *The V.C.s* and was set in a future where combat corps scour the solar system in search of alien invaders named Geeks. In a reader survey in Prog 117, future-war had polled strongly as a favourite type of story so we were delighted to get our hands on the strip. Moreover, this was perfect scripting territory for Gerry. All the war-strip skills he had developed on *Battle Picture Weekly* could be applied to this similar scenario, but set in the far future. The strip was told in the first person, its protagonist narrating the story in similar, deadpan manner to Captain Willard in the film *Apocalypse Now*. After we had coined the catchphrases 'You're hit, you're dead' and 'Suck it in', *The V.C.s* appeared ready to fly, but there were two problems: the strip had no artist and each episode had been written at twice the length of a normal *2000 AD* episode. I decided to sub each episode into two parts myself. In a way it felt like I was back on *Battle*, working with Gerry on a new strip.

As I began this task, I found myself retyping the whole of the first episode, cutting pictures and generally tidying up dialogue as I went along. I knew Gerry would not mind because this was the only way to prepare the strip for *2000 AD*. The deeper I delved into the initial scripts the more I felt like I was on a journey akin to the protagonist Smith, or indeed Marlow, the narrator of the source novella *Heart of Darkness*. I became immersed in the world of *The V.C.s*. It was rewarding work.

The scripts focused on a team of dysfunctional soldiers, trapped in a future-war scenario, united solely by their loathing of their superiors. All I had to do was keep the dialogue terse and the mood dark. Into this mix was sprinkled occasionally knowing references to contemporary culture (song lyrics and suchlike) to strike a chord with the audience. Above all, of course, I made sure to ensure a goodly count of extra-terrestrials being vaporised. Gerry's controlling idea for the strip was stated in the opening episode, where *The V.C.s* shun glitzy labels such as Star Troopers or Space Warriors, explaining that their chosen label of the V.C.s is a private joke: the initials in this case standing for Vacuum

Cleaners, because even having a name as stupid as that is not as ridiculous as warfare itself.

Asking Mike McMahon if he would draw the first episode (designing the characters, hardware, and spaceships along the way) solved the artist problem. What he created was everything we could have wanted and more. There was a buzz gathering around *The V.C.s* and despite its influences it felt fresh and just right for *2000 AD*'s audience. I even contributed some scripts, including a two-part story put together with one of the artists sharing the strip, Garry Leach, whose artistic star was in the ascendance. We liked the idea of the ship's computer copping a hippy attitude, its dull hologram changing to that of a dude with long hair, and shades, wearing a Sergeant Pepperish tunic, its speech patterns peppered with the argot of 1970s counterculture. It was fun.

The other artist sharing the strip was Cam Kennedy, who lived on the Orkney Isles and was perpetually having his roof blown off by hurricane-force gales caused by storms originating in the Atlantic. I know this because he used to casually mention the fact when we spoke on the telephone, much as one might casually mention the late arrival of a bus or train. Despite these violent tempests, Cam always made sure his artwork was posted on time.

Very occasionally, Cam would travel to London to deliver his artwork in person. Dinner would be taken accompanied by whichever contributors were also visiting the office, usually a 'kilter' of fellow Scots. On one occasion, towards the end of the meal, Cam chided the waiter in a jovial way about the cost of the mixed vegetables compared with his locally grown produce. The vegetables were shockingly pricey, it was true, but it was an expense-account dinner and I was paying so I didn't think it mattered. However, a spirited dialogue soon developed between our table and the waiter, and then the manager appeared. I quickly paid the bill and shepherded everyone outside, but as we stood around idly on the cobblestones of Southwark I heard a police-car siren, not unusual for that part of London, but paranoia suddenly seized me. Had the manager called the police in revenge for our questioning the price of his veg? And if he had, how could I protect my artists and writers from what would surely be an interesting conversation. 'I am the law,' would be the copper's opening line, to which someone would surely reply, good-naturedly, 'No, *I* am the law, and for that matter I'm also the judge and the jury!' I could imagine this would be the sentence that would get us all nicked, with our next stop being Clink Street, former home of the notorious prison that gave its name to all others. Then what? Would I be able to claim the cost of my party's bail on my expenses form? It seemed doubtful, although I had heard of some pretty dubious claims in the past. I shared these fears aloud with my Caledonian companions but no one appeared to be listening, and if they were it was obvious they were not in the slightest bit bothered by what might happen, quietly laughing and joking in the dark as they were, unlike me the 'softy Sassenach' quivering in the background. Fortunately, the sirens died away, silence returned, and we made our way back to our respective dwellings.

During a visit to the office by Pat Mills I had showed him Cam's debut artwork on the strip and he was politely impressed. That gave me a big boost and indeed Cam went on to become a mainstay of *2000 AD*, his art eventually gracing *Judge Dredd*. In due course, and on the basis of this work, Cam got a call to present himself at DC Comics in Manhattan. Having given his name 'Cam Kennedy' at the reception he was asked to repeat himself to verify the surname. 'Say again... you are Kenny *who?*' This exchange has passed into comic-book legend and led to the creation of Kenny Who?, a hapless comics artist from the CalHab Zone, whose dreams of making it big on the other side of the Black Atlantic always come to naught.

Both new strips began in Prog 140 dated 24 November. *The V.C.s* ran for thirty-two episodes and once again demonstrated Gerry's ability to keep an audience hooked, returning for more space action, week in week out. Also in that issue we ran a competition to win Dinky models of the *USS Enterprise* and a Klingon Cruiser. The front cover featured the *Enterprise* powering through deep space, allowing *2000 AD* to bask in the hype surrounding the *Star Trek* movie. Inside, *Judge Dredd* featured a four-part story set in the Cursed Earth, and Blackhawk became trapped inside a black hole. The only letdown was Wolfie Smith, whose story involved him battling a beast of darkness called the Wendigore. Or 'playing with his Wendy House', as Robin Smith put it rather cuttingly, because that was about as scary as the strip got.

In the next issue, we switched our focus from space travel to time travel by boldly announcing that it was possible to look back in time. As a kid I had been fascinated by time travel and this interest had continued into adulthood. So when I saw an article in *Nova* magazine on the subject I bought a copy and swiftly decamped to the nearest watering hole, there to learn more. Resolutely ignoring the synthetic, siren-like call of the *Space Invaders* machine (I was never any good at it anyway and much preferred *Missile Command*) I took a large swallow of lager, lit a Marlboro, and turned to the appropriate page, inhaling deeply. By the time I had finished, the kid in me was so excited by the article's contents that I wanted to share it with the readers. I was sure they would be as amazed as I was by the author's contention that, provided they had a telescope powerful enough, and were in space looking at the Earth, they could see back in time. How far back in time would depend on how far away they were; station themselves in the Orion constellation and the light from Earth would be nine hundred years old. In this situation and with their super-telescope pointed at England, say, they would be witnessing life in Norman times. My mind boggled. We had already been running an occasional book-review page (science-fiction related) and planned to feature reviews of film and even bands in due course, so I thought a feature on time travel would fit nicely. Looking for the author's name, I discovered that it was none other than Patrick Moore, the eccentric presenter of *The Sky at Night*. What a coup, I thought. If I can get his permission to reprint the article, not only will the coverline 'Patrick Moore Writes for You' quell the internal mutterings that *2000 AD* was staffed by mavericks (how could we be, when we were hobnobbing with establishment figures such as the esteemed Mr Moore?), but also the article would be thought-provoking to our readers, no doubt prompting birthday requests for 'One of them telescopes that can look back in time, please.'

I contacted Moore and he gave permission to reprint the article, but insisted on sending me his original text, when I could have just copied it from *Nova*. However, when the text arrived in the post (wrongly addressed to *Zodiac* magazine) my heart sank. It was much, much longer than had appeared in *Nova*. Obviously, a sub-editor at *Nova* had cut Moore's original text and he had not noticed. I gave the text to Alan and asked him to sub it down to a similar, manageable length, just as *Nova* had done. I don't think Alan thought Patrick Moore was quite the sort of person who should be writing for *2000 AD* and he set about the text with a certain amount of zeal, his green ink pen moving across each line at speeds similar to those mentioned in the article. When he returned the text to me I saw he had done a marvellous job, making the theory more reader-friendly and working Tharg's home sun, the red giant of Betelgeuse (520 light-years away) into the piece, but I knew I would have to show it to Moore before publication, if only because it was going to appear under his name, and he could hardly fail to notice the prodigious amounts of green ink that now decorated every page. I posted the subbed text to him the next day and waited. His reply was by return. We were not to touch a single word in the piece and it was to run as originally supplied. I was caught in a Mexican standoff. I could have spiked the feature, but I still felt the readers would be intrigued by the theory. What to do? I knew I couldn't be seen to have wasted Alan's time, still less be seen to be siding with Moore. I was foxed until I realised that Moore believed the piece was to appear in *Zodiac* magazine. Brilliant. That's where he would look for it, not in a children's comic, and when he couldn't find it he would assume it hadn't been used. I gravely announced to the office that I was sticking by Alan's version and ceremoniously sent the text to the typesetters. The piece appeared in Prog 141, without comment from any quarter, and everyone moved on.

Once a year it was an editor's duty to take the managing director out to lunch. When my turn came in the autumn I chose to visit Ken Lo's Memories of China, if only because it was the most expensive place I could think of. A company car duly deposited us in Belgravia and we shared some lukewarm conversation over starters of bang-bang chicken and five-spice spare ribs. I am not a gregarious dinner companion and I just minded my table manners, trying not to lodge a chopstick in a nasal cavity or drink from my finger bowl. In the car on the way back, the MD turned and said something rather odd. He asked about Alan. Was Alan a 'union man'? I knew Alan was a man of forceful views, but that didn't make him an activist, which was what I inferred from the phrase. I paused, before pointing out that we were all union men, as membership of the National Union of Journalists was compulsory. In point of fact there hadn't been one dispute since I had joined, so membership didn't seem to matter either way. Silence descended. I wondered if the board feared a revitalised NUJ, armed with serious plans to improve the pay and conditions of its members. If that were the case then probably the word would have gone out from on high to identify potential firebrands. This sounded worrying and, as it turned out, the company and the NUJ were to lock horns in a serious dispute the very next year.

Engrossed in such thoughts, I realised my own first year as editor was drawing to a close. In the canteen at lunch one day I happened to mention that I thought the paper was in quite good shape, what with me being 'a rookie editor an' all'. Embarrassed looks were exchanged. Alan disagreed, without being specific. Colin appeared to share Alan's judgment and I was left rather shaken. Obviously I had been deluding myself. I was glad they were both honest, though, because that lunchtime conversation made me realise *2000 AD* wasn't even close to rediscovering its mojo, despite the quality of the issues following the merger with *Starlord*. I was going to have to raise my game. The objective was a state of maximum Thrill-power, where each strip in every issue would be *zarjaz*. The work we had put into Prog 140 had been a good start, and the coming dawn of a new decade would be a great place to continue.

1980: OF STRIKES AND LAWMEN

1980 WAS TO be a defining year for Judge Dredd, with three stories in particular marking his development into Britain's favourite comics character. The strip's fame was to spread to America, where one top executive from Marvel Comics would proclaim Dredd to be 'the best comic creation since the Second World War'. In the style of American comics, a gang of novel lawbreakers was created to populate Dredd's world, some droll, some homicidal, and some heroic. But of all these villains surely the most memorable is Judge Death.

Death is the antithesis of Dredd, a psychopathic lawkeeper from another dimension, a place where all life is adjudged to be a crime. In his debut story, Judge Death sets about judging the citizenry of Mega-City One, pronouncing, 'The crime is life, the sentence is death.' This motto is followed by his executioner's slogan, 'I just put my hand in and squeeze.' Introducing the story, Tharg told his readers he thought the art was 'some of the best and most sinister comic artwork ever published.' The illustrator was Brian Bolland and rarely can fifteen pages of comics art have caused such a stir. The story unfolded over three episodes, and we in editorial waited until Brian had delivered the third episode before scheduling publication. This was because Brian was putting his life and soul into the art, with its estimated completion date turning from weeks into months. When Brian brought the first episode into the office we goggled in amazement at its sheer perfection. The story had also introduced a new Judge, her name being Cassandra Anderson. Brian's depiction of her was sublime. I did query her left nostril, which was smaller than the other. Brian chided me, pointing out that in real life most people's nostrils were asymmetrical. I shut up, feeling like a nitpicking nose-picker. Whatever delivery deadlines had been set for episodes two and three were quietly forgotten. Work of this standard could not be rushed. For form's sake, though, I still telephoned Brian regularly, doggedly enquiring as to his progress on the remaining pages. The nature of my calls was humorously acknowledged in episode three, where he drew a corpse in a morgue with a toe tag reading: 'MacManus. S. Terminal brainstorm.'

When John Wagner saw the art he was equally impressed, but did grumble that Anderson's high-heeled boots were not suitable for a Judge. Having criticised a nostril, I was not about to query a heel, so I did nothing at the time. But when Anderson returned, in *Judge Death Lives*, her footwear was standard Justice Department issue.

Reports of the artwork quickly circulated within the *2000 AD* freelance community. Visitors would request to see 'the Bolland art' and whistle softly at its beauty. When it finally appeared in Progs 149-151 it silenced even our sternest critics within the company, including the diehard aesthetes who maintained that the art in *Eagle* comic could never be bettered.

The second story that shaped Dredd's development was a three-parter by Pat Mills called *The Blood of Satanus*. I say 'shaped' because at the time details of Dredd's past were still sketchy, even though the title was approaching its third birthday. Yes, we knew that Dredd was a clone of the Chief Judge. Yes, we knew that he had been trained for fifteen years at the Academy of Law, the toughest school on Earth, before being allowed to dispense justice on the streets. Initially this would have been under scrutiny, wearing the white helmet and half-eagle badge of a rookie Judge. When not on the streets we knew Dredd lived a Spartan life, his sole pastime being the study of his law books. In the story *The Return of Rico* (Prog 30) also written by Pat Mills, we had learnt of Dredd's criminal clone-brother – and watched Dredd draw fastest in a shootout between the two. In Prog 116, written by John Wagner, we had learnt that Rico had a daughter named Vienna, whom Dredd felt responsible for. And that was about it for backstory. So when the scripts for *The Blood of Satanus* arrived in the post, I was not unduly surprised when the storyline introduced a woman called Lynsey Peters, of whom Dredd said in dialogue, '*I used to go out with her.*' In the story, a dinosaur has just eaten Lynsey and Dredd is remembering this apparent old flame. 'That's interesting,' I thought. Obviously Dredd didn't have girlfriends anymore, but it was intriguing to think he had once had an emotional connection, similar to the familial one felt for Vienna.

I gave the scripts to Ron Smith's agent and thought no more about it until the art arrived. Looking through the pages I saw Ron had captured the story's black humour perfectly and I passed the episodes to Alan to sub the dialogue, ready for lettering. A while later, Alan called over to me from his desk. He was deeply unhappy. The story's proposal that Dredd had gone out with a girl in the past was 'ridiculous'. The controlling idea of Judge Dredd was that he had been tutored, schooled and trained to serve the Law and nothing but the Law. There would have been no time for emotional attachments. As Alan was living in a farmhouse with John at the time, I took this doctrinaire view to be shared by John. We agreed that Alan would change the dialogue to exclude all references to a previous relationship between Lynsey and Dredd. I supposed that John's view was that Dredd now needed to become utterly impassive, a judicial martinet nicknamed 'Old Stony-Face' by his colleagues and as unyielding as the cast-iron police boxes to be found in Scottish cities.

Alan had described these to me once, explaining how the police would sit in them at night, balefully eyeing the citizens as they passed by. Apparently, if they didn't like the look of you they would call you over for a 'chat'. What happened next would depend on the depth of your civility, not to mention sobriety. It sounded terrifying, with the implied threat of physical violence or sudden arrest or both. But, whatever the spur had been for John's new direction, one thing was certain: the events surrounding *The Blood of Satanus* had ensured that Dredd's character traits were now also cast in iron.

The third story to shape Judge Dredd was *The Judge Child Quest*, a space epic totalling twenty-six episodes. Written by John Wagner and drawn by Messrs Bolland, McMahon and (Ron) Smith, it tells of the search for Owen Krysler, *'The boy with the Eagle of Justice mark on his forehead'*. A pre-cog has predicted Krysler is fated to rule Mega-City One in its gravest hour, thus saving the city. Dredd's quest to find the Judge Child takes him first across the Cursed Earth to Texas City and then into outer space, encountering many bizarre beings along the way. The story introduces fabled members of the Dredd universe such as the Angel Gang and Judge

Hershey, not to mention the Judge Child himself. In addition, it develops Dredd's character, revealing a profound dislike of facial hair. When Dredd orders crew member Lopez to take Oracle Spice, a hallucinogen that may help them locate the Judge Child, Lopez objects, citing Dredd's suspected distaste of his moustache as the real reason he's been chosen. Dredd does not yield and Lopez subsequently dies from the effects of the spice, but not before we witness him hallucinating. We commissioned Brian Bolland to draw a front cover of this scene, with Lopez recoiling in fear as he sees a tortuous vision of Dredd and Hershey standing over him. I had my fingers crossed that there would be no murmurs from management. After all, it could have been argued by an ill-wisher that we were showing someone tripping, which could then have been construed as akin to having a banner on the cover saying, 'Hey, kids, try *these* acid drops!' Upon publication nothing came of it, though, probably because the closest management had got to embracing the counter-culture was using the word 'psychedelic'. But I did get a couple of meaningful looks in the lift, as if to say, 'Don't push your luck, MacManus.'

Judge Death, *The Blood of Satanus*, *The Judge Child Ques*t: these three stories, following one after the other, fleshed out Dredd's world and provided a rock-solid spine to *2000 AD*'s editorial content during 1980. The continuing strips *Blackhawk*, *The V.C.s* and *The Stainless Steel Rat* offered strong support, ticking the science fantasy, comic science fiction and future-war genres respectively. In addition, a short-run strip called *Fiends of the Eastern Front*, whose unique proposition of vampires operating in World War II remains a minor triumph, also went down well with the readers. I contributed a four-part denouement to *M.A.C.H. Zero* in which the long-term effects of Compu-

Puncture Hyper Power are slowly killing him. Zero seeks only to die in peace, passing his remaining days working as a railway porter. I thought this warped example of the negation of the negation, where a character is portrayed as having reached rock bottom by working for British Rail, was entirely in keeping with 2000 AD's darkly comic view of the world, but I'm not sure anyone else got the joke. The story itself was influenced by events surrounding the character of Jim Prideaux in Le Carré's *Tinker Tailor Soldier Spy*. As with Zero, Prideaux has suffered a personal disaster while working for the British secret service. I liked the way both of them sought anonymity in a caravan, each binding their wounds at night behind curtains closed in weary resignation from society. But in truth my farewell to *M.A.C.H. Zero* was a simple story, and had nothing exceptional to offer beyond a picture of a Mickey Mouse phone being demolished and a nicely structured beginning, middle and end. Weaker fare still was to be found in returning strips like *Wolfie Smith* and *Timequake*, which both suffered from run-of-the-mill artwork. Restoring the title's mojo was still proving elusive.

While 2000 AD's editorial content remained constant for the first half of 1980 its staffing changed significantly, so that by midsummer the title had a new sub-editor and a new art editor. Alan left to go freelance in the spring, quickly forming an impressive writing partnership with John Wagner. Richard Burton, whose good looks were more akin to those of Louis XIII than his film-star namesake, succeeded Alan. Richard quickly made his mark by introducing a new young artist to 2000 AD named Steve Dillon. Not only was Steve a talent for the future, he would also reveal himself to be a skilled pool player. It seemed pool was the game to play at the time and before long most every pub had a table installed. My first introduction to the game was courtesy of John Wagner. We came across a table in a local pub one night and we put our money down to play the winner of the current game. I went first and before each shot John called out instructions from his stool at the bar. I was told to, 'Use some top', or, 'Play it with side', or, 'Give it plenty of bottom!' The black ball wasn't the black ball, it was 'the eight'. Two shots were not two extra shots, they were 'two misses', and so on. Despite all this coaching I remained convinced for at least six months that to pot the object ball your cue had to strike the white ball on the side, not in the centre. Robin was a keen pool player too and before long we had organized a *2000 AD* pool team, playing friendlies against Marvel UK staff and a team from Steve Dillon's local pub, the Assembly House in Kentish Town.

Colin and Kelvin departed in May, each to pursue a freelance career. We were fortunate that Kelvin continued to script *The Stainless Steel Rat*. As with Alan, I felt Kelvin was better suited to the freelance life. The constrictions of working for a company, where no one wanted to be seen rocking the boat, suited neither of them. Unemployment was rising fast and the economy had just entered a recession. Magazine jobs were scarce and people were keeping their heads down, clinging to whatever role they had. It was not a time for mavericks.

Upon Colin's departure, Robin stepped up to take over his role as art editor and suddenly we were a new team, eager to pool our talents in the quest to produce the best comic in the UK, not to mention publish something to be admired by our industry cousins in America. We had gained an honorary team member, too, by the name of Tom Frame. Tom had become the regular freelance letterer on *Judge Dredd* and now he was also colouring the centre spreads. Tom took to coming to the office every day, and he made the spare desk opposite mine his home from home. Among many other attributes, Tom was also a skilled pool player and it was he who put me right on how to strike the white ball. In fact, Tom did a lot more than that and in a way became my mentor. He always had good advice, which I received gratefully, especially after the occasional bruising phone call from an irate contributor. On these occasions, his advice came in one word: 'Pub.' If ever there was a fifth member of the *2000 AD* staff, it was Tom Frame.

We had also acquired a new group editor along the way. He was a tall, bespectacled man and, as with his predecessor, had to be shown each issue before we sent it to press. His feedback was delivered through marks out of ten for each strip. I felt like I was back at school when I made the weekly trip with each new issue to his office. Other than that, he did not interfere too much, apart from banning the use of the word 'POP' on a cover. Apparently it was slang for the word 'fart', which, so they tell me, is an offensive term meaning to release intestinal gases through the anus, usually with an accompanying sound. His stable of comics contained *Tiger*, *Battle-Action*, *Roy of the Rovers* and a newly launched but soon to crash-and-burn comic named *Speed*. His editorial philosophy was to populate these titles with articles written by sports stars and celebrities of the day. As such it was not uncommon to bump into Ernie Wise or Eric Morecambe in the lift, on their way to a *Tiger* 'awards' lunch in the directors' dining room. Geoff Boycott, Peter Shilton and the wrestler Big Daddy were other well-known guests; each one's visit subsequently reported in the house journal, along with photos of well-fed executives laughing uproariously at some clever lunchtime quip. (As it happened, *Battle* had boasted its own television celebrity for quite some time. Dick Emery was president of the Airfix Modellers Club and his photo appeared at the top of a weekly feature in *Battle* about kit-building sponsored by Airfix. The connection between a man whose catchphrase was 'Hello, Honky Tonks!' and model-making still eludes me, though.) The group editor was also an expert publicist. Somehow he obtained permission for Tharg to be photographed on the steps of 10 Downing Street. Dressed as the Mighty One, I was supposedly delivering a petition for intergalactic peace or some such nonsense. It was a hoot. On another occasion he persuaded the Duke of Edinburgh to write an introduction to the first issue of *Roy of the Rovers*. This lent credence to speculation that his ambition was to be included in the New Year Honours' List (for services to children's publishing) but such a dream was never mentioned to me.

During the staffing changes our union, the National Union Of Journalists, had been locked in negotiations with management over an improvement to its members' salaries. The offer on the table was a seventeen per cent increase in pay (one per cent below the rate of inflation). The union was holding out for a thirty-two per cent increase, and to press our claim we had voted for a one-day strike. Mandatory union meetings and further one-day strikes were threatened. The company's response was to issue all thirteen hundred journalists with dismissal notices on Sunday 25 April, so that come Monday morning Richard and I arrived at work to find ourselves jobless. The art department, who were members of a different union, were left to their own devices and our future plans for the title were in ruins.

It was a month before we were reinstated. In that time the dispute had a catastrophic effect on the production schedules of the company's magazines. Particularly hard hit was *2000 AD,* which disappeared from the newsstands for five whole weeks, much to the mystification of its readers. The last issue was Prog 164, dated 10 May, and it was not until 14 June that Prog 165 appeared. Alan wrote a spoof Tharg story to explain to the readers what had happened. In his version the droids fall under a spell cast by the Hag of Zrag and they strike for better conditions – at which point Tharg sacks them and editorial production is halted. When the story was published the last page appeared on the back cover and it must have caught someone's eye because I received an urgent phone call from the MD telling me to put on the Tharg costume straight away and go to a more senior executive's office. I was under the impression this was just a show-and-tell visit, but when I entered the office the secretary observed wryly, 'We've just been reading your story about the strike.' She ushered me into the executive's inner sanctum with a pitying look that seemed to say, 'Are you completely mad?' I suddenly realised there might be some form of reprimand in the offing, perhaps even a sacking for gross misconduct. But when you see standing before you a man dressed in a blue ski suit, wearing black motorbike boots, his face covered by a green Neanderthal mask with costume jewellery glued to the forehead, all this topped off with a blond, ponytailed wig, it's pretty hard not see the joke. And so it was for my senior executive. I left the office unscathed, realising that the phone call to dress as Tharg had been a clever way to defuse a potentially dangerous situation, showing as it did that Tharg was a comics concept and not some union firebrand, pedalling anti-management propaganda to the innocent youth of Britain.

The after-effects of the strike were blown away by the buzz surrounding the second *Star Wars* film. Surfing the wave of anticipation concerning the movie's release, we ran a competition to win *The Empire Strikes Back* electronic games and action figures. Brian Bolland drew a fabulously detailed front cover featuring the action figures and its powerful imagery of Luke Skywalker & co just seemed to confirm *2000 AD*'s emerging reputation for Thrill-powered entertainment. While other magazines had used stills from the film, we had gone one better and produced a unique, illustrated image. *2000 AD*'s street cred was boosted further in the very next prog when Pat Mills and Kevin O'Neill unveiled their next co-creation, *Comic Rock*. This was their planned series of strips to be inspired by breaking bands of the day, and The Jam's 'Going Underground' provided the background for the first story. Only one more *Comic Rock* story appeared, but it did mark *2000 AD*'s growing synergy with the music scene of the time.

August saw the much-anticipated publication of the *Judge Dredd Annual*, which was launched with a signing by the writers and artists at Forbidden Planet in Denmark Street, London. This was the science-fiction bookshop Nick Landau had opened when he left IPC. The signing was pre-advertised in *2000 AD* and the queue stretched around the corner into St Giles High Street. I noticed a good proportion of the queue were teenagers and it occurred to me that, unlike other comic readerships, these kids had chosen to keep buying *2000 AD* after the age of twelve. What's more, it wasn't just a signed copy they were after; they were anxious to meet the creators. This was my first appreciation of the growing celebrity of *2000 AD*'s writers and artists. It was clear they were fast becoming big names in comics, but I had no idea they would soon be revered with the same enthusiasm as that displayed by a film fanatic or sports aficionado. The signing started at

2.00 p.m. and the last customer was served three hours later. As they totted up the day's extraordinary takings, a member of staff turned to me and said the signing had saved the shop from a cash-flow crisis. I said I was pleased to have helped, what with having ousted Nick from *2000 AD* the year before. After that, Forbidden Planet signings by *2000 AD*'s creators became an annual event and they were a win-win occasion for all involved. Nick and I went on to meet regularly, usually at the Rasa Sayang in Chinatown, where we would drink Mai Tais and chew satay chicken while swapping industry news and general comics gossip.

By the end of 1980 I had settled on a publishing strategy to promote *2000 AD* at the start of each autumn term. This meant scheduling new strips to start in September and ensuring continuing characters began fresh adventures at the same time. The target was potential new readers, aged around eight or nine, who were just starting secondary school. The plan was they would come across the promoted issue, plastered with the words 'New' and 'Featuring Judge Dredd' at their local newsagent and, enticed by the stunning strips, make a spur of the moment decision to purchase. Having read it and become hooked, they would then spread the word at school, perhaps even taking the issue with them, thereby introducing yet more potential new readers to the world of Tharg and Thrill-power. The title was also promoted each February, to celebrate its birthday. This policy meant the summer progs were not as strong as they could be, only because we were saving the best Thrills for the autumn. This Thrill-power shortage became something of an urban gripe among the title's older fans, but as the majority of the readership was away on holiday once school was over, or else they were playing out late, it seemed foolish to promote the title during the summer.

In the army now... *Battle* launched in March 1975 to great success, featuring characters such as The Sarge (below) and Major Eazy (bottom).

Ace pilot Johnny Red was a popular addition to *Battle*'s line-up.

Art editor Doug Church (on left) and editor Dave Hunt in 1979.

By 1977, *Battle* had joined forces with *Valiant* (left). (Below) John Wagner's first series for *Battle* after going freelance was the violent and uncompromising *Darkie's Mob*, which debuted in August 1976.

With stories such as *Kids Rule OK* and *Hook Jaw*, *Action* was causing waves that would ultimately see it pulled from newsagents' shelves eight months after it was launched.

The crushing power of the Great White's jaws were too much for Red McNally.

YA DUMB CRITTER. I'LL GET YA YET.... AAAAAGGGGGHHHH!!!

Soon—all that was left was the ruins of the rig and the Great White Shark — Hook Jaw!

"SHARKS CANNOT BE TAMED, THEY CANNOT BE DOMESTICATED, THEY CANNOT BE HERDED INTO GAME PARKS AND THEY CANNOT BE EXTERMINATED". J. & P. Cousteau, 'The Shark — Splendid Savage of the Seas' (Cassell 1970)

Action's resident stunt hero *Action Man* tackles the challenges suggested by the readership, including snake-handling and fire-eating...

...making him the public face of what was becoming an increasingly controversial title.

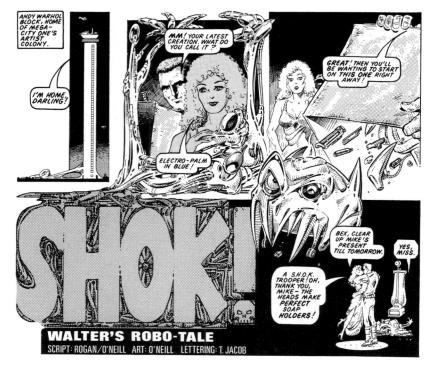

1977, and the being from Betelgeuse arrives on Earth, bringing the gift of *2000 AD*. One year later, and the sister title *Starlord* ceased publication after twenty-two issues and was merged into the prog, bringing with it *Strontium Dog* and *Ro-Busters*.

Bottom left: The one-off *SHOK!* by MacManus (under the pseudonym Ian Rogan) and Kevin O'Neill, which would later form the basis of the movie *Hardware*.

Below: The popularity of the Galaxy's Greatest Comic grows as (from left to right) Brian Bolland, Mick McMahon, John Wagner and Ron Smith sign copies of the 1981 *Judge Dredd Annual*.

The notorious (in the eyes of the Portsmouth Association for Community Standards, at least) page from *The Bad Boys Bust*...

THE PRESS COUNCIL

No. 1 SALISBURY SQUARE, LONDON EC4Y 8AE

ESTABLISHED 1953
Tel: 01-353 1248

Chairman: F. P. NEILL Q.C.
Director: KENNETH MORGAN O.B.E.

Please quote our reference: S8425

FIRST CLASS

S. McManus, Esq.,
Editor,
2000 AD,
IPC Magazines Ltd,
King's Reach Tower,
Stamford Street,
LONDON,
SE1 9LS.

20 Oct 81

Dear Mr McManus.

Further to my letter to the Assistant Managing Director of 1 May 81 I am happy to inform you that Portsmouth Association for Community Standards have now told the Press Council they are not proceeding with their complaint against 2000 AD.

This case has accordingly been marked on the file as Not Pursued.

I enclose a copy of this letter for the Group Editor.

Yours sincerely,

James Dewen
Assistant Secretary

...who would later decide to take no action against *2000 AD*.

DREDD AT THE

He's four years old. He's inspired one Human League song, and another is on the way from Spizz. His fans include Madness's Suggsy, various ex-Specials, around half a million schoolkids and, recently, a fair number of the vast section of the populace who read the national 'newspaper' *The Star*.

He's Judge Dredd, arguably the first home-grown comic-strip character to both garner and deserve a national following spanning the familiar 6-60 age group since 1950's adventurer Dan Dare.

Dredd's the star of the comic weekly 2000 AD, a futuristic Dirty Harry whose main beat is Megacity 1, the vast metropolis which, in Dredd's hypothetical 22nd Century, covers most of the US east coast.

Started in 1977 alongside a short-lived companion paper *Starlord*, 2000 AD has a current weekly sales figure of 120,000, with most of them around the 15-mark age-wise, but dropping down as far as four year-olds and extending upwards and outwards to include everyone from the aforementioned pop musicians, to strippers, soldiers, and unemployed university graduates.

2000 AD differs from its stablemates in the IPC comics division, *Roy Of The Rovers*, *Battle* and *Tiger*, in being totally concerned with things to come. It's also been the repository for some of the most exciting comic-strip art to have come out of Britain in several years, with artists like Brian Bolland, Mike McMahon and the highly psychedelic Kevin O'Neill being at the very least the equals of their counterparts in the American Marvel Comic stable or the French-based Metal Hurlant monthly (*Heavy Metal* in its *National Lampoon*-funded US incarnation).

And it's a lot of fun. The weekly's private mythology insists that it's written, drawn, lettered and inked by a team of robots supervised by Tharg, an all-powerful alien editor.

2000 AD's actual Earthly location is somewhat more prosaic, being some eighty square yards of office space half-way up the IPC tower block HQ on London's South Bank. Tharg's human alter ego is a soft-spoken, bearded young man named Steve MacManus, the comic's third editor to date, previous incumbents having "succumbed to breakdowns or left with recriminations on both sides". Clearly, being The Mighty Tharg is no piece of cake.

The main problem, it transpires, is one of excessive violence, something which the highly popular Judge Dredd seems to encounter (or more often dole out) on a 24-hour basis. What IPC's high-ups haven't cottoned on to is the fact that a good half of the 2000 AD readership are now in their mid-teens, most of them having stuck with the paper since its 1977 start.

"That makes it a bit difficult," says MacManus, "because it's no longer the ten to twelve age group that an IPC boys comic *should* be aiming at.

"So every 18 months or so we get really hammered and everything has to die down again." Despite the mag's overflow into other markets – Judge Dredd's weekly appearance in Saturday's *Star*, plus syndications to Australia, France, Germany and even a few fans in Moscow – another crackdown is just about imminent, says Tharg/MacManus.

He mentions a story about a shotgun killer a few months back which unhappily ran simultaneously with the Reagan assassination attempt as having brought down particular amounts of wrath from above.

IT WAS THE LITTLE THINGS THAT HAD WORRIED HIM AT FIRST... THE WAY HIS FINGERS WERE TURNING INTO TENTACLES, THE SHAGGY HAIR SPROUTING FROM HIS NOSTRILS, HIS RED SCALEY SKIN.

BE PURE

NERVOUSLY HE HAD CONSULTED HIS BESTIARY...

"We've arrived at a minor crossroads now: we could double the price and use better paper and go for a higher market of 16 year-olds and we'd be okay; then we could say, right, it's not for kids. Or we might have to amalgamate with another comic and end up having to water everything down again."

Despite the storm clouds, Judge Dredd's entrenchment as a national icon goes on apace: his second annual's just out, a board game and a watch are on the cards, and there's a Judge Dredd '45 ready to go as soon as a record company (Stiff would be ideal says MacManus) of suitable shape and size comes along. Other projects are at the discussion stage: one's a short support movie, either animated or live action, and a possible radio series is also being discussed.

"That'd be great," says McManus. "Imagine the sound effects – the hubbub of a city with eight hundred million people!"

The other 2000 AD offshoot is the recently published *The Chronicles of Judge Dredd* (Titan Books, £2.95), a collection of the best of the early Dredd stories by writer Brian Wagner and artist Brian Bolland. This started as an IPC project that was ditched for apparently lacking adequate commercial potential and then 'leased' to Titan, an offshoot of Forbidden Planet, the London and New York-based comic, fantasy film and sf megastores, who started out in this market with a series of excellent but somewhat costly Dredd posters.

The Chronicles establish Bolland as one of the country's most imaginative and entertaining artists, his strong lines providing what many fans rate as the definitive Dredd, while a sharply humorous visual imagination will frequently reward Dredd's worldlier supporters with all manner of visual puns and echoes, including appearances within the stories of anyone from The Marx Brothers to Boris Karloff in 'Frankenstein 1970', or a lovingly drawn mad scientist character straight out of the crazy world of *Mad* regular Don Martin.

Steve MacManus, human alter-ego of 2000 AD's all-powerful alien 'editor' Tharg. Below, artist Brian Bolland whose visualisations of Judge Dredd have helped make the futuristic cop arguably the first home-grown comic-strip hero since Dan Dare. Bolland holds the 1980 *Eagle* award for Best British comic artist.

Photos by Ray Stevenson

CONTROLS

Bolland himself, despite such accolades as the 1980 *Eagle* award for best British comic artist, is a remarkably humble man. He much prefers the work of Mike McMahon, (subject of the forthcoming *Chronicles . . . 2)* and says: "I just followed his mutations and tried to make them look more real."

Bolland's career followed the familiar route: drawing comics as a kid, finding himself at art school, and then eventually ending up doing comics again. "I don't think it's a low-down occupation – you can do virtually anything in comic-strips that you could possibly want to do with graphics or painting." He's not put off by the 2000 AD system of a script being extremely specific about the contents of each frame he draws.

"If you draw something just for yourself you just tend to draw what you know you can draw. When you get a new script you'll find you've got to draw someone getting out of a London taxi or a bunch of Italian soldiers coming over a hill. And the first

reaction usually is, Oh God! I don't want to draw this! Then you do it."

Bolland (a Frank Zappa fan, incidentally) recalls 2000 AD's appearance being greeted with suggestions of fascism by the *NME*, and he's well aware of the old saws about the violent aspects of comic-strip art and their possible effects.

"But you usually find that you're pulling in the opposite direction from the scriptwriter. I tend to think that the bloke who writes Dredd sees him as a hero and identifies with him. But I tend to think of him as a bully, and I try to draw him in such a way that you don't feel any sympathy with him at all . . . so you get an interesting tug-of-war going on."

He mentions one story that had a bunch of 'muties' who wanted to raze Megacity 1 to the ground and go back to a simple agrarian life-style, a sort of future tense Greenpeace. "The writer wanted their leader, Father Earth, to look ridiculous. But I saw him as sympathetic – much more than Dredd.

"I like to draw things in a realistic

way. If there's violence, people being shot, I prefer to draw it in graphic detail – and I'll only stop when I'm told to cut down on the blood.

"There's this argument about whether you should stylise violence, turn it into slapstick – do a Marvel Comics," says Bolland. "The other argument is that if you see more and more graphic violence you just get immune to it."

Bolland says he's amazed at how seriously kids take the stories. "They always want to know what the characters do in their private lives." He mentions having attended a convention in the States recently where the majority of the fans' questions boiled down to: "Are The Vision and The Scarlet Witch in 'The Avengers' having sexual relations?"

"And if they accept that they're existing off-frame . . . where does that leave you about violence? Do they really believe people are getting their heads blown off? And do they care?

"And if they do believe it and they don't care, *then* we're in trouble." ■

Above: detail from a Judge Dredd adventure drawn by Brian Bolland. Facing page illustration by the psychedelic Kevin O'Neill.

Casa Mac takes shape with the launch of *Crisis* in September 1988.

Stories such *Third World War* and *New Statesmen* would be collected into *2000 AD Presents...* US-format prestige editions to penetrate the direct market.

Crisis was followed in 1990 by the short-lived *Revolver*. Despite an extensive signing tour – above, Grant Morrison, Brendan McCarthy, Rian Hughes, Peter Hogan and Charles Shaar Murray – the anthology lasted only seven issues. *Photo © Rian Hughes.* Below: *Diceman*, an experiment in interactive gaming comics. Below right: *True Faith*, a *Crisis* series that marked Garth Ennis out as a talent for the future.

The debut of the promotional strategy came with Prog 178, cover-dated 20 September and now priced at 14p. Robin had designed a sleek new *2000 AD* logo and the casual browser could not have failed to be impressed by it and the front cover's bold coverlines announcing 'Five New Stories!' and 'Featuring Britain's No.1 Sci-Fi Hero'. Also on the cover were the magic words 'Free Badge'. This was our first free gift since Prog 3 and the honour of appearing on the badge fell to Judge Dredd. His image was drawn by Mike McMahon, who also drew Dredd on the cover, his Lawgiver gun suitably set to fire bullet No 3: 'Incendiary'. For those who had yearned for a *Dredd* T-shirt, there was now a chance to win one inside the issue. And if they had £2.95 there was an advert urging them to send away for a giant *Dredd* poster, measuring a mighty five feet tall. We staffers realised these merchandising rights had obviously been licensed by some shadowy department, whose existence we were previously unaware of. We were irritated by the thought that strangers were 'getting to play with our toy', but nonetheless pleased the readers were gaining the chance to send off for merchandise. Whatever the deal, it was clear that *2000 AD* was becoming more than just a comic – it was turning into a brand.

The five new stories were actually four brand-new strips, all commissioned to appear alongside the return of *Strontium Dog*. Judge Dredd's quest to find the Judge Child continued in the centre pages. The four new strips each had a different genesis. *Meltdown Man* was written by Alan Hebden and drawn by Massimo Belardinelli. It filled the science-fantasy spot left vacant by *Blackhawk*. Ex-SAS soldier Nick Stone is atomised by an atomic bomb, but then finds himself alive in a parallel world where eugenically bio-formed animals work as slaves for their human masters. Naturally, Stone finds himself leading the animals in revolt against their masters. The strip suited artist Massimo Belardinelli perfectly as his human figures could look weak, but his animal art was superb. The bio-formed creatures in *Meltdown Man*, with their human shape and enhanced intelligence, made for strikingly effective pictures and Alan Hebden's clever script kept the readers coming back for more each week. I had a feeling that *Meltdown Man* played well with younger readers who were just joining the title, not to mention their parents. It certainly became a success, running for nearly a year. The strip was entirely Alan Hebden's idea and he wanted to call it *Yujee*. I thought something more reader-friendly was required, so I imposed the title *Meltdown Man* on him, not realising that if you missed the first episode, where Nick Stone is melted in the atomic explosion, you would spend the next forty-odd episodes waiting expectantly for this intriguing event to occur. Which is exactly what befell one reader who wrote in to enquire, rather acidly, when *Meltdown Man* was actually going to melt.

Tom Tully pitched *The Mean Arena* strip to me. I hadn't been overly impressed with his scripts for *The Mind Of Wolfie Smith*, but this near-future sports scenario seemed well worth considering, not least in recognition of the success of the *Harlem Heroes* strip in Prog 1. The sport, a mixture of paintball, football and American football, was played in sections of specially evacuated towns and cities with two sides stalking each other through the streets and buildings therein. These urban backdrops gave the strip a feeling similar to a film of the time called *The Warriors*, in which a stranded New York gang has to fight its way across rival gang territory in the Bronx and Manhattan, to reach its own hood. I was all for a bit of urban grit set in tomorrow's wasteland and I thought the strip was novel in that its games were to be played between towns and cities in the UK, a kind of 'Great British Face-Off'. Tully lived in Reading and I went down there to photograph backgrounds with him as reference for the artist. It felt like we might have an exciting prospect on our hands, especially if the strip's gameplay were to be imitated by the readership, perhaps playing a cutdown version on their bikes. Unfortunately, the artist struggled with the sports theme and never really got the best out of the scripts. A two-part fill-in by Steve Dillon showed what might have been: his art really brought the strip to life. Encouraged by this, we commissioned another series, with Steve as lead artist, and it ran successfully during 1981. The concept remains a great format for a reality TV programme, assuming the day comes when a TV company will be allowed to show a full-on contact sport, played out on the streets of inner cities, with roving referees carding players for overly violent conduct. The closed-circuit television cameras, envisaged in the strip to monitor every street and alleyway used in the game, are certainly already in place.

Dash Decent was, pure and simple, a spoof on the recently released *Flash Gordon* movie. It was the brainchild of Kevin O'Neill and he brought in writer Dave Angus to co-script it with him. The movie itself was a respectful spoof of the original 1930s newspaper strip and it has something of a cult status among today's film fans. O'Neill's art was lovingly crafted and we judged only Tom Frame skilful enough to letter the strip's dialogue balloons. Admirers of O'Neill's art would have been delighted to find Prog 178 also contained four pages of art for part one of a *Comic Rock* story inspired by the album *Killer Watts*. The strip was also notable for unveiling the character Nemesis, who would later become one of *2000 AD*'s all-time great creations.

The *Strontium Dog* adventures were the product of the newly formed Wagner-Grant writing partnership. They featured Johnny Alpha and his partner Wulf Sternhammer in witty, quick-fire escapades with titles like *Death's Head*, *The Schicklgruber Grab*, *Muties' Luck* and *The Doc Quince Case*. Carlos Ezquerra's artwork gave the stories a cool, space-Western backdrop as the bounty hunters toured alien planets searching for their wanted-poster bounty. With *Judge Dredd* occupying the centre pages, *Strontium Dog* appeared at the front of the paper, becoming the perfect introduction to what *2000 AD* was all about. *The Schicklgruber Grab* remains a classic of comedic science-fiction storytelling, with Adolf Hitler being kidnapped for crimes against humanity and spending most of the strip with a sock in his mouth to stop his ranting and raving. There was nothing quite like this being printed anywhere else. The readers devoured each episode and the Nerve Centre postbag bulged with drawings inspired by the strip. Unfortunately, it was soon to cause outrage in, of all places, the City of Portsmouth.

The editorial content assembled for Prog 178 felt like a step in in the right direction, despite *Mean Arena*'s initial, unconvincing art. The issue wasn't just about the strips, though, we wanted to foster the close relationship we had built up with the readers. They seemed to follow *2000 AD* with a passion not displayed by the readers of *Valiant*, *Battle*, *Starlord* or even *Action*. To this end Robin spent much of his time designing pullout posters for the readers to collect and mobiles for them to hang in their 'Terran dwellings'. The detachable wraparound cover became a specialty of his. Previously, it had been thought that an image could not continue around the spine onto the back cover. Robin challenged that assumption and found printing improvements had outdated it. Alongside these innovations, there were interactive features inviting the readers to design an alien, take part in a reader survey and, as always, send letters and drawings in to Tharg's Nerve Centre.

1980 felt like a big improvement on 1979, but still we hadn't found the title's true mojo. There was something running through the Command Module's Thrill-banks though, something that seemed to suggest that the next twelve months might just be a defining phase for *2000 AD*.

1981: MOJO WORKING

PROG 193 SAW IN the new year with the announcement that *2000 AD* had been voted Britain's favourite comic in the Eagle Awards for 1980. Judge Dredd had been voted favourite comics character, while best artist had gone to Brian Bolland, and best writer to John Wagner (under his pseudonym of 'John Howard'). Once again we published the news on the front cover, as much to advertise the achievement inside the company as to inform the readers, newsagents and general public. In a way it was a tease, another poke in the eye for *2000 AD*'s internal detractors. Their irritation was obvious. This time there were sly suggestions that British comics fans were a bunch of unwashed weirdoes, a cult whose taste in comics was bound to be questionable. I didn't respond. We had won eight Eagle awards in all and I didn't think it too many.

The very next prog saw us go from a high to a low with the publication of a four-part *Strontium Dog* adventure called *The Bad Boys Bust*. In this story by the Wagner-Grant Combine, Bubo and his Bad Boys, vicious alien outlaws with a taste for human flesh, capture and barbecue alive a local sheriff. When I read the script I had my doubts about this scene, with its three-picture sequence showing the sheriff tied to a roasting stick, then the stick placed over a burning fire and then a long shot filled with the sheriff's agonized screams. As editor, I had three choices: amend the picture descriptions so the barbecuing took place off camera; ask the writers to amend the scene themselves; or let the script go to the artist and see what the pictures were like when the artwork came in. I cravenly chose the last option, which only kicked the can down the road apiece because once the artwork came in I was stuck with the scene. Fiddling with the dialogue wouldn't obscure the fact that here was a man being burnt alive. 2000 AD was coming up for its fourth birthday, and we knew many of the original readers had stuck with us, making them all four years older and now in their teens. At this age I doubted the sight of a man being roasted alive would overly upset them. But such logic forgot the new readers, younger kids who had only just begun reading 2000 AD, and whose parents might just take a critical view of the scene. I dithered and then decided to publish and be damned, sending the strip to the printers after conveniently forgetting to show it to the group editor. Following publication there was no outcry, not one internal comment and not one letter of complaint... or so I thought. In fact, the issue had fallen into the hands of a body called The Portsmouth Association for Community Standards who, it seemed, had decided to lodge a complaint with the Press Council. This supervisory body was set up voluntarily by publishers of newspapers and magazines to handle public grievances concerning material published in their journals. The first I knew of its work was when I was called in by the group editor and handed a letter from the Press Council informing him that they were investigating a complaint against 2000 AD. It ended by saying we would be hearing from them again soon. In Fleet Street, hardboiled editors regularly ignored such letters, refuted any subsequent rulings and even published long tracts denouncing the original complainants as enemies of free speech. Alas, I wasn't in Fleet Street. I was in the office of a man whose supposed ambition was to be awarded the CBE. I rather got the feeling that being censored by his industry's watchdog was not part of the game plan. I eyed my old friend the fireman's exit, but there was no escape. A chill suddenly descended on the office and spread outside, causing the secretary to shiver and complain about the air-con 'going wonky again'. Behind a now closed door I offered to take full responsibility should the complaint be upheld. And why wouldn't it be? As we'd seen with *Action*, kids' comics were an easy target for the media. Yes, it looked like Bubo and his dang Bad Boys was gonna get me busted, and busted good.

As we waited for an outcome, I wondered if someone at the Press Council had been assigned the task of reading *2000 AD* regularly, to see if acts of near cannibalism were commonplace in this pernicious periodical posing as a children's comic. If there were such a person, they would have been grandly entertained by the very next *Strontium Dog* adventure entitled *Portrait of a Mutant*. Scripted by the Wagner-Grant Combine and drawn entirely by Carlos Ezquerra, this nineteen-episode epic told the origin story of Johnny Alpha, following his journey from birth to teen-hood before finally becoming a bounty hunter. It was brilliantly written and illustrated, and rattled along at a tremendous pace with nary a chewed thighbone in sight. If *The Judge Child Quest* had been *2000 AD*'s editorial spine in 1980, then *Portrait of a Mutant* was its editorial spine in 1981.

The story is set in twenty-second-century Britain, where much of the island is a nuclear wasteland, ravaged by a series of atomic wars. As the survivors rebuild their lives, children begin to be born with mutations. Nelson Bunker Kreelman, a wealthy politician with designs on total power, foments people's fear of the growing number of mutants and begins to build a serious anti-mutant powerbase. Targeted by a series of increasingly brutal laws, the mutants respond by establishing a rebel army for protection. In this way, the story's battlelines are drawn: Norms versus Mutants. The reader is then presented with a protagonist to follow in the shape of Kreelman's newly born son, who is discovered to have a mutation himself, caused by his mother being caught in a Strontium shower during pregnancy. Kreelman orders the boy to be locked away indefinitely, horrified at the harm news of the child's deformity would do to his political ambitions. As time passes, the boy realises he is a mutant and slowly learns to harness his mutation: intense alpha rays that stream from his eyes and, among other tricks, give him the ability to read minds. Escaping his house arrest, the boy, now twelve, joins the mutant army. Knowing he can't give his real name of Kreelman, he adopts the name Johnny Alpha. As the story progresses, Johnny's mutie eyes make him very useful to the army and he soon rises to second in command. Meanwhile, Kreelman has become Minister of Mutations, drafting a bill that proposes the extermination of every mutant in Britain. In a national uprising, the mutant army attacks Upminster Palace, floating centre of power and home to King Clarkie II. After numerous ferocious battles, a ceasefire is agreed. Kreelman is forced to resign by the prime minister and the king, but the mutant army is herded into exile, sent off-planet into the endlessness of space. There, some choose to join a new agency set up by the Galactic Crime Commission and become search/destroy agents or bounty hunters. The norms name them Strontium Dogs, because *'only a dog would hunt his fellow man for money'*. Meeting his father many years later, at the story's end, Alpha refuses to shoot him, instead condemning him to life in a time loop consisting of the last five seconds of terror when he think Johnny is going to shoot him.

For the younger reader, the main appeal of the story must have been following the youthful Johnny Alpha, secretly imagining themselves to be a teenage rebel with Alpha eyes. For the older reader, there were glorious portraits of mutants with names like Studs Boyce, Clacton Fuzz and the Torso from Newcastle, each bearing a physical disfigurement to match his moniker. Most striking of all was Middenface McNulty, whose modern Scots dialogue, filled with statements such as *'Are ye deif?'* *'Div ya ken?'* and *'Gi'e them scunners laldy'*, no doubt became the new slang in every playground south of Dumfries. It was fortunate that the good people of Portsmouth did not twig that a 'midden' is a rubbish dump containing, among other detritus, human excrement. Among the serial's many delights were the taglines that ended each episode. The office favourite quickly became *'Next Prog: No Snecks Please, We're Brutish!'*

1981 turned out to be a definitive year for *Future Shocks*, with one of these self-contained tales appearing in almost every prog. Over half of the *Future Shocks* published were from two writers who shared the same surname: Steve Moore and Alan Moore. Steve was a founder member of *The Fortean Times* and an established science-fiction writer in his own right. Alan was a new addition to Tharg's stable of script droids, but was mastering the ins and outs of the *Future Shocks* format with dazzling speed. Between the two of them, the Moores crafted sixteen *Future Shocks* during the year; crisp, light-hearted tales with titles such as *Grawks Bearing Gifts, Slashman, Kowalski and Rat, The English/ Phlondrutian Phrasebook, Once Upon an Atom* and *The Regrettable Ruse of Rocket Red Glare*. Previously, *Future Shocks* had been a bit hit and miss, but when you saw the surname Moore on the credit card you knew you were in for a treat. It turned out Alan was a close friend of Steve's and planned to stay with him when he made his first visit to the Command Module from Northampton. Not knowing what to wear to impress the Mighty Tharg, Alan arrived sporting the suit he had got married in. This was a snazzy, silvery outfit set off with a bold red tie and black boots. With his long hair and beard he cut quite a dash and we all took to him immediately. Had I known, I would have worn the Tharg suit in response. We went for a drink and Alan talked about his work for an upcoming independent anthology magazine to be called *Warrior*. After a pint or two he headed off on the lengthy journey to Steve's house in Shooters Hill. There, no doubt, the two of them would relax and discuss, among other topics, their mutual interest in magic. Strangely, Steve did not write another *Future Shock* for *2000 AD* for twenty-odd years, while Alan went on to create some of the title's most memorable strips. Stranger still, that night I dreamt of two candlelit figures cajoling fireballs out of the ether and releasing them through a skylight from where they floated upwards, exploding colourfully but silently in the sky, replicating Van Gogh's *Starry Night*.

In August I went on holiday and returned to discover that *Judge Dredd* had been licensed to the *Daily Star* newspaper. He was to star in a one-off strip appearing every Saturday. It was strange how every time I went on vacation something seismic occurred in my absence but, nonetheless, the news was exciting – one minute the newspapers were slagging us off, the next they were clamouring for our content. In my absence, Richard had been tasked with organising the production of the strip and it was a real thrill to see its debut announced on the front cover of the *Daily Star*. Dredd's fame was spreading and so was the name *2000 AD*.

This had already been evident at a convention held in Birmingham, where *2000 AD* figured prominently in the Eagle Awards. I found myself on stage being handed the award for favourite British comic by the con's star guest who had been flown over specially from the United States. I doubt he had heard of *2000 AD* before, but he had now. I discovered he was an extremely famous comics creator called Jim Steranko, but not being a reader of American comics I'd never heard of him. I bathed in his luminosity all the same and held the award up to the audience. They obviously worshipped Steranko and the room shook with their tumultuous applause each time he announced the winner of a category. I was impressed and found myself beginning to enjoy this world of fandom. Having celebrated at the bar, Tom and I went to the cinema room where all-night movies were being shown for those fans that could not afford to stay in the hotel's rooms. I fell asleep during *2001: A Space Odyssey* and awoke later with a Hal of a hangover.

In October we heard from the Press Council that the Portsmouth Community Association had decided not to proceed with their complaint. I breathed a sigh of relief, equipped now with the learning that the great British public will put up with most things in life, but draw the line at their local bobby being roasted by aliens. Rescued from the prospect of having to tender my resignation, I focused on keeping my head down, not wanting to attract any further attention from management. What I needed was a passage of time without any bloopers. But mistakes were easy to make if you weren't focused. I had heard tales from experienced editors about their nearly publishing an issue without its price on the cover (gulp), without the sponsors' brand logo on the cover (yikes), or even realising at the last minute that the hero on the cover proof in front of them did not actually appear inside the issue (d'oh!).

With six or seven issues to manage at various stages of production such errors were easily made. The final thing to check was the run-on, namely that all the episodes followed on sequentially from the previous issue. This was so embedded in the checking culture that I can only assume there had once been an occasion where, perhaps, episode six of a strip was followed by episode eight, not episode seven. Sid cannot have been amused, I'm sure. Once all these checks had been made, a simple telephone call set the printing presses rolling – and God help you if you had missed anything because the printers were located one hundred miles away, so there was no chance of grabbing an early copy from the press and shrieking 'Stop!' Instead your error would be replicated across one hundred thousand copies and the decision then for the production department would be whether to bin the entire print run, fix the mistake and embark on a costly rerun of the print process, or, more probably, just let the mistake go. Either way, an irate management would be considering how severely the editor responsible should be disciplined, as clearly he 'didn't know what day it was'. Such a scenario was a recurring nightmare for any editor worth their salt.

All year we had been planning the autumnal promotion

in which we would unveil new strips to thrill the current readership and attract new readers. But this time the promotion was going to have an added refinement: no gaps in serials. Such an occurrence was never a problem when episodes were only three pages long, but with the *2000 AD* model of five or six pages there was an ever-present threat of having to drop an episode from an issue because it wasn't ready. Doing this made one look amateurish internally and was hugely irritating for the readers who, having waited all week for the next episode of their favourite strip, were sorely disappointed to find it missing, held over until the following issue.

I came to realise that the only way to ensure an uninterrupted run for a new strip was to stockpile the episodes first. While this solved my problem it was a breach of the last-minute ordering process that had ruled Fleetway comics since the year dot. I banished these thoughts, telling myself this was all about the year 2000. Unfortunately, there was a pecuniary side effect. Stockpiling episodes meant their cost had to be assigned to 'stock' rather than to an issue. As the weeks passed the level of stock grew and grew and pretty soon I had accumulated thirty thousand pounds' worth of strip artwork, sitting in the plans chest, waiting to be published. I knew it was thirty thousand because that was the figure quoted in a miffed memorandum from the MD. He coolly asked if I was aware I holding so much stock? (Absolutely; the plans chest was positively overflowing.) The memo went on to request a written assurance from me that every last page was to be used and not written off – so much for keeping my head down. I inferred that behind the frosted screens in the accounts department there were financial tracking devices monitoring my every fiscal contraction. Fair enough; the company had to have an idea of what its financial status was, even down to the expenditure of a lowly comic editor. Unfazed, I pulled my typewriter towards me there and then and replied politely that I fully intended to use every single page, right down to the very last word balloon. I then put the memo in the internal post and, happily, heard no more about the matter. In due course, though, I realised my stockpiling process had to be finessed, somehow made more cost effective. But for the time being we went stockpile crazy and the first beneficiary of the process was the warped sword-and-sorcery strip *Nemesis the Warlock*.

We had been saving it for the autumn promotion, but cracked instead and began it in Prog 222, dated 25 July, simply because we had no other content available to replace a series that had ended the week before. Tharg introduced the strip by reminding readers of its origins in the *Comic Rock* stories *Terror Tube* (Prog 167) and *Killer Watts* (Progs 178-9). Now the saga of Nemesis and Torquemada, Grand Master of Termight, was ready to be told in full, across seventeen planet-cleansing episodes. The strip must have been a bolt from the blue to the readers. Nothing quite like it had ever appeared in *2000 AD*, and I don't think in British comics either. The fevered minds of Mills and O'Neill had given birth to a wickedly funny, macabre mélange of bigotry and bestiality. In the right-hand corner, wearing the priestly robes and hood, Torquemada, whose mission to purge all alien life would take him from Terra to the stars, and woe betide any traitor he met along the way who gave the alien succour. In the left-hand, sinister corner, Nemesis: the cloven-hoofed arch deviant, clad in alien armour, and leader of the resistance. This was giddy stuff. We weren't in Kansas anymore, and we certainly weren't in the sudsy world of Roy of the Rovers and his fragrant wife Penny.

The strip began with the beheading of an alien and then

carried on purifying deviants with crusader-like zeal. I felt I was walking on eggshells every time I took an episode up to the group editor for his approval. Kevin's artwork was sharply dark and dramatic, at times laced with comic humour, but in tone more often reminiscent of Goya's 'black' paintings, in particular *The Sabbat*, with its depiction of the he-goat Devil presiding over a coven of witches. In her book *Goya's 'Black' Paintings*, Priscilla E. Muller describes the mural's dark atmosphere as 'heavy with action, implicit plot and intrigue'. Much like the strip itself, in fact. But it was episode three, where Nemesis has been caught and strung up by fearful planetary settlers that caused problems. Nemesis remained hanging for three episodes and when I showed the pages to the group editor I thought he was going to ask for these pictures to be redrawn, but (perhaps in anticipation of that request) Kevin had drawn the noose going around Nemesis's 'hideous maw' so we were able to rebut any accusations of us showing a hanging by the neck. Long discussions took place nonetheless and the group editor insisted a safety notice be attached to the first of these scenes warning, '*Nemesis is an alien. No sensible Earthlet would try to copy any of his actions. Be safe, don't be a grexnix.*' This didn't seem the end of the world and things settled down after that, apart from the occasional scene of immolation, but these were drawn in the best possible taste.

Unfortunately, by starting the strip early we'd reduced Kevin's chances of completing the story in one go. We managed to run twelve episodes before Kevin found himself running down Stamford Street to the office, clutching the next episode, desperate to meet the deadline. We decided to rest the strip for four weeks to give him time to complete the last parts, which he did to warm applause from all quarters.

Another strip we had been stockpiling was the return of Judge Death. Readers had been asking the whereabouts of Bolland ever since his last published strip ten months previously and Tharg's eventual reply was that he had been busy drawing the sequel, *Judge Death Lives*. It was five episodes long and by the time he had finished Bolland had drawn thirty-four pages of immaculate comics art. The story began in Prog 224 and introduced Death's Dark Judge accomplices: Fear, Fire and Mortis. The ensuing battle between light and dark was electrifying and as I read the proofs for Prog 224 a tingle went through me: *Strontium Dog*, *Nemesis The Warlock*, and now *Judge Death Lives* – this was mojo territory.

The way in which a strip got commissioned varied. An editor could have an idea and ask a writer to flesh it out into a series. Or a writer could pitch an idea to an editor in the hope of it being commissioned as a series. On the previous comics I had worked on, writers and artists did not collaborate on pitches, but on *2000 AD* there was plenty of room to work as a creative team. The benefit of such a pairing was that a pitch could be made with accompanying character sketches and sample art. *2000 AD* also differed in the creation process in that it regularly sought the opinions of its readers through off-the-page reader surveys. These questionnaires were enthusiastically completed and returned and gave a great picture of the readership, which now seemed to include students as well as the traditional 8-12 age range. It was through this route that the future-war strip *Rogue Trooper* came to fruition. Tharg's reader survey of 1980 had revealed a pent-up demand for a future-war strip to replace the gap left by the conclusion of *The V.C.s* in Prog 175. I turned to Gerry Finley-Day and he came back with a proposal for a strip called *Trooper Tube*, which would feature genetically enhanced soldiers sporting anthropomorphic weaponry that could transform, much like a Transformer toy. I was not totally taken with this and nor was Dave Gibbons, whom we had asked to draw the strip. Dave and Gerry came up to the office for a script conference and between us we came up with the idea for bio-chipped equipment that would contain the psyches of Rogue's three dead comrades. The biochips would be slotted into Rogue's helmet, rifle and backpack, and a micro-synthesiser would turn their thoughts into speech. Rogue's motivation was to find a traitor general who had betrayed his regiment of Genetic Infantrymen to the enemy. I don't think Gerry was used to collaborating with an artist in the development of a strip, though, and the meeting lacked energy. My mind went back to when Gerry, John and I used go to a bistro called Le Bistingo in Fleet Street, and how on the way there Gerry would always walk on ahead. John was sure it was because Gerry didn't want to be seen with us, which seemed speculative, but maybe that's why the script meeting was a little leaden; Gerry just felt uncomfortable. Like Rogue, he was a loner, too. But however he felt, he went away and wrote a first episode, which Dave and I looked at but still weren't happy with. As with the scripts for *The V.C.s*, I retyped the episode cutting pictures, adding pictures and subbing dialogue along the way. Changing the title to *Rogue Trooper*, after the book by Geoffrey Household called *Rogue Male*, I sent the script to Dave for his comments. My phone rang a few days later and it was Dave, saying, 'I think you've got it!' I was delighted, but at the same time my heart sank, I wasn't sure I could retype every episode. But that was in the future. In the meantime we waited for Dave's art to come in and when it did I knew we were onto an absolute winner. The only word I could think of to describe the art was 'warsome'. A promotional pin-up generated huge anticipation among the readers and contributors alike. When the debut front cover and first episode was published it was an instant hit. What's more, Dave's speed was such that he could draw four pages a week and letter the dialogue into the bargain, so there was no need to stockpile episodes. As such, *Rogue Trooper* went live with Prog 228 and quickly became one of the title's most popular strips.

Another artist who was able to draw four or even five pages a week was Massimo Belardinelli. He was what you might call a 'commission-and-forget' artist. Once you had sent him his scripts you could turn your attention elsewhere knowing he would complete the artwork for each episode with praiseworthy regularity and artistic skill. Although we never met Massimo in person, by virtue of the fact he lived in Rome (and even there apparently he was quite the recluse) we all had a soft spot for him and we made sure to keep him busy. He worked through an agency run by an Italian named Alberto Giolliti. Alberto was a fine artist himself and specialised in drawing western comics. He was reputed to have a mechanical saddle in his office, which he sat on so to take reference photos of himself holding the reins or firing a six-shooter or cracking a whip. Following the conclusion to *Meltdown Man* we turned to the Wagner-Grant Combine for a new strip for Massimo. What they came up with was a space comedy called *Ace Trucking Co.* This featured the wacky adventures of alien truckers, told using a comprehensive CB lingo that Alan and John had clearly worked long and hard to devise. The first script arrived with tons of visual character reference torn from all sorts of tax deductible, expensive art books. Ace Garp was the pencil-headed sole owner of Ace Trucking Co. and his crew consisted of Feek the Freak (ship's skeletoid engineer, whose look was based on the Aztec god of the death Mictlantecuhtli) and GBH, former member of the Sha'ka'kan space nomads and ship's troubleshooter. Ghost, the ship's computer, provided a sane commentary to accompany the madcap proceedings. The whole strip suited Massimo down to the ground; you could tell just how much he was enjoying its idiosyncrasies. I put *Ace Trucking Co.* at the front of the paper on page three and kept it there. It was a pleasing way to begin each issue and its comic charm surely drew the horns of any busybody looking to cause trouble. After all, without the accompanying Space Trucker's Dictionary, the whole strip would appear to have been written in a foreign language and words like 'upchuck' (meaning to be sick) would have soared over their heads.

The highpoint of the year was Prog 232 featuring *Judge Dredd*, *Strontium Dog*, *Nemesis the Warlock*, *Rogue Trooper* and the debut of *Ace Trucking Co.* We hadn't been able to launch the new strips simultaneously, but here they all were debuting in the autumn period at least. Outside, royal wedding fever may have been sweeping the country, but on *Planet 2000 AD* we were celebrating the year's other big event. It had taken three years but we had found the paper's mojo. What's more, thanks to stockpiling, we were sitting on a 'lode' more Thrill-power for 1982.

1982: PROG ROCK & FAMOUS FOLK (OOH-ER!)

ONCE A WEEK a thick internal envelope landed with a thud on every editor's desk in the building. The contents were the latest circulation figures for each title published by the company. My focus was the sales of *2000 AD* and its comic stablemates, although it was interesting to follow the fortunes of music titles such as *NME* and *Melody Maker*, both of which appeared to sell a steady 50,000 copies a week. The format of the document was a series of columns containing figures for home orders, export orders, and the total number of copies to be printed (the print run) for each issue published in the calendar year. All the magazines were sold on a non-returnable basis, so a newsagent had to be careful he didn't over-order a title or he would be left holding unsold copies. At the time, most of the comics were selling 80,000 copies a week. Gone for sure were the days of the 1950s when sales of a million a week were commonplace for *The Dandy* and *The Beano*, while *Tiger* and *Lion* would casually record weekly figures of around 300,000 copies. Studying the document became something of an obsession and I slowly came to realise that *2000 AD*'s sales during 1981 had held steady at 100,000. More than that, the other comics had had variable sales, sometimes going up with a free gift or merger, but mainly following a downward trend.

These rock-solid sales began to be matched by a growing buzz around the title. In February, we were just a little star-struck when a freelancer working for the music, fashion and culture magazine *The Face* contacted the Command Module eager to write a piece about the title. In it he wrote about Judge Dredd inspiring a song by The Human League and how fans included various ex-Specials. We'd heard anecdotal evidence of *2000 AD*'s popularity in the music world and so we started a feature page called *Mega-Sounds* to report this to the readers. The page was written by Garry Rice, who had been scripting *Future Shocks* and *Ro-Jaws' Robo-Tales* since the early progs, and who enjoyed nothing better than surreptitiously letting off firecrackers in the office. These explosions caused the nearby staff of *Battle* to wince; they were always expecting the balloon to go up. In contrast, we *2000 AD* droids retained our *sang-froid* and just carried on working as though nothing had happened. When your lead character has a gun that fires six different kinds of bullets, each with a deafening roar, the sound of a firecracker exploding under your desk is about as disturbing as a stifled cough heard at evensong in the next county. Garry's investigations revealed *2000 AD* did indeed have fans in the music business. These included a punk/new wave duo named Spizzenergi, who had released a single called 'Mega-City III'. Buster Bloodvessel, front man of ska revival band Bad Manners, was a fan, as were recent chart-toppers Duran Duran and the nutty boys Madness. Basking in their esteem, we interviewed them all for *Mega-Sounds*, where they appeared photographed avidly reading the Galaxy's Greatest Comic. When Garry heard Lemmy was a fan, he set up an interview with the man from Motörhead at his record company's offices. I had read somewhere that Lemmy threw fabulous heavy-metal parties so I accompanied Garry to the interview, fervently hoping to cadge an invite. My mind boggled in expectation at what would actually occur at such a party, but when we arrived Lemmy took one look at me and said, 'You're scared of me, aren't you?' I must admit that up close he was a fearsome sight and I could not dispute his diagnosis. Lemmy then grabbed the copy of *2000 AD* we had brought along for him to pose with and prepared to rip it apart with his teeth, chewing it up, with no regard for the two metal staples in the spine. Garry's interview and the accompanying photo of Lemmy consuming raw Thrill-power appeared in Prog 278. I loved Lemmy's rocking attitude to life, but I never did get an invite to one of his rocking parties. The synergy with the music scene continued with later admirers including folk-punk dudes The Men They Couldn't Hang and shock-rock band GWAR. There was one sour note during this musical merry-go-round. A record producer, pally with the group editor, planned to record a song about Judge Dredd, with lyrics such as: *'Judge Dredd, he's bad; he's going to break your back.'* He telephoned me, wanting *2000 AD* to plug the song in *Mega-Sounds*, a proposal I politely refused. 'But we're going to chart this one,' he bleated desperately. I stood my ground; the thought of some manufactured foursome prancing around on *Top of the Pops* eulogising Dredd was unbearable. There was a price to pay, though. When the group editor learned of my rebuff he looked very cross and called me a 'stupid boy'. (Sniff!)

One effect of the growing chatter around *2000 AD* was that it became the plaything of departments and people I'd not previously encountered in the company. My first experience of this was when I got called to a room in which a white screen had been set up. A man came in and began to fiddle nervously with a video projector. Slowly the room began to fill up and then there was a hush as someone of obvious importance bustled in and sat in the chair next to me – it was the chief executive. The lights dimmed and to my utter surprise artwork from the *Judge Dredd* annual appeared on screen and the camera began to pan across it, moving from picture to picture. Then, from unseen speakers, 'Ride of the Valkyries' began to blast out. It was a surreal experience that lasted for several cacophonous minutes. As Wagner met Wagner, so to speak. I recalled the company owned a video division, which had distributed the home video of Joan Collins in the film *The Stud*. Was this a pitch to the chief executive for a sequel, perhaps? Was Joan going to appear at any minute (in her role as Fontaine Khaled) draped languorously over Dredd's Lawmaster bike, toying teasingly with his Lawgiver gun in the hope of it dispensing some instant justice? I was not to find out because suddenly the lights clicked on and there was an embarrassed silence. No one stirred, probably on the assumption that any movement would ascribe responsibility for the ghastly presentation that had just been inflicted on the room. After what seemed an age, the chief executive sprang up from his seat and disappeared without a word. We trooped out in his wake and I never heard anymore about the whole bizarre presentation.

On another occasion I got a call to go to an office where a man in a crisp white shirt breezily informed me he was going to promote *2000 AD* through a poster campaign in bus shelters. My involvement would be to provide artwork for the poster and to co-ordinate some goodly editorial content to appear at the time of the promotion. As it happened, we had the perfect piece of art for him, namely the front cover to the first *Judge Dredd* annual. As for the content, I suggested a date for the campaign that would coincide with some new strips starting in the paper. I turned to leave, but as I got to the door he called out in the sort of pained voice teachers use when reminding errant pupils to do their homework. 'I was going to ensure the quality of the stories in the paper would justify his campaign spend, wasn't I?' My blood began to boil. Who the heck did this *nonscrot* think he was, appearing out of nowhere, babbling about bus shelters and budgets, and then questioning my editorial skills? I nearly turned round and upchucked on his aforementioned crispy white. Instead, I continued my exit, muttering, 'Sod you and sod the white horse you came to work on.' (Grrr!)

Meanwhile, the shadowy department that seemingly licensed merchandise to rights to *2000 AD* was clearly having a bumper year. The fifth birthday issue contained an advertisement for colour candles of Judge Dredd and Judge Death priced at £4.95. Subsequent issues advertised products such as *Judge Dredd* colour T-shirts, *Judge Dredd* gold-plated badges and *2000 AD* figurines. The year ended with a *Judge Dredd* board game, designed by Ian Livingstone of Games Workshop, offered through the post for £7.50. It seemed the galaxy and his wife wanted a piece of *2000 AD* – and then the television folk got involved.

Standing in the lift on the ground floor, waiting to be hurtled up to the twentieth, I became aware of a collective intake of breath among the rain-coated suits gathered around me. My vision was restricted but as the lift whooshed up I realised the source of the raised temperatures. A late entrant to the lift had been Julie Burchill, and from what I could glimpse she was wearing nothing more than a flimsy white T-shirt and jeans, despite the outside temperature being well below freezing. Puddles formed around the suits' shoes. I didn't want to dwell on what the liquid might be, all I wanted was to follow *NME*'s star writer as she got out of the lift and introduce myself. It seemed to me *2000 AD* and *NME* had a lot in common and if I couldn't hang out with Lemmy perhaps I could hang out with her, maybe get some tips on living in the media spotlight? But I couldn't leave the lift. I was dressed as The Mighty Tharg and waiting patiently for an audience on the next floor was Paula Yates.

This was the first in a flurry of television interviews where it seemed every week a film crew was camped out in the *2000 AD* office. If it wasn't *The Tube*, down from Newcastle, then it was London Weekend Television's *The Six O'Clock Show*, popping in from their studios across the road. Heck, even BBC2's esteemed *Money Programme* felt bound to send a crew to film Tharg's droids at work. The presenter was none other than former children's host Valerie Singleton, which must have been hard for her, what with trying to reinvent herself as a financial reporter and here she was back in the playground. She was very quiet between takes whereas Paula Yates lit up the room with her personality and badgered Richard on behalf of her boyfriend for 'one of those books with the shiny covers'. It took us a while to figure out she was referring to the annuals. The production team had wanted to play the theme from *Jaws* over a film of Paula riding the lift to meet Tharg, but had baulked when the licensors quoted a fee of $10,000. I was mesmerised by Paula's vivacious charm and would have liked to get to know her better, but it was not to be, mainly because I was wearing a latex mask and was only allowed to converse in Betelgeusian *bon mots* such as 'Borag Thungg' and 'Splundig Vur Thrigg'. (Double sniff.)

Perhaps the oddest encounter with a famous person occurred when Kevin O'Neill rang to say Michael Wadleigh was in London and wanted to have dinner with me. 'Kev,' I said, 'why on earth would the director of *Woodstock* and other seminal rock documentaries, a man who has schmoozed with such stars as Joan Baez and Janis Joplin, the man whose cameras documented one of the great cultural events of the twentieth century, why would this person want to have dinner with a lowly comic-book editor like me?' Kev explained that Wadleigh was in town because he had a film called *Mirrorman* in pre-production here. Kev had been producing design artwork for the film's visual effects and Michael wanted to persuade me to let him carry on working with him. 'But, Kev,' I said, 'you're a freelance. Doesn't he know that?' It appeared not and, seeing the confusion, I agreed to meet Michael for dinner in Covent Garden. It turned out *Mirrorman* was a fantasy science-fiction film. Apparently, *E.T. the Extra-Terrestrial* had just been the hit of the Cannes film festival and other forthcoming science-fiction movies, with names like *Blade Runner*, *Tron* and *Star Trek II: The Wrath of Khan*, were the year's hot tickets. Absorbing this knowledge and after a decent interval, I broke the news that Kevin was a freelancer and I had no control over his work assignments, other than to expect timely delivery of any work he did for *2000 AD*. Michael looked taken aback. I wondered silently if, after his initial stint, Kevin had wanted to end his work on *Mirrorman* and had given '*2000 AD* deadlines' as an excuse. Either way the conversation lost traction after my announcement and slowly ground to a halt over the tinned potatoes. By this time I was completely tongue-tied. I knew colleagues who were such film fanatics that they could have told Michael the name of his gaffer's granny and then got into deep conversation about all things film, but not me. Then, over the syllabub and through the hubbub, I heard my name called. Looking up I recognised two female acquaintances, sat at a table in the balcony area. 'Call them over!' said Michael, brightening noticeably. 'What a cool idea,' I thought. For one night only I would be a *bon viveur*, not 'Mr Tongue-tied Editor'. I would take my party to the Marquee Club in Soho, no doubt bumping into my mates Julie and Paula. Now that would be something. And in the morning I would be the talk of the town, the mysterious man whose appearance at several top nightspots with one of Hollywood's hottest directors had triggered spontaneous applause from patrons and entertainers alike. But I didn't call the girls over. I just waved back limply and watched my meal with Michael Wadleigh fizzle out ... much like Woodstock had done on its last, rain-soaked morning. 'Stupid boy', indeed. (Sob!)

The buzz around *2000 AD* had also intensified in the world of fandom. The comic marts at Central Hall were now taking place every two months and suddenly it seemed that every other attendee was a budding talent whose dream was to work in comics. Since London was a lot nearer than Manhattan (home to DC and Marvel Comics), aspiring artists began to bring their heavy portfolios with them, ready to thrust them in front of anyone who might have industry connections. We had always received unsolicited submissions through the post, but these had usually been script proposals. Photocopiers were expensive and not every youthful illustrator wanted to commit his originals to the care of the post office, so the trip to the capital became the favoured route to a possible commission. The determination of the putative artists to get their work seen was such that professionals were ambushed all over the building. The urinals became a favourite place for a pitcher to lie in wait; with both hands occupied the unfortunate professional had no choice but watch helplessly as a portfolio's pages were turned over one by one in front of him. In time, the typical programme for comic conventions would come to include a designated portfolio session, with aspiring artists queuing up patiently to show their work. Such sessions could last all afternoon and my first experience of this was at a convention in Scotland. The organisers had been in touch with Robin and apparently *2000 AD* droids were invited to attend. Before we knew it, Robin had us all on the train north, there to be met several hours later by our hosts who were beaming broadly and talking knowingly about pints of 'heavy', whatever that was. At the location, the Royal Stuart Hotel, Glasgow, I met an attendee who, rather than proffer art samples, showed me some of his lettering samples. They were very good, nearly to a professional standard. 'What are you doing at the moment?' I asked. 'I'm on the brew,' he replied matter-of-factly. I assumed he meant he worked in a Scottish tea factory, only to be told later that 'being on the brew' was the same as being on the dole. Ah, clearly there was a lot to learn about Scotland, but the little I'd seen already had made me an admirer and I revelled in the secret knowledge that, on my mother's side at least, I was a McAlpine, one of the Highlands' oldest clans.

Come December we realised the year had proved a watershed in the development of *2000 AD*. The stable sales and promotional synergies with the media had enhanced the title's reputation within the company and fortified its position as a leader in the UK comics industry. As it happened, 1982 had also been designated 'Information Technology Year' by the government in a bid to increase awareness of, er, information technology. Naturally, Tharg was on hand to help. In July he introduced a *Mighty Micro Page* to reproduce program art printed out by readers on their microcomputers. By the autumn, advertisements for traditional boys' hobbies, such as stamp collecting and making model kits, had been replaced by adverts for videogame consoles. Philips, Atari and Mattel all had such devices on the market and the accompanying proprietary games enthralled the whole family. In response, Tharg introduced a videogame review page, while in the office a watch that played Pac-Man games besotted us. Little did we know that this new mode of entertainment would eventually bring about the demise of all but the hardiest weekly comic. Instead we felt we were surfing a wave of hot, new electronic entertainment ... a wave that assuredly announced the future had arrived. (Ulp!)

1983: HALCYON DAZE

BY ITS SIXTH birthday, *2000 AD* had accumulated a cast of evergreen characters whose popularity would span the next two decades, propelling the title headlong into the twenty-first century. Supporting these evergreens were a combination of one-off stories under the *Future Shocks* banner and the occasional self-contained strip whose finite ending meant it could not spawn a sequel. Using a more finance-friendly version of the stockpiling process (whereby we began running a strip as soon as an artist had drawn three-quarters of the episodes commissioned) we began to rotate the evergreen stable, with strips being written, drawn and stockpiled, ready to replace the strips running in the paper. For the reader 1982 had dispensed an uninterrupted flow of Thrill-power, featuring storylines unhindered by production deadlines. This halcyon period continued through 1983 with the title's comic-strip universe now catering for most tastes in the genre of what we'd come to call 'speculative fiction'. The dystopian future of *Judge Dredd*, ruled by crime and punishment, was ever present. *Rogue Trooper*, with its dark underbelly and occasional tongue-in-cheek scenarios, had quickly established itself as a new Thrill whose instant popularity also demanded a weekly slot. Space western showdowns were the province of Johnny Alpha's *Strontium Dog*, while space comedy was the realm of Ace Garp's travelling circus, a.k.a. *Ace Trucking Co.* Meanwhile, Nemesis had occupied the sword-and-sorcery high ground with demonic insouciance. This left Sam Slade, whose return in *Robo-Hunter*, after an absence of nineteen months, took him to Brit-Cit. The vaudeville-style storylines that followed included the darkly comic *Beast of Black-Heart Manor*, which left one wondering whether the tricky subject of cannibalism had once again raised its head in *2000 AD*. As an accompaniment to *Tharg's Future Shocks* we had devised a new self-contained series called *Tharg's Time Twisters*, which, like *Tharg's Future Shocks*, also served as a showcase for new talent. However, it was a story about William Shakespeare by veteran writer Chris Lowder that brought a congratulatory memorandum from the MD, who praised the tale and its dialogue, peppered as it was with famous quotes from the Bard's plays. I myself couldn't help reading and re-reading Alan Moore and Dave Gibbons' *Chrono-Cops* tale, with its creeping nuns and temporal trickery. But either way, there was no doubt that *2000 AD* had reached an awesome state of Thrill-power.

Notwithstanding this I was conscious that the Wagner-Grant Combine was responsible for scripting four of the six evergreens. We needed a couple more writers, but finding new writing talent was not proving easy, despite a daily deluge of unsolicited scripts in the post. However, following his success on *Future Shocks*, Alan Moore was now making a name for himself on *Tharg's Time Twisters*, writing nine seminal stories during 1983. Meanwhile, Pat Mills was scripting Book III of *Nemesis* and Gerry Finley-Day had contributed a very successful, self-contained story called *Harry Twenty on the High Rock* that ran for twenty-one episodes and detailed prisoner Harry Twenty's attempts to escape from a prison satellite in orbit above the Earth.

But behind the scenes there had been problems on *Rogue Trooper*. Gerry's scripts were very poorly typed and full of bizarre spelling mistakes, like the word 'escorting' being typed as 'scrotnig'. This did not matter for foreign artists because their agent would translate the scripts beforehand, but it was a problem for British artists. Indeed I had paid Alan Grant a freelance fee to sub and retype the scripts for *Harry Twenty on the High Rock* because they were going to a new, young artist and I didn't want to freak the guy out. (Continuity could be a problem too. Alan told me he came across a Mexican prisoner named Magnifico 7, who died in one episode only to reappear, Lazarus-like, in a later episode.) Having retyped episode one of *Rogue Trooper*, I sent the scripts for the subsequent episodes to Dave as they were, cravenly relying on him to find his way through them, much like Rogue himself having to navigate his way through the chem-clouds of Nu Earth. When Dave had finished and posted his art in I would then sub the script's dialogue to fit the art. This process worked after a fashion, but come Christmas I found I had contracted the Hepatitis A virus from the staff canteen and I was off sick for several weeks. When I returned Richard, who had been deputising in my absence, told me Dave wasn't happy with the direction of *Rogue Trooper* and I don't suppose the state of the scripts had been helping matters either. I saw *Rogue Trooper* as a grim war story enlivened by banter from the biochips. I liked them. They had play value. Obviously, Dave saw the strip differently and this wasn't something I was able to resolve to anyone's satisfaction. I barely had the strength to get to work each day, feeling like I'd been poisoned by a chem-cloud myself, and once there I was not in any shape to broker a change in the strip's controlling idea. In due course Dave left the strip, which was a bitter blow, but fortunately, other artists were quick to establish themselves as *Rogue Trooper* regulars. Colin Wilson, our first artist to hail from New Zealand, had been drawing Rogue alongside Dave. He had made contact with us through Brian Bolland and when I saw his portfolio I knew we could give him some work. Even with the stockpiling process there were times when a *Judge Dredd* script needed to be drawn very quickly and when I required two episodes completed in a month I took advantage of Colin being new, knowing he probably wouldn't turn down the chance to draw Dredd, and decided to commission him. He wasn't on the phone, so I took the scripts round to where he was staying and, finding no one at home, I stuffed them through his letterbox in my usual, thoroughly professional manner. It must have been a double shock for him when he returned, initially to find he had been commissioned to draw the UK's favourite comic character, and then discovering the first episode was wanted in two short weeks. He rose to the challenge admirably though, completing the work on time, and soon he became a *2000 AD* stalwart. Brett Ewins, who had declared Rogue to be 'the best thing to appear in *2000 AD* in a long time', joined the art team with great enthusiasm. Brett had been contributing to *2000 AD* since the early progs, but it was on Rogue that he found his forte. Cam Kennedy completed this talented triumvirate, being a natural choice for *Rogue Trooper* following his fiery art on *The V.C.s*. Indeed I saw Cam as the spearhead of a band of new artists to appear in

2000 AD: a band that included Steve Dillon, Colin Wilson and others, all of them keen to emulate the work of *2000 AD*'s first generation of artists, most of whom had now been drawing for the title for six years. The newcomers had either learnt their craft on *2000 AD* or had arrived fully formed. Cam for example had previously shaken things up on *Battle* with his work on a strip called *Fighting Mann*, while Steve had illustrated *The Hulk* for Marvel UK.

In addition to this second wave of ready-made artists there was growing influx of unsolicited samples from enthusiastic amateurs. When not posting samples of their work they would try to deliver it in person, unaware they would first have to be granted a visitor's pass by the person staffing reception. Fat chance. Most visitors who did make it to the lifts and up to the office arrived in a state of shock, bewildered by the rudeness they had encountered when merely seeking permission to gain entry. That aside, judging whether an artist's work had promise was a lot easier than deciding whether a writer would flourish, but it still took time, with practical advice being the primary feedback. As such all art submissions addressed to 'The Editor' or 'Tharg' were gladly passed to Robin as soon as the post arrived. Phone-call enquiries regarding submission guidelines were also passed his way. As art editor he began the laborious but rewarding task of coaching the more promising aspirants in how to draw for comics, not least *2000 AD*. He helped them come to grips with the techniques used for creating sequential art, how to pencil first then ink, preferably with a pen not a biro, and if you had the skill, why not employ a fine brush. The first commandment in all this was that the artist had to be able to draw the human figure. Only when they had mastered this could they expect to distort a figure for dramatic effect, such as employing the technique of foreshortening. Many samples used foreshortening, but most of the time the artist possessed no obvious anatomical knowledge and the results were always grotesque. Alan Davis was an early beneficiary of Robin's coaching and before long he was lined up to share the art chores (as the Americans say) on *Harry Twenty on the High Rock*. But when the other artist dropped out Alan suddenly found himself commissioned to draw the whole series, delivering five pages a week for the next five months. He undertook this task with considerable aplomb and was soon recognised as a new addition to the second wave of artists. Another beneficiary of Robin's feedback was Cliff Robinson, who developed a style of inking that was so clean you could eat your dinner off it. It was great to see artists like these making the grade, and still the samples kept on coming.

Of course the search was always on for new characters and there were no barriers to entry other than scripting talent and an appreciation of what worked for *2000 AD*. Despite this, new content generally originated from our established writers and it was during 1983 that two memorable strips appeared in *2000 AD*, the first spawned by the pen of Alan Moore and the second fashioned from the pen of Pat Mills. And neither was set in the future.

For quite some time I had been fixated by the notion that a protagonist with the name 'Skitz' would be an interesting addition to the *2000 AD* universe. I imagined the character would have the usual attributes of a *2000 AD* anti-hero; that is to say being taciturn, pessimistic and generally no fun at all except when employing a multi-function future weapon to progress the plot. I thought this might interest Alan Moore and I decided to pitch the notion to him at a comic mart in London. What with one thing and another I wasn't able to convene an actual sitdown meeting; in fact my pitch only occurred as Alan was leaving the mart, with me trailing in his wake. I breathlessly asked if he would like to create a new strip around a character named Skitz. I was about to elaborate when Alan was suddenly swept up by a swarm of fans and he just had time to call over his shoulder that he would see what he could do before he was lost to my sight. Alan must have misheard me that day at the mart because when his proposal for the strip came in I saw that Skitz had become *Skizz*. That aside, *Skizz* turned out to be an anxious alien castaway, marooned in Birmingham and light-years from the helmeted anti-hero I had envisaged. Nonetheless I liked the idea immediately and commissioned Alan to script the whole story. While strips in *2000 AD* were often inspired by popular films of the time, this anecdote proves that the genesis of *Skizz* owed nothing to *E.T. the Extra-Terrestrial*, as often believed, and although the beginning of the strip is uncannily similar that was a pure coincidence. Indeed when Alan later watched the video with Steve Dillon he apparently held his head in his hands after the first fifteen minutes as if to say, '*No one's going to believe I didn't plagiarise this. My career is over!*'

Skizz was Alan's first series in *2000 AD*. When he was writing his early *Future Shocks* I had encouraged him to keep his text boxes to a minimum and let his dialogue tell the story. He took me at my word with one script, which arrived with no text boxes and barely any dialogue either. I knew Alan was letting the pictures tell the story, but I also knew that if I published the art without any words at all my managers would assume I had forgotten to have the pages lettered before sending them to the printer. By this time

they were watching *2000 AD* like hawks, ready to pounce
on any repeat mentions of 'strikes', 'barbecued flesh' or
'trapped wind', so there was no chance of their overlooking
a four-page story with speech bubbles that had apparently
gone AWOL. Reluctantly, I added sufficient dialogue and
some text boxes to forestall any such misunderstanding and
then got the story lettered, making sure to change the script
credit to 'R.E. Wright'. I'm sure this baffled Alan when he
saw the published version, but worse was to come. In the
final episode of *Skizz* there is a scene where Roxy, the true
star of the strip, is saying goodbye to Skizz. In the script
this poignant farewell spanned three pictures, each without
any dialogue. In the last picture, Roxy suddenly grasps the
alien with both hand and kisses it full on the lips. I stared at
the sequence for ages, trying to gauge whether the younger
readers would catch the rhythm of the scene, get the beat of
the pictures. In the end I decided they would not and I added
five words of dialogue to the second picture, so as to pause
the reader before the big kiss. This addition may have helped
some readers but it ruined the scene. Afterwards I decided
that, within reason, *2000 AD* would cater to its existing
readership who, despite growing older by the year, showed
no signs of giving up their weekly dose of Thrill-power.

A new artist named Jim Baikie was attached to *Skizz*.
Spookily, he lived in Orkney, home of Cam Kennedy. I
mused on the chances of two comic artists living side by side
in a windswept archipelago off northern Scotland before
putting it down to a bizarre, *Outer Limits*-type coincidence.
Jim had an illustrative art style, developed for *Look-In*.
This style suited *Skizz* perfectly and when we unwrapped
Jim's art for the first episode we were silenced by its quality.
The drawings were on illustration board, large, not quite

twice up but bigger than we were accustomed to. It looked novel, alien even, and, like the script, decidedly grown-up with not a blaster or costume in sight. We felt the warm glow of knowing a first episode's script and art had fused perfectly and that here was a treat in store for the readers. It was definitely a step forward for *2000 AD* as well: Britain's bestselling boys' comic was now confident enough to feature a story about a female lead whose humdrum life is suddenly plunged into crisis. The more I thought about it the more it made me recall the gritty, present-day strips in *Tammy* and *Jinty*, and that was no bad association... although a trifle spooky in itself.

Sláine was the saga of a teenage mercenary, who would rise to become a king in prehistoric Britain before the Flood. Pat Mills' research into Celtic mythology was prolific, involving the purchase of many expensive books on the subject, which would be filleted for visual references for the artist. Because of this, and other research factors, Pat asked for a development fee to supplement his pay for each script. I'd never been asked to do this before, but I acquiesced and blithely divided the extra cost across the strip's first twenty episodes. Unfortunately, a keen-eyed junior employee in accounts spotted the unorthodox payments and before long management appeared, barking (metallically), 'WHAT IS A DEVELOPMENT FEE? WE DO NOT PAY DEVELOPMENT FEES. THAT IS WHAT THE SCRIPT FEE IS FOR. EXTERMINATE.' I took my lumps and promised not to do it again. Notwithstanding the strip's historical setting, Pat described the relationship between the two protagonists as similar to the TV show *Minder*, with Ukko the Dwarf as the devious conman and Sláine Mac Roth as his brawny minder. There was no 'er indoors' but Pat did propose his wife visually create Sláine, drawing the first episode and designing its accompanying characters and furniture. I thought this was a fine idea: like *Skizz*, this was going to be a different strip for *2000 AD*. Pat's wife, Angie Kincaid, was given the go-ahead and we left her to proceed at her own pace, asking only that we see the pencils before inking began. There was no hurry, but there was disapproval in the office. Robin, as art editor, was unhappy and I don't know if it was because he felt it was a case of nepotism on Pat's part or what, but when the pencils came in objections were raised and there were calls for the drawings to be corrected here and there. I yielded to these demands but played them down, telling Pat we would be sending the pages back for 'just a few minor adjustments'. The art then went back and forth for some time and the to-ing and fro-ing spread to the accompanying cover, which got everybody in a complete tizzy, but to her credit Angie never cracked and eventually the cover and six pages of interior art were deemed good to go, and *Sláine* made its debut in Prog 330 to instant acclaim.

The introduction of *Skizz* and *Sláine* brought balance not only to *2000 AD*'s strip content, but also to the proportion of strips created by the writers. With the return of *Nemesis* in Prog 335, *2000 AD* featured two strips by Pat Mills, two by the Wagner-Grant Combine and one by Gerry Finley-Day... and in development were two new strips by Alan Moore. The future looked bright.

Meanwhile, the company had relaunched *Eagle* the previous year and then relaunched it again in September 1983 with my old friend the spud gun as its free gift. The humour department had launched and closed a title called *Wow!* ('It's a laugh from start to finish') and then tried again with *School Fun*, which pronounced itself *'The first ever all-school comic'*. It seemed that while *2000 AD* was evolving, elsewhere in the wacky world of British comics it was business as usual. And why not? After all, only a chump would question the timeless appeal of a free spud gun... wouldn't they?

1984: MONEY TALKS

AWAY FROM *Planet 2000 AD*, the burgeoning interest in home computing had sparked the launch of various specialty magazines aimed at the trend's youthful enthusiasts. Rather than the spud gun or the flying disc, these 'Newtech' titles gave away cover-mounted flexi-discs and cassettes containing computer programs for the purchaser to run on their BBC, Spectrum, Commodore 64 or Atari machines. In April, IPC launched *Big K*, a monthly that proclaimed itself to be *'Bursting with ideas to help you get the most out of your micro'*. Priced at 85p it was originally called *64K* but the creative team soon realised the built-in obsolescence of such a numeric appellation and chose instead the more generic name it launched with. Doug Church designed the front cover of issue one and it showed a monster recoiling in horror at the sight of an overly smart geek-punk. Presumably, the geek-punk embodied the intended reader and the monster was meant to represent the dangerous characters patrolling the world of videogaming. But the image's message was confusing: why would a monster be scared of a punk? And if it was, why was the punk's attire freshly laundered? I was baffled. What was certain was that

Major General Sir Jeremy Moore, commander of British land forces in the recently ended Falklands war, had been hired to review the latest war games, which I suppose was one way to exploit the national conversation surrounding that far-off conflict.

Big K had an immediate impact on *2000 AD* in that sub-editor Richard Burton was offered a post on the new magazine, which he accepted with alacrity. Richard had been the brains behind *Tharg's Mighty Micro Page* and the film review page, not to mention editing the *2000 AD* annual – I was sorry to lose him. He never complained about the fun made of his alter ego, the droid Burt in the Tharg stories, and I commended him for it. Robin bickered with him from time to time, and some of the exchanges became so heated I found it easier to leave the office until tempers cooled down. Happily, Richard agreed to continue writing the *Micro Page* and so *2000 AD* was able to maintain its apparent expertise concerning all matters digital.

The year ahead was also to see us bid farewell to three of *2000 AD*'s first generation of artists, namely Dave Gibbons, Brian Bolland and Kevin O'Neill. In each case, their eventual destination was the American comic-book market. For a professional with a passion for superhero comics this was the Holy Grail. Among the many attractions was the fact that American comics usually featured just one character or group of characters in their twenty-eight-page make-up, with each title having its own writer-artist team. As such, you got your name on the front, and the glossy covers and full-colour interiors merely added to the sense of ownership and the pleasure derived from producing a quality product. From a recognition point of view the American fans were avid comics collectors, so if your work became popular you were sure to be invited Stateside to one of the frequent comics conventions held there, with your air fare and hotel costs pre-paid by the organisers, or even by your publisher. And as a final inducement there were rumours that some titles might soon pay a royalty according to sales, instead of the usual practice of a paying flat fee under the terms of a work-for-hire contract.

When it was his turn to leave, Brian Bolland took me out to the local café to break the news that he would be working for DC in future. I was very touched and have never forgotten this simple act of politeness. I wished him well; indeed, we wished all our departing artists well. Their contribution to 2000 AD's early success could not be overestimated. The big topic of conversation surrounding their departure was the exchange rate. As they were to be paid in dollars everyone was hoping the rate would equalise at which point, as Kevin O'Neill jokingly put it, they would throw a 'Parity Party'.

The titles now publishing under the 2000 AD banner included the weekly, the two annuals, the Sci-Fi Special, and the Daily Star strip. In addition, selected early strips were now being repacked for the American market as a monthly publication, each sporting a brand-new Bolland cover. The reprint albums in Britain had grown in number to more than twenty, while the still mysterious merchandise department can't have believed their luck when they got to license a software company to produce two Strontium Dog computer games (each priced just under £8.00), one for the Commodore 64 and the other for the Spectrum 48K.

One proposal to strengthen the publishing arm of the brand was the idea for a standalone Judge Dredd comic. This would be fortnightly, thirty-six pages long, with glossy covers. A dummy was prepared, with artwork drawn from scripts supplied by the Wagner-Grant Combine. The scripts featured *Judge Dredd*, *Psi-Judge Anderson*, *Blood Cadet* (a story about a trainee Judge), *HellTrekkers* (an update of the long-running television series *Wagon Train*), and *Bad Company*, a nifty reworking of *Darkie's Mob* from *Battle*. A single-page humour strip called *The Blockers* completed the dummy, which was then handed to management to ponder. No one doubted the quality of the product, nor its consumer appeal. A survey in *2000 AD* showed the readers were excited by the notion of such a title but there was disagreement over the price they would be willing to pay, ranging from 25p to 60p an issue. I was encouraged when the publisher called me in to talk me through the business plan, all written out in longhand, and he revealed 45p as his chosen cover price. This suited me fine. It was twice the price of *2000 AD* but the same price over a month. If the readers were happily coughing up £4.95 for a *Judge Dredd* candle and £7.00 for a *Judge Dredd* boardgame, then surely they could find 90p a month for two trips into Judge Dredd's world? Unfortunately, and after due deliberation, management chose not to share my conclusions and the project was shelved.

2000 AD itself was now priced at 22p, and with weekly sales of 100,000 it was generating annual circulation revenues of £1,144,000. Half of this sum went to the wholesaler, leaving the remainder to pay for the print, and paper and to fund the editorial budget. The (meagre) staff salaries were not included as they were costed centrally. Despite these deductions, I estimated the title was making £200,000 profit a year on its copy sales alone. I really got a feel for the value of the actual brand when I discovered that a copy of Prog 1 was fetching £6 in the collectors' market.

This was an increase of 7,500 per cent on the 8p purchase price charged just seven years previously.

All this financial activity surrounding the title began to create tensions among the contributors, not least because of the company's continuing policy of acquiring all rights in their work. The terms of this policy were set out on a payment docket the contributor received along with their cheque. To bank the cheque they had to endorse the terms, which were repeated on the back of the cheque. The docket template was used across the company's magazines and it contained tick boxes stating which rights had been 'granted' by the originator of the work. These boxes ranged from the aforementioned, ever so humble 'All Rights' to the haughty 'One Use', meaning the company was being granted one use only and would retain no rights in the work thereafter.

It was galling to see the 'One Use' box, brazenly sitting there in plain view, the unspoken message to the lowly comic-book editor being 'Look, (lick even) but don't tick'. We could only guess what mighty personages had the clout to demand One Use before deigning to take the dust cover from their typewriter or remove the lens cap from their Nikon. Perhaps it was the preserve of Fleet's Street's finest scribes, negotiated when they felt the need to slum it with a contribution to one of the women's magazines in order to settle an unexpected bar bill at El Vino's or the Press Club. Not being greedy, most comics contributors would have eagerly settled for the 'First British Serial Rights' option, which gave the company first publication rights in Britain but no other legal ownership. On *Starlord* I had seen a script written by Pat Mills on which he had explicitly typed '1st BSR Only'. I was startled that he had managed to extract this deal from management, but the next time I saw the script I noticed the words had been heavily crossed out by an unseen hand and thenceforth the standard deal for freelancers reverted to all rights.

The job of filling out the dockets was a weekly one, undertaken by the editor and triggered by a stack of contributor invoices. It began with a weary sigh as you heaved your typewriter in front of you, before loading a docket and doggedly typing the contributor's name and address, work supplied and fee payable, taking such details from the invoice. The docket was in five parts: the top copy went to the contributor, a blue copy was placed in the relevant issue when the work supplied was printed, yellow and green copies were kept by accounts. Finally, there was an anonymous white copy which some suspected was sent direct to the Inland Revenue, enabling them to pounce if the contributor did not declare the fee specified. Each docket then had to be signed by the editor and authorised by a manager, who must have winced at some of the sums being earned because, despite the grant of all rights in the work, scripting comics was good money, especially if you could build up a set of six or seven strips, each requiring a weekly episode. To disguise this, the more prolific writers wrote under a number of pseudonyms, although the evidence was there to see if the manager had ever noticed that several of the writers appeared to live at the same postal address.

While writers made more money because of their faster output, artists could sell their art to collectors and make up the difference. Previously, the company had stored finished artwork as a matter of policy, but this was slowly revoked, beginning with a stormy meeting between artists and the company lawyer Mr Peter Mason (fondly nicknamed 'Perry' by plaintiffs and defendants alike). Despite this victory for the artists, and the money-making opportunities for the writers, the time soon came when I received a phone call from a senior *2000 AD* freelancer expressing the view that if the company did not introduce a contract for contributors, one that would enable them to share in the exploitation of their work, then their creative talents would be drawn inexorably to the American comic-book industry. It was a prophetic warning that, when relayed upwards, fell on deaf ears.

Meanwhile the *2000 AD* line-up was about to be enhanced by two seminal strips written by Alan Moore. He must have thought me an odd editor, what with my misguidedly tinkering with his freshly delivered scripts, and then propositioning him in the street. Now, here I was on a Sunday afternoon, calling him up to talk about work, no doubt disturbing the casual study of the local paper or some such. The backstory was that I had taken the make-up book home for the weekend and was staring at it on the bed, planning which strips would run in the title during the coming months. Scheduling, as the task was known, was a job best done away from the endless interruptions of the office environment – interruptions that ranged from irate contributor phonecalls, complete with sobbing noises in the background, to squabbling staff, to artists' agents tottering over Blackfriars Bridge, eager to bat the breeze after a liquid lunch, to being called downstairs to tell visiting bands that they could not come upstairs because there wasn't enough space (to which one band member dressed as John Lennon, responded rather cleverly, 'But Tharg deals in space, doesn't he?'), to feeling the Big Hep return, coursing malaria-like through my veins, or just gazing grumpily out of the window, wondering if the building really was a disguised spaceship then where the feck was Ornella Muti?

The purpose of my call to Alan was simple: among his *Time Twisters* he had written a comedy called *D.R. and Quinch Have Fun On Earth*. All Alan's *Time Twisters* had been popular with the readers, but D.R. & Quinch were far and away the most obvious candidates for a follow-up series. 'Dennis the Menace with a thermonuclear capacity,' was how he described them in one interview. And that's what I had realised I needed as I sat there on the bed: a comedy strip to balance the drama of *Judge Dredd*, *Rogue Trooper*, *Sláine* and *Strontium Dog*. Alan, gentleman that he was, kindly agreed there and then (rather than berate me for disturbing his Sunday) and when Alan Davis came aboard to reprise his role as the artist/creator, D.R. & Quinch returned to *2000 AD* with the aforesaid thermonuclear impact. After all, who could resist a series that contained episodes with titles like *D.R. & Quinch Go Straight*, *D.R. & Quinch Go Girl Crazy*, *D.R. & Quinch Get Drafted*, not to mention the definitive *D.R. & Quinch Go To Hollywood*, complete with its running Brando gag 'Mind the oranges, Marlon'.

The second strip from Alan was called *The Ballad of Halo Jones*, a story about a teenager marooned in a man-made habitat moored off Manhattan in the fiftieth century. Remembering my vow not to tamper with his scripts anymore, I extended this pledge to the front cover that had been drawn to accompany the first episode. Usually, we pinned cover artwork to the office wall and had a cover session, whereby we swapped suggestions for appropriate coverlines to accompany the imagery. In this case, though, I telephoned Alan (from work) and asked him what the coverlines should be. 'Where did she go? Out. What did she do? Everything,' came his reply. Ian Gibson was the artist/co-creator on the strip and he had visited with Alan to envision the background to Halo's world. I had known Ian since he first came into the *2000 AD* office to deliver some artwork from Spain on behalf of one of the agents. He had been wearing a cowboy hat at the time and exuded the same easygoing charm as the actor James Garner in his roles as Maverick or Jim Rockford in *The Rockford Files*. It was clear Ian's art was influenced by the free-flowing style of the Spanish artists and his work on *Halo Jones* was exquisite. To me, Halo was a natural extension of Roxanne O'Rourke in *Skizz*, both protagonists being galvanised by a crisis in their otherwise humdrum lives. The first episode's storytelling must have perplexed some readers, though, and their subsequent appreciation of the strip can't have been helped by the fact that the next episode did not appear for four weeks due to another NUJ strike. Fourteen of the sixty-eight magazines published by IPC were suspended during this latest dispute. They included *Woman*, *New Scientist*, and *Ideal Home*. *Melody Maker* and *2000 AD* also failed to appear on the newsstands. A permanent casualty of the strike was a new launch named *Scream!*: 'It's the creepiest comic ever. Dare you look inside?' proclaimed the advertisements. I had welcomed its arrival and was looking forward to some healthy competition, but *Scream!* was cancelled shortly after its raucous launch, its demise being blamed on the strike. The title, and its top three stories, was merged into *Eagle*, but this was no consolation to the staff, who now found themselves stranded in the dreaded comics limbo.

Staying true to my word about not tampering with Alan's work, I delegated the supervision of *Halo Jones* to Richard's replacement, a livewire Londoner by the name of Simon Geller, who had given up a perfectly respectable job on *Oh Boy!* magazine to join us. For me this was the final proof that *2000 AD* was hot. Here was a proper journalist working on a proper magazine, presumably with a great career in consumer magazines ahead of him, and yet he was ready to say goodbye to all that and cross over to 'the comics'.

Staff who joined *2000 AD* were inducted into the secrets of generating Thrill-power. It was a matter of 'getting it' and Simon got it straight away. He also got on famously with Robin, which was nice, and had a fabulous way with coverlines and snappy trailers for the next issue. 'Disguise in trouble, Dredd loses face' was one of his coverlines. Another was 'Mutants! Mayhem! Mistletoe!' As Sim-1 (the droid name he was given), Simon took charge of ensuring Alan's dialogue for *Halo Jones* was correctly lettered and matched to Ian's artwork, a task he undertook with zealous intent. Normally, one gave the letterer the art and script, with a strict deadline for completion, and that was it. Not so with Simon. With the letterer before him, Simon would stand *en garde* like a fencing teacher, ready to make foil-like thrusts with his pen to indicate exactly where the lettered balloons and boxes should be positioned on each of the artwork's pictures. The idea was to ensure the reader enjoyed the perfect picture-strip experience. It was always quite a performance and Simon must have enjoyed all the jabbing and thrusting because soon after he actually took up the sport of fencing, which, *à mon avis*, was rather endearing.

While Robin admired Simon, he took issue with my news that an artist named Bryan Talbot was to take over *Nemesis the Warlock* from Kevin O'Neill with effect from episode three of Book IV. Robin did not care for Bryan's style, it was 'fannish' apparently, but to me the art perfectly suited Book Four's Victoriana setting and Gothic overtones. Bryan wanted to deliver his artwork in person, but not in the office, so we agreed to meet at Café Pacifico in Covent Garden.

There, noshing nachos and fajitas, I admired Bryan's art, being careful not to spill my *muy grande* jug of Dos Equis all over it. Bryan was also down in London to deliver some private commissions of an erotic nature, which he nonchalantly held up for my comment. Behind us sat David Essex, clearly rehearsing his lines for his role in *Evita*, and I often wonder what he made of the two hombres holding XX beer in one hand whilst casually examining XXX artwork in the other. *Caramba!* After lunch, I took the artwork back to the office where it was scowled at by Robin and handed to the art assistant who, a short while later, cheerily informed us that (in his opinion) Bryan had not left enough room for the *Nemesis* logo. ¡*Ay, caramba!*

Despite the problems 1984 had thrown up, my state of mind was good. *2000 AD* was running smoothly, we had attracted new blood on editorial, and I had even found time to script a two-part *Rogue Trooper* subtitled *Major Magnum* and then have the joy of seeing Cam Kennedy illustrate it. Mike McMahon had taken *Sláine* to the next level with a new style of drawing, and new creative talent had come through the door in the shape of Peter Milligan, Mike Collins, Mark Farmer, Geoff Senior and Trev Goring to name but a few. By Christmas, the traitor had been located in *Rogue Trooper* and *The Stainless Steel Rat* had returned. Meanwhile, the *HellTrekkers* strip had been rescued from the Dredd dummy but was now credited to (pseudonym alert) 'F. Martin Candor'.

Away from *Planet 2000 AD*, though, the year had been dire for most Britons. Unemployment was over three million, *TitBits* magazine had closed, and the comedian Tommy Cooper had died on stage, just like that. Who got his fez I do not know, but I always got his act.

1985: THIS SPACE FOR SALE

THE RUMOUR WAS an ugly one. Each comic's art department was to be disbanded and the staff redeployed to a central art studio, which would service all the comics. As art editor, Robin was understandably nervous. The rumour sounded ridiculous to me, especially in the case of *2000 AD*, whose strength in part had always been its dedicated art staff.

Someone suggested the comics in the Youth Group were being prepared for sale. In actual fact, by now the comics *were* the Youth Group, all the teenage titles having been spun off into a separate department. The previous year's industrial dispute had cost the company millions of pounds. When the directors had formulated their business plan for 1985, perhaps they had thought to sell part of the business to recoup some of the losses. Admittedly, the comics had always looked out of place in the overall stable of magazines, but why include *2000 AD*, the golden goose, with its sparkling financial performance, unless that selfsame factor was the bait?

With little hard evidence to go on we could only await developments. Fortunately, visits to a pub called The Rising Sun kept us from dwelling too long on what unpleasantness the future might hold. The siren-like call of the Sun's newly installed pool table was irresistible. If we were to be sold, we would be sold potting the eight ball with panache and to hell with the pub clock reproachfully showing 2.30 p.m.

Back in the office, the year had begun with a strong line-up featuring *Judge Dredd, Nemesis, Ace Trucking Co, The Stainless Steel Rat* and *HellTrekkers*. Prog 401 saw the return of *Rogue Trooper* in the story *Regene*. Having settled his score with the Traitor General, Rogue returned to Milli-Com (the orbiting Souther HQ) and set about having his three bio-chipped buddies made whole again. This new storyline ran for six episodes, all drawn by Cam Kennedy, who was bidding farewell to the strip in fine style before graduating full time to *Judge Dredd*. Cam's replacement was Spanish artist José Ortiz, who preserved Cam's gritty style, but found himself following artist Horacio Lalia, who was drawing *HellTrekkers* in the preceding strip. This made the back of the comic look reminiscent of the early issues, with its artwork coming from Spain and the Argentine. I should have paginated those issues more carefully.

Prog 405 contained a prologue to *Halo Jones Book II*, which began proper in Prog 406 and ran for ten episodes. This story, in which Halo finds work as a stewardess on a luxury space liner, would later win a clutch of Eagle Awards including favourite character, story most worthy of its own comic, favourite story of 1985, and favourite writer (being Alan). Ian Gibson didn't win favourite artist, but he had drawn himself in episode seven, as a pest badgering a female partygoer. Had there been an Eagle Award for 'best covert appearance in one's own strip' I am sure Ian would have walked off with it. In May *2000 AD* celebrated its eighth birthday with the arrival of Judge Anderson in her own strip (rescued from the aborted *Dredd* dummy) drawn in the main by Brett Ewins but with supplementary episodes supplied by Cliff Robinson and Robin Smith.

While Cliff Robinson had been coached and brought along by Robin, the two artists who drew Sláine in the serial *Time Killer* came courtesy of Pat Mills, who had put the word out in freelance-land that he was looking for new talent on *Sláine*. The artists were Glenn Fabry and David Pugh and between them they drew twenty-two episodes, Glenn drawing eight and David fourteen. Bryan Talbot had recommended Glenn, thus rescuing him from a summer job pumping gas near his home in Shepperton. Drawn with a 0.25 rotring pen and liberal quantities of black Uno ink, Glenn's early work clearly showed he was going to develop into a major talent. David, I wasn't so sure about. I could have suggested one of the proven Spanish artists draw the strip instead, but Pat was looking for people who could properly express the lead character's psyche and not to worry too much if their artwork was not yet fully formed. I was all for giving artists the chance to develop their talent in public and both artists' initial samples had certainly captured the Celtic life force of the strip. Nonetheless, when David's first episode arrived in the post, sandwiched between thin board with my name on it, I was nervous. I knew the others would be unimpressed if the work was not up to *2000 AD*'s standards and when I peeped inside I was disheartened. The work certainly had energy but I just couldn't get on with it. I put the package down by the side of my desk, fearful to show it around, and slunk off home. The next day I got in early ready to reappraise the art, thinking perhaps I had been a bit harsh, only to find the package had gone. I knew immediately what had happened. The cleaners had been round the night before, assumed the thin cardboard package was empty and removed it. I guessed David would not have kept copies (no artist did) and realised I had a problem. This was a thirty-storey building. The night before, each floor's numerous wastepaper baskets would have been bulging with paper and parcel packaging. The sweat began to pour off me. How do you explain to an artist that you have lost six pages of his art, six pages that took him two weeks to craft lovingly, and all because you were too scared to show it to your colleagues? I hurtled down to the ground floor looking for where the cleaners might have put together a pile of black bags waiting for collection. I found it and began to tear the bags open. First one: nothing. Zilch. Niente. D'Oh. Second one: nothing. Zilch. Niente. D'Oh. Then, a most odd feeling took hold of me: I was looking in the wrong place. Circling the building I came across a huge skip; it was massive and could only be accessed by a custom ladder. I climbed up and peered in. It was three-quarters full, awash with cardboard boxes, postal packets and suchlike. Stepping in, I forlornly began to pick through the debris. Again, nothing. This was daft: thirty storeys of rubbish rocked under my feet, which were sinking slowly into the debris. I was getting catcalls from staff arriving for work and odd looks from people in office windows above me. Then, the strange feeling returned. Slowly, my eye was drawn to a far corner of the skip. I saw it lying there immediately, the thin card parcel with my name and address, glaring crossly at me. Deliverance. The feeling of relief was so intense I damn nearly had my very own warp spasm there and then, settling instead for a roar of triumph that echoed around the skip. Some unseen Celtic force had guided my actions that morning and from that moment on I always treated Sláine Mac Roth and his artwork with the utmost respect.

As the year passed it occurred to me that if there was a clandestine plan to sell the comics then someone had better hurry up because no matter how well *2000 AD* was doing the rest of the stable was contracting fast. Not that we wanted anyone to hurry up, but the indications to do so were everywhere. After thirty years of publishing, *Tiger* had merged into *Eagle*. Declining sales had forced *Battle* into an uneasy alliance with a toy company to promote the company's new range of action figures under the banner of *Battle Action Force*. Over in the humour department the joke was on *Whoopee*, which had been merged with *Whizzer and Chips*. *Buster* may have celebrated its twenty-fifth anniversary, and *Roy of the Rovers* may have been scoring at newsagents across the country, but the existing model of publishing comics for children was looking decidedly dodgy. A flood of roleplaying games and adventure gaming books had now joined videogaming in the battle for prestige in the playground, not to mention the battle for pocket money. The next generation of readers was turning to different forms of entertainment, leaving comics publishers with ageing readerships. The upcoming move by *Viz* comic, from local to national distribution, would change the comics publishing landscape forever.

Despite the competition, *2000 AD* continued to flourish. The editorial line-up hummed with Thrill-power and Tharg was now receiving four hundred letters and drawings a week. Each month seemed to bring a new artist, whether it was through a writer's recommendation or Robin's 'Academy' or an artist's agent, or just someone who had smuggled themselves past reception. Among the new intake were talents like Will Simpson, Barry Kitson, Jeff Anderson and Kim Raymond. There was also a welcome return by

John Higgins, whose colour work would later gain him a crack at painting the movie poster for the *Judge Dredd* film.

At the newsagents, the *2000 AD* brand was grown by the addition of three 'new' titles. The first of these was the American *Judge Dredd Monthly*, which we discovered was now on sale in the UK priced 60p. (Perhaps this was why our proposal for a *Dredd* monthly had been rejected?) The only new aspect of the monthly was its American size and new Bolland covers. Otherwise it was a reprint vehicle, albeit the strips had been coloured. The second addition was an album collection of *Judge Dredd* strips selected from the *Daily Star* and keenly priced at £1.25. October saw the launch of *The Best of 2000 AD*, which was to be a monthly compendium of classic strips from Prog 1 onwards. Demand from new readers for stories they had missed was intense. Not all of these newbies knew about buying the reprint albums from the specialist outlets, and probably couldn't have afforded to anyway. *The Best Of 2000 AD* solved their problem for a mere 65p a month and I had great satisfaction in selecting the appropriate strips for their monthly reading pleasure. Once I had chosen the material it was the easiest thing in the world to put the magazine together. All I had to do was search out the printer's film (which had been used to make the plates for the initial printing), mark it up as *The Best of 2000 AD*, Issue 1 Page 1, etcetera, and send it to the printer. The whole process took about thirty minutes and the printed product sold in huge quantities, but under the work for hire contract no reprint fees were payable to either the writers or the artists.

The comic collectors were doing rather better. Prog 1 was now worth £12 and later issues were acquiring resale values of their own. Meanwhile, the shadowy merchandising department continued to rake in the cash, this time by licensing a *Judge Dredd* roleplaying game. Still none the wiser as to the department's staff or location, I began to imagine it as being hidden away down one of the many corridors occupied by the women's magazines. There, camouflaged in Icelandic-style sweaters, and sipping tea from Radio One mugs, I envisaged two jokers called Nigel and Tarquin, singing songs while they worked, their favourite being a rendition of 'My Favourite Things' from *The Sound Of Music.* In their version, however, the 'favourite things' became the favourite 'stings' of a homicidal maniac whose chosen hunting ground was the humble bathroom. Their first verse went like this:

Loofahs that are lasers
And taps that are tasers
Soap bars slicing sharp as razors
These are a few of his favourite stings!

A second verse was a work in progress, attended to between signing contracts and fielding transatlantic telephone calls from excitable movie folk in Manhattan, eager to transfer *Judge Dredd* from page to screen.

Bathmats that break legs
Shampoos that scorch heads
Mouthwash that melts pegs
These are a few of his favourite stings!

The rumour that we were to be sold was strengthened when we heard we were to be relocated to a nearby building. The prospect of being forced to work in an art studio naturally proved unattractive to Robin and after six years' unstinting service he chose to leave, departing in November, keen to concentrate on his career as a freelance artist. We supported him with a commission to draw a ten-part series called *Bad City Blue* and threw in lots of cover commissions as well. Robin's departure was announced in Prog 439 with a farewell Tharg story in Prog 443. We had not always seen eye to eye, but the circumstances surrounding his departure felt wrong.

The year was ending badly. Maybe I should have stood up for the art staff and demanded that the team remain inviolate, but I was beginning to feel misused myself. In true comic fashion, a black cloud had anchored itself above my head. We were losing talent to America, the heart of the comic was about to be ripped out, and we were being packaged for sale. Fun? This wasn't even funny. As winter closed in my mood darkened. Somewhere out there was a spiv with a barrowload of creds, eager to cash in on *2000 AD*. Yeah, Christmas was coming and the golden goose was going to get fecked.

1986: IN THE GLASS OF DARKNESS

'YOU CAN *WRITE*, can't you, Steve?' My interlocutor was Brendan McCarthy and we were sitting in the gloom of The Rising Sun. Brendan had been enriching *2000 AD* with his distinctive art since the early progs. Brendan was elusive, often disappearing for long periods to work on a film or television show, or one of his own projects, and then suddenly reappearing, perhaps to propose a front-cover image or to enquire about any scripts that might interest him. In this instance he had just delivered his artwork for a *Judge Dredd* script and was now describing one of his own projects to me, questioning whether I could do some writing on it for him. I was prevaricating, and it was this that had prompted his curt, 'You can *write*, can't you?' The truth was the black cloud that had been sitting over my head since Christmas had refused to budge and by now it was summer. I was down. I was really down. I had even lost interest in playing pool. As we sat there I could see the table at the back of the pub, standing vacant. Normally, such a sight would have set my pulse racing and my hand reaching for the 20p coin that would secure the table while I called to the bar for a pint of froth and prepared myself for a session of 'winner stays on'. Not that day. Not that summer. In addition to the huge frustrations at work, my personal life had gone down the tubes. First, I broke up with Miv, then I met and broke up with Francine, despite many cosy evenings spent together in the rowdy company of the pool crew in The Rising Sun (where, initially, and after a few pints, I would struggle in the gloom to tell the difference between Fran and her identical twin Georgina, often with highly embarrassing results). Yes, I was wearing my heart on my sleeve that summer, stubbornly ignoring Peter Milligan's sage advice not to do so.

The *Dredd* pages Brendan had just delivered were for a script that perfectly suited his style. It was called *Riders on the Storm* and began in colour on the centrespread. Brendan had drawn a vivid, sci-fidelic front cover to accompany the script and it spoke to the whole gamut of my 'Ticket to Ride' emotions. The cover showed a woman standing in the rain, cradling an umbrella in one hand and brandishing a *Mad Max*-like weapon the other hand. She looked happy, free as a bird, wearing earrings in the shape of guitars and sporting the ace of spades tucked in her waistband. Beside her, Brendan had drawn a lyric from the Beatles' psych masterpiece 'Rain' and the whole effect was mesmeric. As he talked me through the cover, Brendan had enquired with a straight face (that quickly broke into his familiar grin) whether I would be bold enough to pluck the ace of spades from its resting place? By way of reply, I smiled for the first time that day and turned to answer the phone.

Of course, to the outsider looking in, they being the reader and anyone who cared to gaze enquiringly over their shoulder, everything appeared to be going swimmingly on *Planet 2000 AD*. The new year had been greeted in style with the advent of *Halo Jones Book III* and the title had celebrated its ninth birthday in May. Core characters Judge Dredd, Sláine, Strontium Dog, Ace Trucking Co and Nemesis were all engaged in new adventures, many of them seminal, while Halo had established herself as one of *2000 AD*'s most endearing characters, earning accolades along the way and inspiring a stage version that would receive glowing reviews at the Edinburgh Festival.

As well as featuring Judge Anderson in a new adventure and the debut of *Bad City Blue*, the birthday issue introduced *Sooner or Later*, an idiosyncratic strip created by Brendan and Peter Milligan. It began at the front of the issue before moving permanently to the back page. Peter had scripted thirty *Future Shocks* by the time he turned his talents to *Sooner or Later* and it was obvious he had a big future ahead of him. For my part, *Sooner or Later* was the back-page humour strip I had wanted since the demise of *Dash Decent*. Although *Sooner or Later* was a departure from the normal fare served up in *2000 AD*, its cheerful anarchy reminded me of *The Bash Street Kids* and you can't have a better reference point than that.

Brendan and Pete were part of what I called the 'Brentford/ Hanwell Set,' the other members being Brett Ewins, Garry Rice, Jim McCarthy and Tony Wright. With Brett drawing *Judge Anderson* when *Sooner or Later* began, the set attained a position of influence in the pages of *2000 AD* that would grow in the months to come. Brendan would follow *Riders on the Storm* by drawing a four-part *Dredd* that introduced British Judges, for which he designed their uniforms and armour. Peter, Brett and Jim would fashion the long-running future-war strip *Bad Company*. In addition, Pete would create the strip *The Dead* and later he would collaborate with Tony Wright on *Tribal Memories*.

As it happened, Peter was not the only recent recruit to *2000 AD*'s stable of writers. 1986 saw John Smith, Neil Gaiman and Grant Morrison all have proposals for *Future Shocks* accepted and published (you wait for one new scribe to come along and suddenly three arrive at the same time). In due course, both Smith and Morrison would go on to create new characters for *2000 AD* while Neil would later find instant fame writing *Sandman* for DC.

John Smith had been submitting *Future Shocks* scripts to me for some time before I accepted one. I got it drawn and lettered and published it in Prog 473. John followed that up with two more submissions that were accepted and published (Progs 478 and 490). Neil Gaiman preferred to pitch his ideas down the phone and if I liked one he would script it. I turned down one about a giant pizza because I didn't like pizza. Perhaps if I had seen a synopsis it would have been more to my taste. One morning the phone rang and it was Neil. During the course of the conversation he mentioned that one of John Smith's *Future Shocks* was plagiarised. Hmm. I called John and he accepted that this was indeed the case. When I enquired why, he told me he wanted to see if I would buy something that had actually been bought before (in other words, could I tell good from bad?). I wasn't too bothered about the plagiarism, I was more pleased I had passed the script appraisal test. Heck knows what Sid would have said, though.

The first *Future Shock* I bought from Neil was called *You're Never Alone With A Phone*. It was his second *Future Shock* in Prog 489 that really struck home. It was titled *Conversation Piece* and it was a model of concise storytelling, leading to a very neat and apt ending that expressed mankind's inherent desire to push the self-destruct button. But if the year belonged to anybody it was to Grant Morrison. Grant was one of the would-be contributors who managed to smuggle themselves past reception and make their way up to the office. He entered with a smile, admired the view and then leaned his slim build against the glass cabinet we had bought to display the licensed merchandise. Grant's soft Scottish burr was a pleasant change from being harangued by the occasional irate contributor or manager and I listened attentively as he outlined some ideas for *Future Shocks*. Anyone who could magic himself up to the twentieth floor was all right by me, so there and then I commissioned him to script his first idea. Between March and October, Grant submitted eight more *Future Shock* ideas and we published them all, each of them highly original and a foretaste of his scripting talent to come.

By the time Grant's first *Future Shock* was published we had been relocated. The move was a jolt, exchanging the plush amenities of King's Reach Tower for a crumbling ruin called Irwin House. This sorry excuse for an office was soon renamed 'Vermin House' on account of the fleas in the carpets and the rodents gnawing away at the skirting boards. With our art team disbanded, Simon and I found ourselves sharing an office with the editors of *Battle Action Force* and *Roy of the Rovers*. Down a very long corridor was the newly established art studio, a gulag-like affair filled with glum art staff interned for the duration. If you wanted anything done – a coverline lettered or the letters page pasted up, or your sketch for a next prog advert put together – you had to take your job to the studio manager who would assign it to whoever was least busy at that moment. Since different staffers had different design styles the new production process signalled the end of *2000 AD*'s consistent design look and the fonts used on the front cover began to vary wildly, from comic to gothic to art deco and back again. It was pitiful.

My fellow editors had similar misgivings about the move, but when these became common knowledge the MD called a meeting and brusquely informed the room that *2000 AD* was contributing three quarters of the group's profits and as such their titles (and jobs) were not exactly guaranteed. It was divisive and embarrassing.

As the year wore on the Thrill-power generated by the ninth birthday began to decline and I had a suspicion the title was looking a little tired, or maybe it was me, after eight years' editing. My mood was not brightened any by an advert for *Judge Dredd* pyjamas that appeared in Prog 495. The design was shoddy and it stank of a fast-buck merchant cashing in on Dredd with not the slightest regard for the character's integrity. It was inexcusable.

The one bright spot in all this was working with Simon, especially when dreaming up coverlines for the front covers. One *Metalzoic* cover (Prog 485) showed a muscular robot working out. Simon immediately came up with 'Pumping Iron – Brawn To Be Wild'. In the story, the robot discloses that he has operated on his own brain. We thought this would make a good word balloon and so we got 'I operated on my own brain!' lettered on the cover. When the issue was published we realised, simultaneously, the balloon should have read: 'I operated on my own brian!' It was maddening... but not as maddening as the day Simon told me he was leaving *2000 AD*.

Alongside his *2000 AD* duties Simon had been busy editing *Diceman*, a new concept in fantasy gaming, all executed in picture strip, with fast-moving combat systems.

Diceman was the brainchild of Pat Mills. His scripts for the magazine's sixty-eight page issues featured the reader in the role of Sláine, Nemesis, an ABC Warrior or Judge Dredd. I thought *Diceman* was a brilliant addition to the *2000 AD* brand, but the company must have thought otherwise because they closed it in October after five issues. I don't think they were ever really behind the title in the first place, which was a shame. By this time, I sensed Simon had begun to feel weary like me and the demise of *Diceman* finally prompted him to leave. As it happened he had received a phone call from a former colleague on the teen magazines, Maureen Rice, who was now the editor of *Mizz* magazine. She told him to apply for the job of deputy editor and that was that: he applied, got the job, and was off.

With Simon gone I felt like the last man standing. There was speculation that Robert Maxwell was going to buy the Youth Group. This was turning into a nightmare. I was sleepwalking into the glass of darkness. Peter Milligan stopped by and began talking about The Smiths. I'd never heard of them. I didn't seem to have heard of anything recently. But when I did hear their lyrics they rang true. Grud knew I was miserable now, too. I had reached my own negation of the negation. On impulse, I decided to follow Simon out of the door. And so it was the next morning I handed in my notice. Just like that.

LA BARCA RESTAURANT in Lower Marsh, behind Waterloo station, is one of the few London eateries where it is still possible to have classic dishes such as Steak Diane, Crêpe Suzette and zabaglione prepared at your table. Back in 1986 it had only recently opened and it was there that I found myself at a hastily convened lunch with the MD. My resignation had clearly set alarm bells ringing. 'Exterminate' had now become 'placate'.

Presumably, from the MD's point of view, the news that I was leaving must have been the last thing he wanted to hear. My departure would leave the golden goose with no staff at all. Stuffed, in fact. With the company on the brink of being sold, the thought of *2000 AD* flying on autopilot must have been petrifying.

As I sipped a ginger beer and chewed morosely on my macaroni, an offer was put on the table that was intended to keep me on the payroll. I had mentioned that I planned to tour America when I left, and the offer on the table took my trip and turned it into a busman's holiday. I would use the trip to research the American comic-book market and return with a strategy to penetrate it, using superheroes created and published in a British title. Before leaving, I would induct a replacement editor. The MD had played his cards well, providing me with a way back from my emotion-led resignation. It was an offer I could not refuse, but in a moment of rare cunning I attached one condition: creators would share in the financial exploitation of any strips they created for me. There was silence as each side studied their cards. Then came the acceptance, in principle. I had played the winning hand.

Having edited four hundred issues of *2000 AD*, I chose Prog 500 to be my swansong. It went on sale at the end of December, neatly rounding off 1986. I was still on the way out, but I had been handed a return ticket, one that I tucked carefully into my metaphorical hatband... right next to the ace of spades.

1987: PART ONE: YANKEE DOODLES

'YOU KNOW WHAT they're going to do to me, don't you?'

This blunt enquiry came from Rick, whom I'd met with Kadee (introduced as his 'old lady') on a fishing trip the day before. We were in Key West. Kadee had over-tanned her feet during the half-day excursion and now she was the Sunburnt Kadee, stranded in their motel room, moaning pitifully. Rick had come over to meet me at La Concha, where I was staying, and told me that the place had a rooftop bar, which Kadee had espied while driving down Duval Street during their arrival. It was on this rooftop bar's terrace that we were now standing, looking towards Mallory Square, its attractions thronged with vacationers soaking up the nightly sunset celebration. The air was warm and slightly damp. Our frozen margaritas added salt to the mix.

'Who?' I asked, not getting his drift.

'The guards at the correction centre,' Rick answered brusquely, looking straight ahead.

'Uh, no,' I replied innocently. It was all coming back to me now. As she had turned lobster red before my eyes, basking on the deck of the boat, Kadee had told me how Rick was shortly to serve time for an offence he had been convicted of. She didn't say what he had done, just that they had come down to Key West to party before he reported to the correction centre. I was back on the same page.

'They're going to hand me a broom,' Rick said with the dull confidence of someone who had patronised the facility before. I said nothing. 'Then, they're going to tell me to sweep the hall with it,' he continued in a flat tone. This didn't sound so bad and I said as much, trying to brighten his mood. 'Only, I'm not going to do it. I'm going to throw that broom right back at them. And you know what's going to happen next?' The opening scenes of *The Shawshank Redemption* flashed through my mind. Suddenly, I got it.

'Er, not exactly,' I answered in a small voice. There was a silence. Down the street, the tip bell in Sloppy Joe's rang loudly to signal another greenback gratuity being slid across the bar. I stood very still. Rick turned to me, his eyes watery. 'They're going to take that broom and they're going to beat the ever-living crap out of me, right there and then,' he said. I swallowed hard. 'But when it's over,' he continued, 'they'll never ask me to sweep the halls again.' His eyes had tears in them now and we both took embarrassed swigs from our balloon-sized glasses. I offered Rick my condolences and the conversation moved on. Rick told me Kadee was from Palm Springs and she thought my British accent was 'cute'. But for the sunburn, he intimated, she might have sought to get to know me better. I smiled. The phrase *'No snecks, please, we're brutish'* came to mind. After all, this was America, land of the free but also the newly observed HIV. After several more drinks we parted, me bidding Rick good luck with the broom, he bidding me good luck with my trip. It seemed a lifetime since I had arrived in the States, but in fact it was only the week before, Monday 23 March to be exact, that my TWA flight had touched down at JFK airport.

I had left Irwin House late on the previous Friday, plunging into the darkness as I closed the door on my editorship of *2000 AD.* I had worked ten-hour days ever since the first week of January for no other reason than to keep myself busy and to make sure I left the title in good shape. Prog 500 had turned out to be the perfect issue with which to bid farewell. *Bad Company* kicked off the leave-taking and I was pleased to have suggested to the writer Peter Milligan that one member of the company be convinced he was fighting in World War II, not in the twenty-second century. Pete liked the idea and Mad Tommy Jones was born. Having worked on *Battle* for so long, it was nice to have conscripted a typical Tommy into the *2000 AD* universe. Meanwhile, Pat Mills had brought out the big guns to salute the occasion: *Sláine*, drawn by Glenn Fabry, and *Nemesis* drawn by Bryan Talbot, looked stunning and continued the mordant mood set by *Bad Company*. The Wagner-Grant Combine weighed in with a decidedly dark *Dredd* script featuring a psychopath, her mind inhabited by two distinct identities: the one, female masseuse Prunella Belchard, the other, homicidal maniac 'Keef'. Brendan McCarthy and Steve Whitaker drew the strip with gusto and it completed the dark tone of the issue, mirroring as it did my own sense of darkness. In recognition of the numerical landmark, we were allowed to exceed our print and paper budget with the addition of separate, glossy covers. Robin agreed to freelance design a wraparound cover for the prog and it featured specially commissioned headshots of twenty of the title's top characters. We spent ages rearranging the headshots, much like doing a jigsaw, before finally settling on an agreed line-up. All that was left to do was to ask Tom Frame to letter 'Prog 500: 1977-1986' on the cover. It looked *zarjaz*.

For my very last act as editor, I bought a strip from Grant Morrison called *Zenith*. Brendan McCarthy had designed the character's look for him and I asked Grant who he wanted to draw the actual series. This had been my standard question on new strips for some time, since by now every comics writer in the UK knew the name of every artist (thanks to creator credits) and it was easier if they chose their partners rather than be assigned one by editorial (as in the good old/ bad old days). Grant mentioned a new artist named Steve Yeowell. Steve had drawn a *Future Shock* written by Neil Gaiman and I had instantly liked his economical style. *Zenith*'s real-world doings as a superhero-come-pop star quickly established Grant and Steve as a class act in the *2000 AD* stable of contributors. Had I been half-awake I would have put Zenith aside, saving him to be one of the superheroes to unleash on the American comics market on my return. But I wasn't and that single error of judgement was probably responsible for hindering the success of the very project I was in America to research.

As I dallied in Key West, monopolising the tip bell in Sloppy Joe's, being refused participation in the daily wet T-shirt competition and turning up too late for the Hemingway lookalike contest (or was it the other way around?) I began to wonder how Richard Burton was getting on. Richard's stint on *Big K* magazine had come to an end when the title closed after just fifteen months, leaving him in limbo until a transfer to *Battle* came through. Richard had then rejoined *2000 AD* to take over from Simon. Following my decision to leave, I spent the winter helping him prepare to take over from me.

In the *2000 AD* universe, Richard's fate on *Big K* had been recorded in a *Tharg* story where he ended up being turned into a paperweight. As I knew only too well, editing *2000 AD* was no lightweight task and I had wanted to give him the best start possible, hence the ten-hour days to help him settle in. I hoped he was coping and I felt a pang of jealousy now that he had the best job in British comics. Still, he may have had Irwin House but I had an internal flight to San Francisco, and I took it the very next day with great expectations.

'*My husband woke me after our wedding night to say our marriage was over.*'

Felicia was a petite, Spanish lady, who had somehow found herself getting hitched while on vacation in the States. Initially she had loved the country, telling me excitedly how it was not unusual to receive a camera in the post, sent for free by kindly insurance folk in Des Moines, or wherever. But now the picture was tainted. I gathered from her comment that on their wedding night her louse of a spouse had decided she didn't measure up to his sexual expectations and had said as much in the morning. I felt intensely sorry for her. We had met on a tour to Monterey and Carmel, she being on vacation from Buffalo after the collapse of the marriage and me too pussy to hire a car, even though I had passed my driving test shortly before leaving the UK. After exchanging glances in the people carrier as it cruised down Highway 101, we had bumped into each other outside a coffee shop during the stop in Carmel and had got talking. Following that encounter we hung out for the rest of the day, our sudden friendship observed with knowing smirks by the Midwestern family that comprised the rest of the carrier's contingent. Back in San Francisco we asked the guide to drop us off in Chinatown, where we ducked into the nearest restaurant, our ears burning. Felicia's fortune cookie that evening promised her a 'life full of good moments' and it was then she told me about the breakdown of her marriage, her story punctuated by sorrowful looks at the paper lanterns swinging innocently outside on Grant Avenue. It seemed we'd both been through a crisis recently. I walked her back to her tiny hotel room on Union Square and, cheering up, she suggested we go to Baker Beach the next day to enjoy its views of the Golden Gate Bridge. Nothing would have pleased me more, but I was booked on an early flight to the wasteland that was to prove to be St. Louis, there to collect a credit card waiting for me *poste restante*. If I didn't collect it, the card would be 'returned to sender', leaving me flat broke just two weeks into my trip. I cursed my bad planning and berated myself for leaving it so late to renew the card. Regretfully, I said goodbye to Felicia and set out to find my way back to my room on Market Street, being sure to avoid the rear of the Hilton hotel where the disenfranchised of the American Dream chose to gather in great seething pools of anguished humanity.

As I walked I, too, felt anguished and vowed that however my project to create a new title turned out, at least it would be well planned. What the strips would be about, who would write and draw them could wait. The first step was to devise a means of overcoming the format obstacles that lay in the way of the project. And these were many. American titles were uniformly twenty-four pages long, wrapped in glossy covers, and all printed at the standard American comic book size of approximately 160 mm wide by 26 mm deep. As a rule, the fans expected each title to feature one character or group of characters, the stories being supplied by a known writer/artist team. Then there was the small matter of frequency, with the American comic-book market revolving around titles publishing on a monthly basis. The whole publishing model could not have been more different from the British model, with its weekly frequency, larger size and anthology content, mainly in black and white. Not to mention the newsprint paper. I knew a title produced at the smaller American size would disappear on British newsstands and a monthly frequency seemed risky for a new juvenile launch trying to establish itself in the market. I felt more like a publisher than a lowly editor; unless I could devise a smart solution to these marketing problems the project would be dead in the water.

'Pah! You not even handsome!'

These words were spat at me by a woman who had perched herself next to my barstool and taken umbrage when I politely declined to buy her a drink. The woman looked to the barman for support, but he said nothing and went on polishing glasses. Lacking his backing, my critic got down and disappeared behind a curtain, muttering further facial epithets as she went.

I was in Los Angeles, having arrived that evening by Amtrak from Oakland. During the trip I had palled up with a portraitist and, being strangers on a train, we had adjourned to the restaurant car downstairs where we found two staff wearing pristine white tunics and serving drinks. Squeezing behind a small table we ordered beers to help pass the long hours that lay ahead. We drank as though we had just been rescued from the parched landscape we were travelling through and I must have nodded off, because when I awoke my new pal was nowhere to be seen. On enquiring about his whereabouts, I was told by the tunics he had been 'cut off'. My blank look drew a translation. To be cut off, apparently, meant one's presence at the bar was no longer welcome. In addition, any attempt to purchase a beverage would be refused. Thankful I had not been included in this draconian ban I went to order my usual six o'clock margarita, only to be told, 'And that goes for you, too, sir.'

Stung by this rebuff, I had ascended the stairs with as much hauteur as I could muster, determined to find a bar that would serve me just as soon as I had found the accommodation I had booked in LA. The place was deliberately chosen because it was said to overlook MacArthur Park, made famous in the song written by Jimmy Webb and first performed by the Irish thespian Richard Harris. Having checked in at reception, which consisted of a dimly lit cubbyhole staffed by a leery man operating from behind thick iron bars, I had stepped into the night, which was how I came to find myself in the bar that evening, just a short distance away, still the worse for wear.

Looking around I had noticed that all the women were wearing the same style costume and all the males were heavily tattooed. After a while it dawned on me: in my stupor I had stumbled into a hostess bar. Bearing in mind I had already been metaphorically cut off that day and fearing my critic had gone to fetch someone to finish the 'Pah' job on my physiognomy, I tipped the barman and left, being extra careful not to knock over any tables on my way. The next morning I threw open the curtains in full expectation of the wondrous sight that would be MacArthur Park, but the scene that greeted me was a massive disappointment. The park was desolate. No 'cakes left in the rain', no 'men playing checkers', no 'dresses foaming like waves', just rubbish, lots and lots of rubbish. Heaven knew what was to be found at the bottom of the sludgy mess I took to be a lake, probably a body or two, courtesy of a couple of contract killings by my fellow drinkers from the previous night. Boy, had I chosen the wrong part of town to stay in. I drew the curtains and retreated into my hangover, turning my thoughts to another form of contract: contracts for contributors.

It was all very well my having negotiated that contributors to the new title would share in the revenue, by way of royalties and reprint fees, but the fact was the company possessed no contract for such a business arrangement. In contrast, not only did American publishers offer a contract but the terms were a model of simplicity. The contributors were paid for each page they created for the particular comic book they were working on, and this fee was considered an advance on royalties. The royalties were calculated as a percentage of the cover price multiplied by the number of copies sold, with the resulting figure split between the writer and artist team. The newly established 'direct sale market' (comprised solely of specialist comic-book shops) made the royalty calculations even simpler: publishers printed only what the specialist comic-book shops ordered, these outlets having guaranteed not to return unsold copies. So if the combined orders came to 50,000 copies and the cover price was $1.00 then the creative team immediately knew they would share a percentage of $50,000 dollars. The safety net for any specialist shop which over-ordered a particular title was the thriving market in back issues. This was driven by collectors, diligently combing racks and racks of back issues, seeking to fill gaps in their treasured collections as detailed on each one's 'wants list'.

How could I replicate that arrangement in British comics, where a title had up to ten contributors per issue, with some bound to demand a bigger share of the pot due to their character's supposed greater popularity? And our market was sale or return, relying on a formula that deducted the unsold returns from the original print order, in order to arrive at a final sales figure. This was always a snail-like process that took ages to complete, with the circulation director seemingly quite happy to report that the sales figures he was presenting were only his 'first stab' at what the final figure might be, as though this was more than enough information with which to plan ahead.

I was beginning to have regrets. Not only was I doing the work of a publisher, but now it seemed I was the finance director and chief legal officer to boot.

'I love myself and everyone else; in return everybody loves me.'

I was back in Key West, ensconced this time in the Kon-Tiki apartments, where I was sitting with 'Bella' and her bicycle, it propped up against the door, the handlebars stickered with what I was to learn were affirmations of self appreciation. Earlier that evening I'd been minding my own business and had entered a dim sum restaurant. After the waitress had taken my order, the blonde diner in front of me had suddenly spun round and announced with a winning smile; 'You're English!' Before I could reply she had moved her plate and wine glass to my table and suddenly my party of one was a party for two. It turned out Bella was a fellow Brit, hence her desire to get together and hear all the news from home. As we talked, I could not help noticing how physically toned she was: she had an athlete's figure and I wondered what she was doing in Key West. I got the lessons on affirmations when she chose to walk me back to my apartment, her favourite affirmation being the aforementioned, 'I love myself and everyone else; in return everybody loves me.'

As it happened, my own dictum of *'No snecks please, I'm brutish'* was wearing thin by now and so was my steely resolve to remain celibate. After much earnest talk about affirmations and tyre pressures, I gave an exaggerated yawn and told Bella I was going to bed, silently expecting her to join me after a decent interval. But when I awoke I found the bike gone and Bella with it. There was a note, which read: *'I came in to look at you but you were asleep and I didn't want to wake you. Besides, this HIV thing's a killer – B.'*

In a curious postscript to our encounter, while making my way to the beach the next day I had passed a nondescript building and noticed Bella's bike parked outside. At that moment, a door had flown open and for the briefest instant I glimpsed inside. There was a go-go dancer gyrating energetically for what looked like a crowd of naval ratings. The dancer looked like Bella. Now I knew how she kept her body so toned. I paused, as if to go in, then carried on. Our moment had passed, and in any case I was due to leave that afternoon.

In my mind, though, I wished her well with her affirmations and decided to choose one to help guide me through my project. I chose, 'I recognise the barriers to achieving my goals and I move around them, over them and through them.' Suddenly, the project looked a little more achievable than it had. I was a convert.

* * *

'If we're going to have to share a bed, then I need to buy some pyjamas.'

I had met up with Felicia again and this time we were in Toronto, having driven over the border from her place in Buffalo. Unable to get back due to a fault with the car, we had suddenly found ourselves in need of somewhere to stay the night. It turned out the only room to be had in town was at the Westgate, where I duly flashed the American Express card I had picked up in St. Louis. The deal was done. What we did not know was the room had only a double bed and not the two singles Felicia had expected, hence her urgent desire to acquire some nightwear. She went off to see what she could find at the hotel shop and in her absence my thoughts turned to the notion of a standalone *Judge Dredd* magazine, a notion I had been pondering since my arrival Stateside.

I knew I had been sent to America to plan a Brit invasion of home-grown superheroes, but I was keen to have another crack at developing Dredd's catalogue as well. After all, his world had outgrown the playpen that was the six pages a week in *2000 AD* – there were secondary characters demanding their own strips, and there were exciting new locales like Brit-Cit just crying out to be explored. In addition, there was talk of a motion picture and if that were true then the commercial case for Dredd having his own title was obvious.

As I sat there on the double bed, the magazine's format and strips quickly fell into place. The idea of a standalone title had always been a winner, but this time it would be a fifty-two page monthly, not a fortnightly. Dredd's huge fan base would happily wait that long for each issue. The Wagner-Grant Combine would be the creative force behind the title, supplying learned consultancy and winning scripts. In return, they would enjoy a financial contract of my creation that

I hoped would soothe even the most furrowed Caledonian brow. There was just one problem: John and I had fallen out before I left for the USA. Unless our differences could be resolved the project would never see the light of day on my watch, and it was all the fault of Robert Maxwell.

Before I had left England, the rumours that this would-be press baron was interested in adding the Youth Group to his publishing empire had been gathering strength. He was known to be ruthless. A report by the Department of Trade and Industry had found he was 'not [in their opinion] a person who can be relied on to exercise proper stewardship of a publicly quoted company'. Meanwhile, stories about his impulsive behaviour were rife; some funny, and some not. There was the time he supposedly mistook a motorbike courier for a member of his staff, and sacked the bemused rider on the spot for being scruffily dressed, regally handing him a wad of notes from his wallet in settlement. Most pertinent of all, this was the businessman who had a policy of buying companies and then sacking half the staff, explaining to the other half that it was the only way for them to keep their jobs. And those 'fortunate survivors', gathered before him to learn their company's fate, would blindly stamp their feet and cheer the charlatan.

It was during this mood of creeping paranoia, when we expected to learn any day that the deal had been done, that John Wagner had called from the innocence of freelance-land and requested that I propose a strike in support of a staffer pal who he felt had got a bad deal from management. I couldn't begin to imagine what retribution Maxwell would unleash in response to news of a strike vote, but I was pretty sure such action would play into his hands and jobs would be lost with a lot of grief suffered all round. I would have explained this gently to John, but unfortunately it was Bad Steve who had answered the phone. Bad Steve was curt, took no shit from anyone, and had a tattoo on the inside of his lip that read '*Duck my Sick*'. Bad Steve had begun to take form in the glass of darkness. I had watched his schizo-ethanolic coalescence with the same fascination as one observing the growth of a third ear on their forehead. Bad Steve wore the same attire as his hero Dr. John the Night Tripper, complete with customised top hat. He would take over during moments of stress and the results were always highly embarrassing. During the negation of the negation, he had appeared at a *Rogue Trooper* album signing and passed out halfway through. He only knew he had passed out when he awoke to find the signing over, the venue empty, and the store manager standing over him, wearing a concerned expression. The first freelance to feel the wrath of Bad Steve had been the artist Jim McCarthy, who had telephoned the office enquiring about work and was brusquely told there wasn't any. 'Well, it's a good thing I'm a freelance,' said the startled contributor. Even Bad Steve couldn't argue with this logic and went back to picking his feet. Now, here he was about to converse with John Wagner. I listened in trepidation. It was a brief call. John made his pitch for a strike and Bad Steve refused him point blank. This prompted John to call Bad Steve 'a little shit', and hang up. Bad Steve just shrugged and returned to his *Mister X* comic, which he held was the coolest strip in the world. Yes, it would take time to get John Wagner back onside and for that reason the *Megazine* (for that was the witty title I had come up with) would have wait its turn.

My thoughts were interrupted by a peremptory knock on the door. It was Felicia. She was clutching a package that suggested her trip to the hotel shop had been successful.

Not saying a word she disappeared into the bathroom and emerged a short time later, wearing a kimono. 'It's all they had,' she said crossly. I could see this was turning into a bumpy night and in an effort to lighten the mood I asked her for a menu, enquiring innocently what sauce came with number sixty-nine. The chilly look she shot me by way of reply was the polar opposite of 'come hither' and no further words were spoken. Before putting out the bedside light I turned my overheated imaginings back to Judge Dredd. What was it he wore to take his mind off something? Ah, that was it: *'Boots. Tight boots.'*

Some weeks later, I awoke in the middle of the night in a dingy, West Coast motel and chose to visit the communal lavatory down the corridor. As I slipped noiselessly out of my room, I found the night manager standing stock still outside. Only his cologne proved he was a human and not a statue. It was unnerving. What were his intentions? Had my snoring woken him or he did he have designs on my pale British bod? I pretended not to notice him and padded off into the gloom, thankful to find he had gone when I returned. But it was at that moment I realised it was time I was gone, too. I had been Stateside for twelve weeks. I had seen America with its tearful divorcées, penitentiary-bound perps and kooky go-go dancers, and these encounters had helped me ponder the obstacles that confronted the project. But there was more. I had also begun to envisage a larger programme, one that went beyond publishing just the one title.

Two days later, the dawn's early flight found me landing at Heathrow, ready to tube it into London. It was cold and damp for a June day, but my state of mind was good. The black cloud had been banished and the future beckoned.

1987: PART TWO: RETURN OF THE MAC

THERE HAD BEEN a great big party in my absence. Realising Prog 520 heralded ten years of publishing, the company had thrown a *2000 AD* bash at the Limelight Club in London's West End, inviting all and sundry to celebrate. If they'd waited a few weeks I could have joined the fun, perhaps appearing as the surprise guest, but it seemed it was a case of 'out of sight, out of mind' as far as my invite was concerned. As I got back into the habit of getting up and travelling to the office each day, I realised I was going to have to work hard to retain the influence I had previously exerted.

During my trip, Richard had hired a former Marvel UK editor named Alan McKenzie to assist him, and the pair would go on to edit *2000 AD* for several years. The title also needed a visual revamp and Steven Cook was handed the freelance task of redesigning it, together with creating a new logo. These changes, along with improvements to the paper quality, made the title look eminently stylish. From my position on the sidelines, it was heartening to see a dedicated team in charge of *2000 AD* once more. Sales were strong and the introduction of *Zenith* in the summer caught the smiley mood of the time. The title's future looked bright indeed.

In fact, the whole comics market seemed to be buzzing, driven in part by the dazzling success of the American mini-series *Watchmen* and *Batman: The Dark Knight Returns*, which were repackaged in the UK by Titan Books and marketed to an uneducated audience as 'graphic novels' by Titan's new publicist Igor Goldkind. Titan were also set to publish a 'dole-playing' graphic novel by Pat Mills and Hunt Emerson called *You Are Maggie Thatcher*, which was in the best traditions of British satire. If ever there was a time to launch a new comic, surely this was it.

As I studied these developments in the market, I received word that the MD was anxious for me to report on my trip, with particular regard to the story ideas I had come up with. I sent back word that I had not actually come up with any story ideas, which was true, and apparently this did not go down at all well. It had been a risk sending me to the States, and such a decision had had to be approved by the board of directors. 'I'm sending Steve MacManus on a mission to America,' had been the MD's bold statement to the assembled personages at one board meeting, and here I was twelve weeks later, nicely tanned but otherwise with seemingly nothing to show for his trust. I was able to manage expectations by referring ominously to the many obstacles that lay in the path of the project and how solving these had taken up all my time, involving me in assuming the varying roles of publisher, finance director, legal officer and production maestro, which I thought was pretty good value for my paltry editor's salary. This did appease the MD somewhat and a short time later I duly presented my report complete with solutions.

The new title would be thirty-two pages, printed on good-quality paper and in colour throughout. The title would have only two strips, each fourteen pages long, and it would be fortnightly. Using this frequency, each strip's episodes could be combined every month to produce material to fill two, twenty-eight page American titles. To give the strips and their four creators equal billing, the new title would be a flip comic, with two front covers. The cover price would be 65p, twice the price of *2000 AD* but the same monthly outlay as for that title or an American import.

It would be introduced to the British market as being '*From the Makers of 2000 AD*' and it would be in proportion to the American comic-book size, so the strip content could easily be resized for that market. The strips would be pitched to one of the big American comics publishing companies to publish under their imprint, thus leveraging their domestic marketing muscle. British creators were hot and the content on offer would be superhero driven, so who could possibly refuse?

My ideas went down well. What I was proposing was a very different publishing model for British comics, but also one that fitted the American model perfectly. The MD began to ask about strip ideas, what would actually be in the title, but I neatly side-stepped the question by stating that we could not commission any content without a contract for contributors, as agreed at La Barca. After some discussion, it was confirmed that the creation of such a document would be my first task.

It was at this juncture, 7 July to be exact, that we heard the Youth Group had been sold to the British Printing and Communications Company for £6.8 million. *Roy of the Rovers, Eagle, Buster, Battle, Whizzer and Chips* and

2000 AD were now the proud property of one R. Maxwell. Before long, BPPC was renamed Maxwell Communications Company and our little part of that empire was named Fleetway Publications. In what seemed a generous golden hallo, we staff were invited to transfer the pension rights we had built up with IPC to the BPCC pension fund, with the carrot of an immediate 16.9% enhancement to our benefits being dangled before us. Many of us decided to take up the offer... a fateful decision if ever there was one.

Initially, though, there was no immediate effect on our working lives. On one occasion, one of Maxwell's sons turned up, gathering us together and telling us how pleased 'Dad' was to have added the group to his portfolio, but other than that nothing seemed to have changed. We remained in the same premises and our titles continued to be distributed by IPC's in-house team known as Marketforce. It was in this period of relative calm that I began work on the contract. Thankfully, Alan Sugar had just produced the Amstrad PCW 9512 home computer, which was perfect for word processing and it was by using this device, purchased with my own money, that I was able to put the document together without going completely mad. It was a long, hard slog. Alan Grant had suggested I get hold of a guide produced by the Society of British Authors, which outlined what prospective writers should expect in negotiations with publishers, and I did. I also got hold of a standard American comic book contract issued by DC and a more liberal contract offered by a new Marvel imprint named Epic. What I ended up with was a fusion of the three and something that was perfectly serviceable for its intended purpose. The essence of the contract was that Fleetway would still retain the copyright in any commissioned material, and the four creators would still get paid a flat fee for their work, but they would also share an 8% royalty on every copy sold above the title's break-even figure. At a cover price of 65p this would equate to each creator receiving 1.3p a copy. Not world-shattering amounts of money, but at least the concept was there. What creators really wanted though was a means to get at the back end, and this was provided for by way of reprint fees (paid as a page rate), revenue from syndication (35% of net receipts), and standard book-publishing royalties for work collected into a graphic novel. There was also provision for a percentage of revenue derived from any audiovisual exploitation, such as TV, film or radio shows. This included the holy grail of any character-driven contract, namely a share of the merchandising rights. All these terms were embedded in the contract and the final draft was similar to the standard deal that was on the table for anyone wanting to work in American comics. I eventually finished the contract and sent it to Pat Mills, who replied that it was a good introductory offer. Pat by this time had produced *Marshal Law* for Epic and *Metalzoic* for DC, so he knew what he was talking about. I showed the contract to the MD who approved it, but ended the meeting by claiming it lacked a particular clause, which made it invalid. I chose to ignore this. We had a contract acceptable to contributors, didn't we? And anyway, I wasn't a bleeding lawyer!

I was now ready to approach writers and artists to work for the new title. For the moment, I kept the notion of a larger publishing programme to myself. In my head, though, the plan was to produce a range of British comics for *2000 AD*'s older readers, devotees of what we were now being told was 'sequential art'. These were individuals who either wanted more home-grown content or strips with more adult themes. After all, a ten-year-old who had bought Prog 1 and stayed with the title ever since would be aged twenty in 1986. Why wouldn't such a dedicated reader want more content from the makers of *2000 AD*? The plan would also stem the artistic brain-drain to America because the Fleetway contract would be the bait to keep comic creators at home. There would be three areas for them to work in: fortnightlies, monthlies, and a line of graphic novels.

I gave the plan a name: I called it 'Casa Mac'. If all went well, I would be responsible for writing a new chapter in the history of British comics. Getting carried away, I saw myself being fêted for unleashing a new wave of creativity in what the French termed 'the ninth art'. These were heady dreams. All I needed to realise them was content for the first title, and then for that title to be a runaway success. That couldn't be so difficult, could it?

1988: A CRISIS IN COMICDOM

WHILE SALES OF American comic books were booming, thanks to the emergence of the direct-sale market, British comics were in a state of flux. John Brown Publishing had turned its recently acquired adult comic *Viz* into one of the biggest-selling magazines in the country, and Fleetway had published a decent enough rival in the shape of *Oink!*. Apart from this, though, the market resembled the curate's egg. *Battle* soldiered on, stoically sharing its trench from time to time with dubious characters transferred in from Civvy Street. *Roy of the Rovers* looked like he had the legs to play in a couple more World Cups, and *Eagle* continued to fly high. On the other hand, independent titles that had burned brightly were suddenly extinguished. Dez Skinn's award-winning *Warrior* was one such title. Overall, the future of the mainstream market, at least, seemed to lie in either the adult humour category created by *Viz,* a category that was soon to overflow with inferior imitations, or the younger licensed titles category. Such titles featured a mixture of comic strip and text pages based on a popular film, TV programme or range of toys. One such licensed product was *M.A.S.K.*, which was based on an animated TV series, that in turn was based on a line of toys produced by the American company Kenner. It was into these turbulent waters that I was going to launch my title. My only concern was the superhero angle, but the popularity of *Zenith* was proving that, done right, such a genre would be welcomed by British readers.

The MD's directive that I develop briefs for writers was not how I would have begun the strip-creation process. I would rather have put the word out that we wanted to create a superhero title and then seen what ideas were fed back by the freelance community. But I figured I owed the MD some compliance with his wishes and so I knuckled down to have a few initial thoughts of my own.

I was hindered by the fact that I had no great knowledge of American comics in general nor of the superhero genre in particular. There had been the briefest period when I had nearly become a fan, finding myself collecting DC comics bought from the local sweetshop, but that budding passion had wilted the day I discovered the drawer I kept them in had been cleared by an unknown hand. As it happened, the first concept came easily enough, perhaps because I had no preconceived notions about superheroes. The premise was simple: by the middle of the twenty-first century each American state would have its own superhero. For local colour, Britain by this time would have become the fifty-first state in the Union, complete with its own *Übermensch*. The strip's dynamic would revolve around the interaction of these fifty-one characters, which I thought was enough starter material for any writer worth their salt. I asked John Wagner what he thought of the 'each-state-has-its-own-superhero' theme and he liked it. We were sat in Le Bistingo again, our strained relations slowly being repaired over plates of mussels and flagons of white wine. What I should have done there and then was offer the strip to John. But the MD had said he wasn't keen for me to use the Wagner-Grant Combine on the new title and I had pretended to accede to this demand (knowing full well that I had them lined up for the as yet unmentioned *Judge Dredd* title). Bearing both points in mind, I said nothing more to John, savouring instead the pleasure of my idea meeting with his esteemed approval.

Development work on the second strip did not progress quite so easily. I had been playing around with another group of characters, a team of sorts, but nothing really coalesced into anything halfway decent. For the writer, I had asked Pat Mills if he would like to work on the new title and he had agreed. We bounced ideas back and forth on the telephone, much like tennis players warming up, and time passed.

Pat had firm ideas on one subject, though, and that was how the title was going to be promoted. We knew we had the *2000 AD* audience as a shoe-in, for the first few issues at least, but we also knew we wanted to reach a wider audience. The new title wasn't going to have a free gift; such giveaways were for kids, weren't they, so how to reach the new audience? As a solution, Pat proposed that someone be hired specifically to promote the title in the lead-up to its launch. I liked his thoughts. A dedicated PR guy, huh? That sounded interesting. I'd be getting a chauffeur next. It was then Pat suggested I talk to Igor Goldkind, who might know someone in the PR field, which was how I came to find myself sitting in the Conservatory café in St Giles High Street, just around the corner from Titan's basement office. As mentioned, Igor had promoted *Watchmen* and *Dark Knight* for Titan, and as it turned out he was looking for a new challenge. We seemed to get along fine. I knew his West Coast accent and persuasive telephone manner had opened many media doors previously closed to the comics community and that he had already accumulated an impressive list of press contacts. Such an operator would be perfect to create a media buzz around the launch. I met with Igor again a week later and I made him a financial proposition to come and work for me for two months. He accepted. After all, it's not every day someone offers to double your pay cheque.

This was fun. I had power. I had no deadlines, no staff to worry about, just me and a select band of freelancers getting ready to lay the foundations of Casa Mac.

By now, I had commissioned John Smith to develop the first superhero idea. We had decided to call it *New Statesmen* and pretty soon John delivered episode one. John had taken the superhero theme and made it realistic, proposing that the New Statesmen's talents were the result of genetic engineering. Some Statesmen would have 'soft' talents and others 'hard' talents. The strip was set in a dystopian future (naturally) and began with one of the New Statesmen seeking election to the White House. The script's fourteen pages were not entirely reader-friendly, but I figured the reader would have the tenacity to suspend judgement and let the story unfold. I had not read *Watchmen*, but I knew *New Statesmen* was working the same dark, adult territory. It would be familiar ground for American fans, and played to the theory 'familiar equals liking and liking equals buying'. As far as I was concerned, obscurity was the new black. All we needed now was an artist, someone who could draw seven pages a week, which is a mammoth task for any illustrator. I had to admit, if the fourteen-page format had an Achilles heel, this was it. In America, using a penciller and an inker to share the art chores solved the problem, especially when a third person was hired to colour the artwork, and here was I, casually expecting someone to do all three jobs. I knew help would have to be shipped in at some point, but additional artists could not join the strip without character and design references, so the first artist would have to draw at least the first couple of episodes for continuity's sake.

As construction continued, Igor's influence on the title's development was proving to be decisive. One morning, I got a call from Pat Mills about the strip we had been batting back and forth. He'd been chatting with Igor and discussing the negative cultural and social impact of American food corporations operating in South and Central America. Pat came straight to the point and said he wanted to make the strip political. This was a bolt from the blue, but as I stood there, cradling the phone in my hand, I thought, *'Why not?'* After all, had Pat not brilliantly described the horrors of trench warfare during the First World War in his seminal strip *Charley's War*? So I said yes, and before long Pat had outlined the essence of the strip which I thought had the best title ever: *Third World War*. Effectively, the strip would examine the involvement of major corporations in Developing World politics through the filter of a story set fifteen years in the future: 2000 AD to be exact. In this twenty-first century scenario, a corporation named Multifoods establishes an ostensibly benevolent outfit called FreeAid to do good works in the third world. In fact, FreeAid is more like a paramilitary group, set up to protect the corporation's business interests. The evils of FreeAid are explored through the knowing eyes of the strip's lead character Eve, who has been unwillingly conscripted into the corps. Alongside Eve is fellow draftee Paul, a practising pagan, who equally isn't fooled by FreeAid's propaganda.

Their fellows include Trisha, a born-again Christian; Gary, a Rambo type who actually enlisted, and Ivan, a punk. The strip's premise was fresh and exciting. Again, all we needed was an artist. For the moment, I put that concern to the back of my mind, as there was the pressing matter of who would design the look of the title, its logo, colour scheme, typeface, etcetera.

I was keen that one of the features of the new title would be its design. It had to match the look of even the slickest newsstand magazine. In this respect, I got lucky, very lucky. Igor had mentioned a designer he knew named Rian Hughes. In fact, Rian had been in to show me his art samples and I had suggested he get in touch with Grant Morrison as I suspected the two would combine to produce something quite striking in the future, which they later did. In the meantime, I asked Rian if he would like to have some design ideas for the *Third World War* logo. At that stage, the title was still meant to be a flip comic, with two front covers, and I thought it would be cool to have two designers working on it, one at each end. For the *New Statesmen* strip I looked no further than Steven Cook, whose work on *2000 AD* had produced such pleasing results. Rian and Steve got on well. Casa Mac was taking shape nicely.

Amidst all these developments, I mentioned to Nick Landau at Titan that I had the idea of writing a book about my time on *2000 AD*. Nick suggested I meet up with Neil Gaiman, who was apparently considering his own book, this one about Alan Moore. Perhaps we could write something together. So we met at the Prince William Henry in nearby Blackfriars Road. I had not seen Neil since the previous December and it was good to catch up with him, but when we began to talk about my book I was seized by a feeling of self doubt, as if I didn't know what the hell I was talking about. It was almost as if we both came to the secret conclusion that I was a babbling idiot, the word 'JACKASS!' appearing in a joint thought balloon above our heads. I fretted about this for quite some time afterwards and then put out it out of my mind. After all, wasn't it so that I was no longer a prisoner of the glass of darkness? Wasn't the sun shining outside? Surely there was no reason to be doubtful unless... unless Casa Mac was being built on sand...

At this point I wanted to emphasise the title's novelty as a flip comic by calling it *50/50*, but this was rejected on the grounds that impersonal numerals were not sales-friendly. This didn't seem to bother *The Observer,* which shortly afterwards came out with a supplement called *20/20*. Nonetheless I still needed a title and it was then that Igor suggested the name *Crisis*. It worked perfectly and was grudgingly accepted by management. But the idea of *Crisis* being a flip comic was judged a step too far, on the grounds it would confuse the newsagents, causing them sleepless nights pondering which way round to rack this newfangled double-sided nuisance. So rather than the title being known as *2000 AD Presents 50/50: Third World War* and *2000 AD Presents 50/50: New Statesmen*, we now had *2000 AD Presents Crisis* and that was that. One consequence of this was that Rian Hughes now found himself designing the *Crisis* logo, front, inside and back covers, while Steven Cook carried on with the *New Statesmen* gig inside the title. Despite these false starts, their early visuals looked great and the finished product was a design triumph.

Very quickly, we had found our artists, too. Carlos Ezquerra had always been fast, exceptionally talented and an excellent storyteller, so it was obvious that we would lure him away from *2000 AD* with the offer of working on *Third World War*. His character visualisations and work on the first episode, which told of a 'friendly' relocation of a peasant villagers going tragically wrong, was perfect. On *New Statesmen* we were lucky again to get our first choice, Jim Baikie, whose style suited the strip perfectly. Before long, their pages were flowing in, giving Igor the visuals he needed to unleash his PR campaign, funded by a generous marketing budget.

Initially, *Crisis* was promoted with the slogan: '*Crisis is coming: Can you handle it?*' Later, potential readers were invited to '*Meet the Psychos, five teenage members of "Market Force", the Psychological Warfare Company. They're out to win the hearts and minds of the people in a global Vietnam drama where the only victors are the big business multinationals of tomorrow.*' This was the trailer for *Third World War*. Meanwhile, *New Statesmen* was being described thus: '*In a society transformed by genetic engineering, where man's dreams of playing God have finally been realised, in an America where each state has its own superhuman operative, in a world where England is the fifty-first state, these are the New Statesmen.*' Bubbling under all this was the concept that *Crisis* was a political comic, a notion that was only half true at best, but one which the press lapped up.

Crisis went on sale with issue dated 17 September 1988. The media coverage that followed far exceeded what a new magazine might expect, let alone a comic. Periodicals as diverse as *Time Out*, *The Scotsman*, *The Jewish Chronicle* and the *Economist* all carried reports of the title's arrival. The *Economist* took the view that *Crisis* was a leftist political tirade while the *Scotsman* declared it 'fresh'. Either way, Igor's campaign was a single-handed *tour de force*, one that reaped thousands and thousands of pounds' worth of free press. And the fans were not forgotten, with a creators' signing tour arranged to visit the newly established specialist comic shops that had sprung up in Reading, Bristol, Birmingham, Manchester, Leeds, Sheffield, Nottingham, Cambridge, Belfast, Glasgow, Edinburgh and London, making twelve cities in nine days. Alerted by advance radio interviews and generous local-press coverage, the fans queued in their hundreds to get their copy of the first issue signed, an act which was expected to greatly increase the issue's face value. This fervour was rock and roll territory. The press campaign continued to gather pace and culminated in a powerful *Crisis* presence at the United Kingdom Comic Art Convention, held in London and attended by over a thousand people. Coincidentally, another new title was being launched at the convention, an independent magazine called *Deadline*, funded by Tom Astor and edited by Brett Ewins and Steve Dillon. Such was the intensity of Igor's campaign though that I believe the *Deadline* crew felt that *Crisis* was trying to suppress the effectiveness of their own launch campaign. Nothing could have been further from the truth. We welcomed *Deadline*. The more the merrier. Casa Mac needed neighbours, the noisier the better. Similarly, the convention organiser, Frank Plowright, may have felt the *Crisis* team was subverting his role. After speaking at an early morning *Crisis* panel, and somewhat the worse for wear from the previous night's libations, Bad Steve had happened to stagger into Frank as they left the stage, nearly causing Frank to plunge to his doom, a collision I believe Frank took to be deliberate and clear proof of Fleetway's ruthless plan to dominate British comics.

Back at the office, change was in the air. Out of the blue, the editors of *Roy of the Rovers, Eagle, M.A.S.K* and *Buster* were offered the chance to package their titles, working from home as freelancers. This wasn't quite the Maxwell method of firing half the staff when acquiring a new company, but it had the same effect in that when the dust had settled Fleetway's staff had been reduced to a rump of just fifteen people. Aside from the managing director and the managing editor, there were a couple of bods each in production, marketing, accounts and advertising, the rest of the numbers made up by five others, being myself, Richard, Alan, Igor and Steve Cook. And it was amidst these ruins that I was hoping to build Casa Mac.

The contrary press coverage didn't matter, the main thing had been to get people to sample the first issue, and as December dawned we received early sales figures. The first issue had sold 80,000 copies, a triumph at 65p by anyone's standards. Soon after, there was a rumour Titan planned to buy 10,000 of the unsolds and everything looked hunky dory.

Christmas was coming, the year was ending, and *Crisis* had been conceived, created and launched. Pausing for breath, I flew to Key West where I planned to spend three days behaving in the most politically incorrect manner I could think of... starting with banging the bejesus out of Bella from the bar, while the back wheel of her hastily discarded bike spun slowly to a stop in a bed of bright pink bleeding hearts.

1989: YEAR OF THE CATS

'WHY SHOULD I throw good money after bad?' This pained enquiry was made of a marketing staffer who, while visiting the MD in his den, had dared to suggest a relaunch for *Crisis*. What was vexing the MD was a slow-motion collapse in sales. Issues two and three had not performed nearly as well as issue one, and by spring the title was reaching only 30,000 readers, a far cry from the celebratory backslapping of the previous autumn.

Another matter that was undoubtedly irking the MD was the fact that we had been moved across town to Camden, there to share an office with a stable of magazines published by Maxwell Communication Corporation. The stable included titles such as *Knitting Weekly* and *Wedding & Home*. This was an ill fit indeed. At IPC, similar upmarket titles had been shielded from we comics riff-raff by being located on different floors, but at MCC we were to share the same floor and our arrival was greeted with some bemusement.

Our new building was a former cigarette factory, built in the 1920s for the Carreras Tobacco Company, and decorated in the Egyptian style popular at the time, complete with two large statues of cats guarding the entrance, symbols of the Egyptian goddess Bastet we were later to learn. As we settled in we sensed there was some kind of power struggle occurring in the boardroom and the cats' brooding welcome each day did nothing to dispel the feeling. Ignorant of the actual details, we staffers contented ourselves with revelling in the fact that Camden was a far nicer location than Southwark, with plenty of pleasing places to eat, drink and generally besport ourselves in boisterous fashion, which we did diligently each evening after work.

Shortly after our arrival, a meeting of several middle-management MCC suits was called to discuss the future of *Crisis*, and I was invited to attend. I got my defence in first, loudly declaring that social commentary, such as that found in *Crisis,* appealed to young adults and I cited a recent song by Enya as evidence. The song was called 'Orinoco Flow' and it had been a chart hit. When asked why this particular song was evidential I replied that, 'It was all about saving the whale.' The ardour of my defence rather took the wind out of the meeting's sails and an embarrassed silence descended, followed by a timid exodus from the room. After all, who could argue with the man who had overseen the sale of five million copies of *2000 AD* each year for the past eight years? In fact, I had misheard the lyrics; Enya wasn't trying to save the whale at all. She was actually singing, *'sail away, sail away, sail away'*. Fortunately, the suits were as ignorant of the song's true message as I was, otherwise a good deal of sniggering would have taken place.

The conversation around *Crisis* was concluded when the MD decided, albeit reluctantly, to release £20,000 to relaunch the title. The case had been made that newsagents had been racking the title wrongly, putting it with the

children's comics. In view of this, the relaunch involved
placing advertisements in trade papers like *Magazine Week*
and *The Newsagent* encouraging newsagents to set aside
a separate shelf for comics aimed at older readers, naming
Crisis, *Deadline* and *Viz* as examples. Additionally, 50,000
copies of *Crisis* were to be inserted in the *New Musical
Express*, whose demographic supposedly matched *Crisis*'s
intended audience. Editorially, it was decided to replace
the two-strip format with three strips each issue. This was
achieved by reducing the page count of *Third World War* to
twelve pages an issue and using the fourteen pages left by
the conclusion of *New Statesmen* to bring in two new strips.

Crisis had been attracting a pleasing amount of mail and
submissions from those comics buyers who actually liked
the title and during our deliberations over what strips to
relaunch with, Igor had come across a synopsis from a
reader named Garth Ennis, who hailed from Belfast and had
proposed a story called *Troubled Souls*. It was a submission
that stood out from what some editors unkindly call the
'slush pile', featuring as it did ordinary people trying to
lead a normal life during the Troubles and what happens
when one of them finds a gun has been dropped into his
lap. The synopsis read well, but surely a novice reader could
not possess the technique to turn a proposal into comic
scripts. Garth proved us wrong when, within two days of
our telephoning him, he submitted the script for episode
one, perfectly formatted, paced and executed as though he
had been scripting for years. Excited, we invited Garth and
his chosen artist, John McCrea, over to London for further
discussions. On meeting them I felt old for the first time in
my life. I was only thirty-six but the creators stood before
me were no more than teenagers. I liked their easy-going

charm and we got on well, despite the age difference. John McCrea's sample artwork for the story suited it perfectly and I commissioned *Troubled Souls* as a twelve-issue series there and then, merely encouraging the pair to make sure any historical references were factually correct.

For the other strip, Igor suggested contacting an up-and-coming writer named Myra Hancock. After telephoning Myra, she proposed an idea she had been developing for another adult title called *Escape*. It was a contemporary soap opera about a young female carpenter and the people who lived and passed through the flat she shared in Camden. The title *Sticky Fingers* related to the lead character's previous pastime of occasional thieving, a habit she was trying to break. Drawn by David Hine, *Sticky Fingers* seemed right at home in *Crisis*. Its light-hearted approach was given depth by its characters, people living on the margins of city life. Meeting in the local pub, I tried to persuade Myra to add more plot to her free-flowing scripts, mostly drawn from her own experiences, but without much success. It seemed this new generation of writers had firm ideas about their work and did not brook any interference. 'They won't take a telling,' as John Wagner said to me of another new young writer whom he was coaching to script *Judge Dredd*.

With *Third World War* returning Eve and her fellow FreeAiders home to Britain, *Crisis* was now a title featuring strips set in the UK. It certainly felt more balanced and I wasn't too worried by the comparatively small readership. We had the American collections to generate a secondary revenue stream, plumping up the bottom line, and that prospect was encouraging, although initially we had struggled to find a publishing partner in the US.

Both *Third World War* and *New Statesmen* had been

taken to the Bologna Children's Book Fair and handed to Marvel executives for their consideration, which led to a polite refusal. DC dallied and then followed suit, despite a rumour they had bid £4 million to buy *2000 AD* outright. This left us with Fleetway's fledgling Stateside operation, Fleetway Quality. The jovial, two-man outfit that ran the company solicited the strips to the direct-sales market as five-issue mini-series, priced at $2.25 each. Once the orders came back, the strips were printed in Spain and air-freighted direct to the States. It was a great moment seeing both strips collected into the prestige American format. Whatever the size of the UK audience, the experiment of using *Crisis* as a producer of comic-strip material to be collected and marketed in the USA had worked.

Back at 'Maxwell Towers', the rumours of a boardroom powerplay were made flesh when we learned the MD had left (taking his shades with him) and we were to be managed by the fresh-faced executives in charge of MCC. It was the end of a magazine career spanning several decades, but perhaps the MD wasn't too sorry to leave. Working for Robert Maxwell cannot have been easy given the man's peremptory manner and sudden changes of mind. An example of this was the story that Fleetway had planned to launch a flagship football magazine to challenge the bestselling title in the market, namely *Shoot!* owned by IPC. As in the film *Citizen Kane*, the top staff at *Shoot!* had been approached and persuaded to transfer their allegiance to the prospective new title, handing in their resignations on the way. Then, just before Christmas, Maxwell decided to cancel the project, leaving the MD with the unenviable task of breaking the bad news to the eight potential new arrivals that they were now jobless and effectively stranded.

One of our new management team's early decisions was to hire a publishing director to look after the day-to-day running of Fleetway. The PD's first encounter with the realities of managing *2000 AD* came when John Wagner made an appointment to see him. I was invited to attend in my newly created role as group editor of the *2000 AD* Group, consisting of *Crisis*, *2000 AD* and its satellite publications. The meeting was a short one. John arrived bearing as much *Judge Dredd* merchandise as he could carry and down it went on the PD's desk: the boardgame, the figurines, the apparel, the reprint albums. SLAP! BAM! BOOM! KER-THUNK! John's message was clear: neither he nor his co-creator had seen a penny from the sales of the merchandise. What was to be done? The PD, a dead ringer for Richard Branson but possessing more gravitas, did not flinch and to his credit he agreed that this was an invidious situation that needed to be rectified. The meeting ended on that bold statement, and within a year a contract making allowance for all contributors to share in any exploitation of their work was introduced. It was a brave, far-sighted move, and I applauded the PD for it.

Following this prickly introduction to the wacky world of comics publishing, the PD soon found himself in more comfortable surroundings with the arrival in the summer of Simon Bisley as the artist on *Sláine*, which was now being printed in full colour. Simon's first work for Fleetway had been on *ABC Warriors*, drawing the strip in line. He rang the office one day to let us know the pencils for the next episode of *ABC Warriors* were completed and he was about to ink them. 'What with?' asked Bad Steve brusquely, for it was he. Simon laughed, intimating a cheese sandwich or some such, at which Bad Steve gave him a lecture on professionalism and hung up. Simon told me later that the admonishment had helped him recognise the need to adopt a more disciplined approach to his newfound occupation as a comic-strip artist. By the time he got to draw *Sláine* he had clearly achieved this and it led to the consistent creation of fully painted artwork that quickly became the talk of the comics world and indeed the wider publishing industry. Unfortunately, when some other contributors tried to imitate Simon with their own fully painted artwork, their initial efforts were not executed with the same skill or awareness of the *2000 AD* printing process, so that for a long time afterwards much of the title's colour artwork resembled a dark brown mess known to the more acerbic readers as *Fleetway Mud*™. Nonetheless, the general opinion among London's media movers and shakers seemed to be that when it came to comic strip art, Bisley was the biz and that was that. *2000 AD* bathed in the reflected glow of such accolades and to be the title's publishing director that summer must have been a very pleasant feeling indeed. However, the autumn was to prove neither as mellow nor fruitful a time.

When the figures for the *Crisis* relaunch issue came in, it seemed the marketing campaign and editorial changes had stabilised the title's sales. We knew now that *Crisis* was never going to be a money-spinner, but it did appear to have established a market for older readers. And what was rewarding was how *Crisis* was becoming a destination for new British talent. The debuts of Messrs Smith, Ennis and McCrea were quickly followed by episodes of *New Statesmen* and *Third World War* being drawn by newcomers Sean Phillips and Duncan Fegredo. Sean's first professional work was completed when he was just a shy fifteen year old, but his big break came on *Crisis*. Duncan hailed from the north and wore the permanent but endearing expression of someone who has just been told they've won the lottery. These two talented tyros were followed by a host of similarly driven artists, people like Glyn Dillon, Floyd Hughes, Steve Pugh, Robert Blackwell and South African painter Philip Swarbrick. Some cut their teeth on the title's one-off story slot, which mixed downbeat tales of discrimination, political repression and the like with humorous recollections of awkward teenage encounters, such as meeting a girlfriend's parents for the first time. Over forty of these tales would be published in *Crisis*, many showcasing new writing talent as well, introducing scribes such as Mark Millar, James D. Robinson, Si Spencer, Malachy Coney and Alan Mitchell. Pretty soon, the office became a meeting point for such contributors, first handing in their scripts or artwork then heading off to the pub and the Camden Brasserie, where occasionally a novice member of the party would end the evening passed out in the doorway of the shop next door.

In the autumn, the title's strip content was strengthened further by the publication of a ten-episode strip by Garth Ennis titled *True Faith*, this being a religious satire on his schooldays. We chose Warren Pleece, another newcomer, to illustrate the strip. I had immediately liked Warren's art when I first saw it his own publication, created with his brother Gary, called *Velocity*. As soon as I read *Velocity* I knew I had found my personal comic-strip nirvana. I was bowled over by its troupe of sleazy, end-of-pier stereotypes written and drawn with comedic brevity that made me want to ingest each page as though it were a Class-A drug. I dreamed of publishing it for them commercially, bringing it to the wider, older audience we were all trying to capture. The three of us met a couple of times to discuss ways and means of doing this, following the example of John Brown with *Viz*, but I didn't possess the business acumen nor personal drive to realise the dream and the opportunity was missed.

Crisis was beginning to cook with the inclusion of *True Faith* and I planned to turn up the creative heat by including a strip called *Skin*. Brendan McCarthy had suggested *Skin* to me over tapas at El Parador one day. He described a strip about a fourteen-year-old skinhead he had known in his youth, who had been born disabled by the sedative thalidomide. Brendan advised me the story would be full on, with plenty of swearing and so forth, but I thought, 'Well, either we can do comics for older readers or we can't.' Peter Milligan scripted the story and Carol Swain supplied the colour. When the first batch of pages came in they were red, raw, and angry. I was electrified. I scheduled *Skin* to appear in issue thirty, starring alongside *True Faith* and the continuance of *3WW*. The line-up was provocative and I hoped *Crisis* would become a talking point, which is what happened, but not the way I expected.

We sent the first episode of *Skin* to the repro house and turned our thoughts to the next issue. The process with the repro house, as with all repro houses at the time, was for them to photograph the artwork and send the resultant film to the printer, who would turn the film into lithographic printing plates. The next thing I knew, the production manager was banging on my office door, saying the repro house had called her to complain about *Skin*. It transpired they were refusing to process the pages on account of the content, which they found offensive. This quickly escalated into the pages being sent back to the office for the PD to read through, while I sat in a nearby chair wondering where the hell a repro house got off, censoring text and image. For sure, they would be only too happy to process pages for an adult sex mag, but dare present them with a comic strip containing adult themes and this was their reaction. I was nonplussed. Matters worsened when the company decided not to publish *Skin* on the advice of legal counsel, who deemed that there was a considerable risk of it being found obscene in a court of law.

ROBERT CRUMBS! I had been spared the dock of the Old Bailey! No doubt my fate there would have been to be found guilty and punished with imprisonment, *pour encourager les autres*, just like the punishment handed down to the editors of *Oz* issue twenty-eight, the Schoolkids issue. What a mess.

In the end, Fleetway released a statement to the effect that while *Skin* was cleverly conceived within the skinhead vernacular, mass-market comics were not yet ready for such material. The creators received the news with weary equanimity and that was that.

The cancellation of *Skin* was a blow, but the construction of Casa Mac was not going to be hindered by the priggish tastes of one Midlands repro house. On the contrary, I recalled Bella's affirmation about 'circumventing barriers to achieving goals' and ploughed on. My state of mind was good. A year had passed since the launch of *Crisis* and the title had found its niche. It was time to start work on the next section of Casa Mac, this time launching not one but two titles.

1990: KA-CHING!

AS ANY PUBLISHING director will tell you, strike lucky and the business becomes as close to printing money as you can legally get. Such was the case when Fleetway won the licence to publish the *Teenage Mutant Ninja Turtles* comic in the UK. A cartoon of this American publishing phenomenon was already being aired on the BBC, causing Turtlemania to sweep the land, albeit under the safer title of *Teenage Mutant Hero Turtles*. The comic launched as a fortnightly in January and it took off in a way not seen since the arrival of the *Eagle,* breaking publishing records with each issue as sales soared beyond the half-a-million mark. Fleetway's revenue on each copy was half of the 50p cover price, out of which all they had to find was a royalty for the licensor, plus the cost of the print and paper. Shrewdly, the right to syndicate the material across Europe had been acquired as part of the licence, thus capitalising twice on what was now a mega brand. As profits mounted, directors strolled the corridors with broad smiles. 1990 looked like being a bumper year for all concerned.

It was during this mood of financial euphoria that I presented my second-stage plans for Casa Mac. I proposed launching two titles: the aforementioned *Judge Dredd* monthly, and a follow-up to *Crisis* called *Revolver*. Both titles were given the green light without hesitation. There had been a minor query from the PD about the laboured sales of *Crisis*, but Igor had loyally covered my back by joking that everyone was allowed 'one turkey'. Not that *Crisis* was a turkey, but his point was well made and I appreciated his support.

At this point I realised I needed to staff Casa Mac, and the first step was to hire an editor who would have the talent to take the twinkle in my eye that was *Revolver* and make something of it. I chose Peter Hogan, a man of my age, who possessed a deep knowledge of comics in general and whose CV detailed a long and varied journalistic career. Peter had his finger on the pulse of what was trending at the time, unlike me. When I chided him for spelling the word 'delight' as 'Deee-Lite' in an editor's welcome letter, he gently informed me that Deee-Lite was an American dance band, whose track 'Groove is in the Heart' was a worldwide hit and as such he was making a referential pun. Ouch! This was another 'save the whale' moment. To his credit, Peter did not snigger at my ignorance and the word 'jackass' did not appear in a thought bubble above his head. He did, however, purse his lips.

In need of an assistant editor, Peter recruited Frank Wynne, a delightfully loquacious Irishman, who spoke fluent French and had an encyclopedic knowledge of European comics. Frank was pals with another new recruit, namely Michael Bennent, who had taken over the editorial duties on *Crisis*. Michael's appearance had a Cupid-like effect on several members of staff and it was not unusual for me to be buttonholed at the photocopier by one of these secret admirers, shyly asking whom the new hunk was. In fact he was the nephew of famed Hollywood film star Johnny Weissmüller, which probably accounted for the all-round swooning that took place during the first week of his arrival.

The last recruit to Casa Mac was a recent arrival from New Zealand, named David Bishop. For form's sake I had put an advert for the *Revolver* assistant editor job in the *Guardian* and David had applied and been interviewed. Afterwards, I told him that he had not got the job, but that I would bear him in mind for another project I had in mind, namely the *Judge Dredd* monthly. David agreed to wait and in fact came aboard a short time later as my assistant editor.

With Casa Mac staffed up, we were ready to commission. It was a heady time; *Revolver* was planned for launch in the summer and the *Dredd* monthly in the autumn. Everyone was genuinely enthusiastic and there was broad agreement that our intended audience had a mean age of seventeen, with plenty of aspirational readers to pitch to as well. From where I stood the editorial bases were loaded with talent and it seemed inconceivable that we would not bat at least one run.

Meanwhile, *2000 AD* had collected the ten episodes that comprised book one of *Sláine: The Horned God* and published them in a sixty-four page paperback priced £4.50 and marketed as a *2000 AD Graphic Novel*. Some commentators chafed at the term, preferring to call it a trade paperback, or comic album, as the Europeans did, but whatever the semantics it looked absolutely stunning with its high-grade paper and laminated covers. *Time Out* magazine reviewed it saying it was 'Sumptuously drawn, a Celtic Conan with a feminist mythology', and it promptly sold 25,000 copies. Ka-ching! This publishing feat was repeated when book two was collected up just as soon as the last episode had appeared in *2000 AD*. Double Ka-ching!

The buzz around comics and the supposedly nascent graphic novel market had already attracted the attention of mainstream book publishers. Penguin had entered the fray with *Maus*, *Barefoot Gen* and *Tank Girl*. Other publishers followed suit. Titan was still the major player, but only had the licence to publish black-and-white collections of *2000 AD* strips. Now that many of the title's strips were appearing in full colour, and we expected more colour material to be drawn for *Crisis*, *Revolver* and the *Dredd* monthly, we decided to recruit a graphic-novel editor, someone who would oversee a publishing programme collecting the best strips these titles could offer and presenting them to new and old readers alike. Once again we looked no further than Titan, this time hiring a studious fellow named Steve Edgell. His arrival, among other things, brought the number of new recruits who sported a ponytail to three. At least none of us had succumbed to that summer's other fashion accessory, namely the blouson jacket. Edgell's assiduous stewardship saw the graphic-novel publication of *Chopper: Song of the Surfer*, *Troubled Souls*, *True Faith* and *For a Few Troubles More*, all priced around £6.00, as well as UK collections of *Third World War* and *New Statesmen*. The first edition printing of *Chopper* was distinguished by the fact that the letter 'r' of writer John Wagner's surname was missed off the spine, so that it looked like we had a new scribe called John 'Wag-knee'. The PD laughed when he noticed it, but this did nothing to console the editor and his ponytail twitched sorrowfully.

To promote *True Faith*, Igor sent the graphic novel to several religious groups as well as his normal group of press contacts. *New Musical Express* reviewed the book as 'a brill kitchen-sink religious terrorism thriller', but others were not so taken by its tale of a disillusioned plumber who is radicalised by a group of church arsonists and embarks on a campaign of fiery retribution following the sudden death of his wife. Complaints were made and there were rumours that these had been brought to the attention of Robert Maxwell. True or not, the fact was that *True Faith*'s 5,000 copies were suddenly recalled, withdrawn from sale after only two months. Once again I was nonplussed. Bad Steve was more forthright, declaring he was getting tired of this interference and wished Maxwell would 'take a long walk along a short pier'. That glitch aside, the fact was we were now in the business of selling the same material twice and Casa Mac's balance sheet was all the healthier for it.

Revolver really had been nothing more than a twinkle in my eye. All I had was the title. Originally, it was to follow *Crisis* as a fortnightly, employing the same two-strip format. But instead we opted for a monthly frequency, with even better-quality paper and a length of fifty-two pages per issue. The thought process behind these changes was that the title would resemble the very anthology comics I had started out on, serving up an eclectic array of strips with the difference being (USP alert) that it was for older readers. Foreign publishers would have the choice of reprinting the strips in their territories as they saw fit.

Very early on, Grant Morrison had mentioned an idea he had to revisit the character Dan Dare. This became *Dare*, the strip he and Rian collaborated on when I had put them in touch with each other. It seemed an obvious choice for the new title. Just as *2000 AD* had launched with *Dan Dare* for publicity purposes thirteen years previously, so *Revolver* would employ the same sales tactic, coincidentally on the fortieth anniversary of Dare's creation. In this case, though, the treatment of Britain's most famous comics icon would be radically different. In Grant's version, Dare is a forlorn figure, wistfully penning his memoirs. Spacefleet has been privatised, Digby is jobless, Professor Peabody has taken her own life, and the Mekon is up to his evil ways, controlling a puppet prime minister looking very like Margaret Thatcher. As the pages began to come in from Rian, I marvelled at the creative team's reinterpretation of the strip. It seemed to me that *Dare* was good enough to sell *Revolver* on its own.

Rian was also responsible for the design of *Revolver*, a wise choice following his innovative work on *Crisis*. His design influence on *Revolver* has been likened to drawing on various bits of the sixties, from early-decade advertising to late-decade psychedelia, to create a 'sixties retro-modern' style. Whatever the case, the effect was striking and he became much sought after in the world of advertising. In fact, his distinctive style was soon to be found everywhere you looked, on adverts in the tube, in print, and posters. When he told me he had even been invited to redesign Virgin Atlantic's in-flight safety cards, I knew his career had really taken off.

The next story to be chosen came at the suggestion of Igor, who proposed a strip about Jimi Hendrix, taken from *Crosstown Traffic*, the biography of Hendrix by Charles Shaar Murray. I loved the idea. *Purple Days* was the result, described by Charles as the missing chapter from his book. Floyd Hughes, who had written and drawn a revealing one-off in *Crisis* about his experience as a black teenager seeking to join the Metropolitan Police, came aboard as artist and for the second time I thought here was a strip that could sell *Revolver* on its own.

Other strips were commissioned by Peter in quick succession. *Rogan Gosh*, a toothsome proposal from Brendan McCarthy and Peter Milligan that explored cosmic enlightenment over a couple of lagers, *Happenstance & Kismet,* by Paul Neary and Steve Parkhouse, featuring two characters with consequential names and the bizarre events that befell them, and *Dire Streets* by Julie Hollings, featuring the goings-on in a houseful of students. Artist Shaky Kane held court in the centre pages, and that was the line-up. Whatever you thought of the stories, you certainly could not ignore the art. *Revolver* was an explosion of colour from cover to cover.

As launch day approached, Igor was stuck for a selling line for the new title, something that would neatly sum up its eclecticism without sounding pretentious. I suggested the slogan *'Where Dan Dare meets Jimi Hendrix'* and he liked it immediately. I liked it, too. It spoke of a place that fused the world of the comic strip with the exuberance of the music scene. The timing seemed perfect.

Meanwhile, in the office adjacent to *Revolver*, work had been going on to fashion the content of the *Dredd* monthly, using the now-confirmed title of *Judge Dredd the Megazine*. At this point my relations with John Wagner were back to their cordial best and he and Alan Grant came aboard as consultant editors. The word went out to creators: *'Show us your take on Dredd.'* The only criterion was that proposals had to be set in Dredd's world and make a good story. The strip ideas poured in, everybody was energised by the idea of getting to play in Dredd's sandpit. However, caution prevailed for the launch issue and the scripts were mainly the work of Wagner. He scripted both *Young Death*, being the boyhood of superfiend Judge Death, drawn by new discovery

Peter Doherty, and *America*, drawn by Colin MacNeil, which examined the state of the American Dream in the harsh light of the Judge system of rule. His other contribution was *Beyond Our Kenny,* drawn by Cam Kennedy. Alan Grant scripted the lead *Judge Dredd* strip, drawn by Jim Baikie, and Garth Ennis scripted *Chopper: Earth, Wind and Fire*, following the exploits of champion skysurfer Marlon Shakespeare, drawn by John McCrea. The issue included a spoof newspaper section called *The Mega-City Times*. The whole project came together very easily, although great pains were taken to get the package right. The last thing we wanted was to fumble this particular pitch. The title didn't need explaining to potential readers, they already knew Dredd's world, nor did it need presenting to the newstrade, who were well aware of the character's popularity. As well as starring in *2000 AD*, he also starred in his bestselling annual and had recently added a *Mega Special* to his canon.

In the interim, *Crisis* had released a special issue devoted to the work of Amnesty International and their fight to publicise worldwide abuses of human rights. At one point, export copies destined for South Africa were delayed over concerns about fourteen South Africans being held on Death Row, whose plight formed the basis of one of the strips. Solicitors representing the group, known as the Upington 14, were worried that the strip would have an adverse effect on their appeal against a judgement of 'common cause'. It was only when they saw an advance copy that they gave their approval for shipping to resume. The issue was launched with a panel at London's Institute of Contemporary Arts, where writers Mills and Goldkind skilfully fielded journalists' challenging questions about Robert Maxwell's view of the issue (no one knew).

Busy with its weekly schedule, *2000 AD* was unearthing new art talent like Kevin Walker and, later, Dermot Power. Both these painters would find their talent leading them to work on the *Judge Dredd* film as storyboard and concept artists in the art department at Shepperton Studios. At a charity auction in aid of Great Ormond Street, I bid £500 for a page of Dermot's work and had it stored temporarily in the hospital's vaults, the canvas being too large to carry home. When I eventually got round to enquiring about its retrieval, I was told it could not be found. Gah!

Come June, *Revolver* was ready for launch with a cover price of £1.65. The creators were rounded up and sent on a seven-city tour, taking in specialist comic shops in Sheffield, Manchester, Edinburgh, Glasgow, Dublin, Birmingham and London. Their mission was simple: to publicise the most expensive comic in history. The message to the fans was: '*Buy this cool comic and store it carefully in an acid-free plastic bag.*' Or as roving comics correspondent Stuart Green put it, '*Revolver*. Safe. Top. Baggy.'

October saw the launch of *Judge Dredd The Megazine*, with its classy gatefold cover and slick design by Sean Phillips. There was some blowback from the artist community about the design's use of imagery, created by previous *Dredd* artists, but otherwise the general reception was overwhelmingly positive. Dredd finally had his own regular magazine.

The publicity campaign for the two launches climaxed at that year's comic convention in London. I had got into the habit of ducking conventions, simply because I had come to realise that these occasions were the only time the freelance community could get together and swap industry gossip, not to mention discuss their respective editors and publishing houses. The last thing they wanted was an executive listening in to these conversations or indeed inviting themselves to late-night capers behind closed doors.

But there was to be a Fleetway party on the eve of the convention at a vodka bar in Soho called the Moscow Club. I attended. There, the PD announced to a room packed with alcohol-fuelled contributors that in future they would share financially in any reuse of their work. He was roundly cheered, with a few contributors attempting some impromptu Cossack-style dancing on the bar. I then took the microphone and, at Igor's suggestion, announced that the other good news was I had been promoted to managing editor. For some reason this drew a puzzled silence. The effect was a little deflating and it was no surprise when Bad Steve appeared a short while later, manning the club's doorway. He proceeded to spend the rest of the evening barring late arrivals and potential gatecrashers with equal scorn, accompanied by a snarl straight from the Eastern Front. It was highly embarrassing. He turned up again the next day, this time at the convention bar, where he got loaded with brand-damaging brio, causing newcomers to the comics scene, theatre producers and the like – whom Igor was keen to interest in mutually beneficial projects – to review his sorry state and say to Igor, 'Is this really the managing editor of *2000 AD*?'

Despite such antics, the fact was that as the year came to a close Casa Mac was throbbing with the same intensity as the year's house-music scene. Three titles were in the marketplace, accompanied by a rip-snortin' line of graphic novels. The initial construction stages of Casa Mac had been completed and plans for more of the same were on the table. In addition, I had met and married my divine co-worker

Angela, and all the office droids came to the reception, where the *Revolver* team flashed many a peace sign and a trio of Thai brides giggled happily on a sofa. A wedding card featuring Judge Dredd, specially drawn by Steve Dillon, was passed around and soon it was filled with fulsome good wishes for the future. The proceedings ended with an hilarious speech from me and a hoarse cry from Bad Steve, lying under the buffet table, encouraging fellow guests to join him in getting 'rat-arsed'. Yes, the groove was definitely in something and all that was needed now was a doorbell that went *Ka-Ching!*

1991: KERSPLOSH

1991 WAS TO prove a watershed in the history of Fleetway, as a tide of events reshaped the company's publishing plans and staffing. In the beginning, though, the directors were cock-a-hoop when the company was awarded the licence to publish Disney material in the UK, following a short beauty contest in which Fleetway pitched for the business against the incumbent licensee, London Editions. The pitch had been based around transforming the face of Walt Disney comic magazines in the British market. Once successful, a Disney group was set up to fulfil that bold pledge. Following the triumph of the *Teenage Mutant Hero Turtles*, Fleetway was becoming licensed to thrill, and why not? The licensed title model was making more and more sense. The arrival of desktop publishing programmes for the Macintosh had greatly simplified the business of blending text and image to manufacture magazine pages, enabling all the content to be created in-house. Now, all you needed was a licensor's style guide, containing proprietary imagery, fonts and logos, and off you went, with no burdensome budget for freelance scripts and art. Combine a generous promotional spend with a modicum of marketing nous (a foundation certificate in marketing seemed to suffice) and your property was ready to take to market.

Naturally, *2000 AD* was still the company's prize asset, celebrating fourteen years of publishing with continuing lucrative sales. The news that the *Judge Dredd* film was to go into pre-production made the brand even more valuable. A licensing company was hired to exploit the merchandising rights, dividing the property into 'Classic Dredd' (being the comic character) merchandise and 'Movie Dredd' merchandise, targeting the same juvenile audience that had lapped up the *Teenage Mutant Hero Turtles*. Some serious money was there to be made, provided the producers could keep the film's certificate below a 15.

During all this excitement about a movie in pre-production, the company got in touch with Palace Pictures over a recently released film called *Hardware* that looked suspiciously like the strip *Shok!* that Kevin O'Neill and I had collaborated on for the *Judge Dredd Annual*. The suspicion led to a meeting where representatives from both sides gathered to watch a tape of the film from the beginning, with me having the tape paused whenever I spotted a similarity, at which point I would solemnly hold up a copy of *Shok!* pointing to the event in question. When I pointed out the twenty-sixth similarity this seemed to snag some sort of legal tripwire and the tape was hurriedly stopped to allow the legal people to confer. An agreement was later signed in which the parties agreed on the terms of a licence to Palace Pictures of all film rights in the strip and an inclusion in the credits acknowledging Kevin and I as the creators of the source material. On release, the *NME* called the film 'A *Terminator* for the 90s' and, following worldwide distribution, the film later rated number eleven on *Variety*'s top fifty video titles, beating such movies as *Robocop 2*, *Another 48 Hours*, *Back to the Future III* and *The Hunt for Red October*. In view of the success of the film, Kevin and I were offered a small ex-gratia payment (we had signed away all rights) of £1,400, which we grudgingly accepted after Bad Steve had scornfully declined a derisory first offer.

Meanwhile, the graphic-novels programme contained fifteen titles scheduled for release during the year, all but four of them *Dredd* related, one of the exceptions being *Hewligan's Haircut*, which Igor sent to Vidal Sassoon for comment, prompting the response 'This is not the sort of thing we want to be involved in'. Singer songwriter Betty Boo was more complimentary, declaring she wished her haircut was 'As nice as [artist] Jamie Hewlett's'.

The jewel in the crown of the graphic-novels programme was *Judgement on Gotham*, a crossover title featuring Judge Dredd and Batman that would be released simultaneously on both sides of the Atlantic. I had seen the title as a pillar of Casa Mac since I had first written to DC suggesting we revive an earlier plan to team up the two comics icons. The Wagner-Grant combine had supplied the script and there was no need to look any further than Simon Bisley for the art, a project he would occupy himself with all summer.

It was against this backdrop of seemingly endless good news, which included the arrival of a daughter whom we named Kathryn (an event that prompted an unexpected three hundred pound cash gift from John Wagner being 'for the baby'), that we learnt *Revolver* was to cease publishing with issue seven. Sales, apparently, were not in keeping with the business model and the title was said to be sinking fast. Peter took the news as well as could be expected and coaxed Frank to the café to inform him. It was hard to figure why the title had fallen below its break-even sales figure. It looked to have everything going for it, not least consumer goodwill, particularly among the fans, who would later vote it their favourite new publication of 1990. It had great scripts, art and design and seemed very much of the moment. We speculated whether it had got proper distribution in the first place, or perhaps the vaunted adult shelf had failed to materialise and *Revolver* had been racked down with the kids' titles, where its chances of being purchased would have been slim indeed.

There wasn't much time to ponder what the truth was because Casa Mac was looking shaky and the foundations really began to tremble when *Crisis* published its final number, issue sixty-three, in October. Again, declining sales were cited as the cause. It had gone monthly with issue fifty-four, and under Michael Bennett's editorship had begun to feature strips bought in from Europe, including, I was astonished to see, one written by Federico Fellini. I was enjoying reading the title and it had some great home-grown strips, too, written by Grant Morrison, Mark Millar and John Smith: *The New Adventures of Adolf Hitler*, *Straitgate* from Smith and *Insiders* by Millar. Mark was very much the newcomer, and when he first appeared in the office one gloomy afternoon I thought someone had turned the overhead strip light on. He was luminescent. He was also enthusiastic, witty, and possessed of an indestructible self-confidence that allowed him to cheerfully dismiss some of his stuff as being a trifle flimsy, despite the readers lapping it up.

The demise of *Crisis* and *Revolver* was a body blow. During a game of pool I heard a rumour from my opponent, a flame-haired staffer working in finance, that *Revolver* had cost the company 750k. This was no fun for anyone. As it happened, *Judge Dredd The Megazine* had had a successful launch and was selling a steady 45,000 copies, but that didn't really soften the blow and indeed it may have contributed to the demise of *Revolver* in that its launch cannibalised that title's sales. I began to realise my only hope of preserving my hard-won credibility was for *Judgement on Gotham* to make so much money that the company would be thrilled to reinvest in Casa Mac, using a less risky business model perhaps, but nevertheless continuing to back the idea of comics for older readers. But such hopes were to be dashed when everybody's plans were overtaken by events.

In October, Gutenbergus, the Danish company that owned London Editions, bought into Fleetway Publications in a joint-venture deal. They were clearly unhappy at losing the Disney licence as a result of the beauty contest, and a joint venture was a way back into the UK market. Then, on November 5, the body of Robert Maxwell was recovered from the Atlantic, off Gran Canaria. He had been on his motor yacht, cruising the Canary Islands, and was believed to have fallen overboard, an event that was not noticed for some hours. In the weeks that followed an examination of the Maxwell Communication Corporation accounts showed the company was hundreds of millions of pounds in debt, and it subsequently went into administration. It was no surprise therefore when we learnt that Gutenbergus had bought the other half of Fleetway from the administrators, for a knockdown price of five million pounds, with plans to merge the company with London Editions to form Fleetway Editions.

In the midst of all this, we launched *Judgement on Gotham* with a signing in December at the Virgin Megastore in

Marble Arch. Fans began queuing at 7 a.m. and by opening time five hours later the queue stretched down Park Lane to the Dorchester hotel, eclipsing the crowd that had gathered the previous week for a signing by David Bowie. The signing lasted three hours during which time 1,400 copies were sold at a cover price of £4.99. Here was my saving grace, my lifeboat... except *Judgement on Gotham* was being distributed by MacDonald & Co. Publishers, a sister company within Maxwell Communication Corporation. It quickly became evident that the chances of seeing any revenue from MacDonald & Co. in the foreseeable future were practically nil, due to the financial turmoil engulfing all the companies within MCC, and until order could be restored there would be no bonanza to refinance Casa Mac – if ever.

As the storm passed, I came to realise that the company's new owners would focus the business on publishing licensed titles for children, with little interest in older readers. An early casualty of the new thinking was the graphic-novels programme, which we heard was to be outsourced to a proper book publisher, granting them the licence to publish in graphic novel form any colour *2000 AD* Group strips they fancied. This prompted the departure of Steve Edgell, who followed recent departure Michael Bennent out of the door. They were treading in the footsteps of Peter and Frank, who had already left, all four of them now in search of gainful employment.

Casa Mac had been a bold experiment. We had launched three titles in the UK, sold into the US market, developed a graphic novels list, not to mention championing creators' rights. I looked on the people who staffed, wrote and drew for Casa Mac as pioneers. But was there a market for older readers in the first place? In my mind the answer was definitely 'yes', but the number of potential purchasers was no more than fifteen to twenty thousand people. These numbers would be bestseller territory for a graphic novel, but were not enough to support a monthly comic-strip title.

Late that December I was sitting with David in the flotsam of what had once been Casa Mac. I did not know what the future held, other than I had fluffed my chance to shape it. As we sat there, perusing unsolicited scripts sent to the *Megazine*, I suddenly snorted.

'What's up?' David asked.

'This guy doesn't know how to spell "harass",' I replied.

David looked at me quizzically, but I gave no explanation. Instead I began to chortle quietly inside, filled with a bittersweet yearning for it to be 1973 all over again.

AFTERMATHS

'HALLO, STEVE. IS this one of those "Friday afternoon fuck-you phonecalls"?' The voice at the other end of my telephone belonged to a member of the American public-relations team that was in London to handle the publicity for the *Judge Dredd* motion picture. This wasn't 1973; it wasn't even 1992: it was the autumn of 1994 and the film had recently gone into production at Shepperton Studios. For a moment I was lost for words. This was my first introduction to La-La Land and I had no idea that everyone in Hollywood spent Friday afternoons telephoning each other with the greeting *'I just called to say fuck you.'* How quaint. Had I known, I would have worn my cussing boots to work that day.

Although taken aback by the expletive-laden greeting, I was able to carry on with my call, which derived from the fact that I had been put in charge of approving all the *Judge Dredd* movie merchandise for what was expected to be the box-office hit of 1995. My call concerned the creation of a movie style guide for prospective licensees. I had already produced a style guide for Classic Dredd, which, while having specially commissioned art by Cliff Robinson showing Dredd in various action poses, was not entirely well received by some colleagues in the office. What they didn't understand was that the whole (admittedly slim) guide had had to be written and designed in a massive hurry immediately after the film was announced. The style guide for the movie was to be different. An inordinate amount of care was to be taken over it, with an American art director being flown over specially from Manhattan to oversee its creation. I was to be her guide and wordsmith. The art director had some really original ideas on the actual look of the style guide, spending long days at Shepperton before falling asleep on the back seat of the cab returning her to London. Chris Cunningham, whose special make-up effects and design talents greatly enhanced the film, solved this problem by constructing a makeshift shelter in his office, which became his overnight residence for the duration.

When the style guide was delivered from the printers, I sent a copy to the MD's office and took myself off to the pub to celebrate. About ten minutes later the MD appeared, clutching the style guide. He was delighted with it and bought me a celebratory drink. I had to agree it looked amazing, brimming as it was with the movie imagery that had transferred Dredd's world from page to screen. It was so spiffy it even won grudging acceptance from the critics of the earlier Classic Dredd style guide.

The style guide was launched by Fleetway's licensing agency at a gathering of all the film's prospective licensees. The licences on offer covered the whole range of potential tie-ins, featuring apparel, comestibles, trading cards and publishing, not to mention the lucrative videogame and master toy rights. The interest was already building, with one potential licensee offering £75,000 for the right to put imagery from the movie on the packaging of its leading brand of cereal. (In this case the bid backfired as the sight of the grotesquely made-up movie villain Mean Machine Angel, sneering across the kitchen table, was to prove enough put anyone off their morning bowl of puffed wheat.) Before long, samples of proposed merchandise began to arrive: sent first to the licensing agency, then biked over to Fleetway marked for my attention. These samples included a proposed selection of party cakes (which never made it to the supermarket shelves) and a full-sized pinball machine, customised to feature famous Mega-City villains and landmarks, which was duly installed in the MD's office.

My highlight of the approvals process was getting to read the actual film script. Not that the producers were going to pay any attention to my comments anyway, but I did write copious notes to them on the approvals form, mainly concerning the need for the Judge to keep his helmet on. These notes, I am sure, were no sooner read than turned into a paper dart and launched into L.A. airspace, from some thirty-third floor window, with the epithet *'Fuck off, Steve Mac!'* scrawled on them.

In the run-up to the film's release, I attended several preview screenings, each time trying to convince myself that here was a great motion picture: the huge budget was up there on the screen for everyone to see for sure, but something had got lost in translation from British comics creation to American cinematic adaptation. After a special screening for all *2000 AD*'s contributors and their partners, one of them told me she had become so enraged by the film's depiction of Dredd that she had gone to the cinema's toilets and lit a cigarette in an attempt to set off the smoke detector, hoping to cause an evacuation and so halt the screening. At the official premiere, we found ourselves being addressed beforehand by the director, Danny Cannon, who apologised for Stallone not being present, acidly referring to the probable cause being a 'belly-ache'. One gathered it had not been a happy shoot. At the party afterwards, Simon Bisley introduced me to the creators of the *Teenage Mutant Ninja Turtles*, but it was so dark and the music so loud that meaningful conversation (such as 'It's turtley cool to meet you, dudes!') was out of the question. There was a V.I.P. section, but it was cordoned off and I had no inclination to try to enter it uninvited. In the end, sapped by the whole movie experience, I left early, nearly tripping over Bob Geldof, who was sitting on the steps outside and looking a little bit fed up himself.

How much better, I thought on the way home, if John Wagner had been approached to write the script in the first place. On a trip to the set he had been offered a fee to rewrite a section of the script but had wisely declined. I recalled how he and Pat Mills had once co-operated on a treatment for a *Dan Dare* film, which I had read and loved, despite having no particular affinity for the character.

Bearing this thought in mind, it seemed obvious that Fleetway should endeavor to retain greater control over any future audio/visual development of *2000 AD* characters. The only other character that had been optioned for a film was *Rogue Trooper*. I happened to mention my thoughts over a glass of red wine to Harley Cokeliss, the film producer who had optioned *Rogue Trooper*. I pointed out that Fleetway's parent company, Egmont, had a film and television division called Nordisk Film. Wouldn't it be great if Fleetway could set up something similar, keeping any a/v development of a character 'in-house'? Harley liked the idea and, with two fellow film industry movers and shakers, approached Egmont. Exploratory meetings took place in the boardroom, whose content I was not privy too, and before long Fleetway Film and Television was established. Its mission: to bring the stable of 2000 AD characters to the attention of Hollywood studios, with the intention of attracting funding for their development as motion pictures or television series.

It was at this juncture that some legal eagle ruled that such documentation as existed, evincing Fleetway had the right to represent the characters, was insufficient and would probably have 'fuck off' written on it by the first hardboiled Hollywood entertainment lawyer it was shown to. As such, a new assignment document was produced and presented to creators, with the necessary explanation of FFTV's aims and intentions, complete with proviso for the creators to get at the back end should the development of their project make it to that magic phase of film production known as principal photography.

The development process began with the creation of a four-page pitch folder for each character, being a dummy's guide to the character's world and motivation. The pitch folders were to be taken to Los Angeles and handed over at meetings, arranged in advance, with senior executives from the major studios. During the writing and designing of the pitch folders, I was invited to the occasional FFTV breakfast meeting at Claridge's. While I made sure to order one of London's most expensive full English breakfasts, my tablemates limited themselves to a pot of tea, either to drink alone or with which to wash down a host of vitamins, minerals and other food supplements, neatly lined up like a string of pearls on a side plate of the very finest bone china. At one of these meetings, it sounded like there was an attempt to influence the future editorial direction of 2000 AD itself and this brought Bad Steve to the table with painful results.

I listened with interest, forking down my full English as fast as I could, as he began banging a bowl of castor sugar on the table, screaming that no one was allowed to influence the direction of the title except the editor. As a fine coating of white powder settled around us, the two execs got up and one said to the other, 'You shouldn't let him talk to you like that.' I assumed they were heading for the washroom to clean up, but after a while I realised they had left the building altogether. Umbrage had been taken. Unfortunately, Bad Steve returned to harangue the executives at a lunchtime meeting the following week, and my role in FFTV began to flicker much like a 1920s movie. It was no surprise then when I learned of a cosy dinner at The Ivy, to which I had not been invited, where a select group of FFTV bosses had wet the baby's head and touched forefingers together, all chiming, 'EEEEE-TEEEEE.' Nonetheless, I managed to stay on board long enough for the pitch folders to be completed and waved off to the West Coast with many a farewell of 'Knock 'em dead, Johnny!' and 'Sock it to 'em, Sam.'

'LIGHTS! COMICS! ACTION!' This was the nature of the coded telegram I expected to receive, sent triumphantly from the Beverly Hills Hotel, announcing the storming of Hollywood by FFTV and foreshadowing the next British Invasion of American culture. But no such communication came. The plain fact was, after weeks of deliberation, Hollywood decided to pass on FFTV's wares... all of them. The only subsequent interest shown was in a strip called *Black Light*, created by Dan Abnett, Steve White and John Burns, but this came from a Pan-European production company and led to fears of any finished product turning out to be a complete euro-pudding. It was almost as disheartening as the slow realisation that the *Dredd* film was not going to be anything like as successful as it should have been and this was borne out by it failing to make an impression at the American box office, although doing reasonable business overseas.

Having failed to establish two comics titles aimed at older readers, and having witnessed the failure of Hollywood to recognise the clear potential of *2000 AD* characters as cinematic or televisual properties, it seemed there were few new projects for me to pioneer. One potential avenue of exploration had proved a dead end in 1992 when I had ventured to produce an anthology for the exact same age group that comics had addressed as a matter of course at the start of my career: namely the 8-12s. I knew I was out of touch with the needs of this audience and I required someone youthful to help me devise the title and its *raison d'être*. I could not ask David Bishop for help, I had handed him the editorship of the *Megazine* with a brief to discover and develop the next generation of British comics creators – a task he was to complete with aplomb. Fortunately, I was recommended a twenty-two-year-old named Glenn Rice, who just happened to be the younger brother of Garry Rice and Maureen Rice, making a thrice of Rices to have come into my life. Nice. Glenn didn't need a CV: he had nephews of the right age, and a passionate love of comics tempered by a critical faculty that weeded out any pretensions to recreate what he had read in his not so distant youth. He was also on first name terms with Brendan, Brett and the rest of the Brentford/Hanwell set, and so had an understanding of the needs and daily worklife of a freelance comics creator. Had he been born in Manhattan, I have no doubt Glenn would have fared well at either Marvel Comics or DC, but he wasn't.

We fed the concept of a new anthology for 8-12s to the freelance community and pretty soon we had been pitched (and readily commissioned) a bunch of unusually cool comic strips. Among them were a soap opera featuring talking dinosaurs, a comedy featuring a laconic, elephant-headed detective, and a young dude called Billy Whisper, who manages to purchase the presidency of the USA. The creative teams behind these strips made a veritable list of who's who in comics then and now: Pat Mills, John Wagner, Mark Millar, Carlos Ezquerra, Clint Langley, Brett Ewins and Jamie Hewlett. New boys Roger Langridge, Dave Stone and Paul Peart joined them. After a couple of false starts, Glenn and I arrived at the scenario that all this cosmic content was being beamed to the readers from a satellite orbiting Earth called *Earthside 8*. On board the satellite a collection of editorial characters, all dreamed up by Glenn, contributed an enjoyable sense of playful misbehaviour to the party. I had high hopes for the dummy, which was subject to the company's new publishing strategy, namely that the post-prandial greenlight process was out, and instead the dummy would be researched to test the market. Fair enough. I was looking forward to hearing what the next generation of 8-12 year olds made of the dummy. Alas the research company had obviously struggled to find anyone in the target audience who actually read comics and when we arrived to view the research we found six monosyllabic youths, whose appreciation of the dummy was that it was 'All right'. Perhaps the truth was that the age group in question had never acquired the technique of reading a comic, i.e. from left to right, and who thus had never got to experience the pleasure of following a weekly strip. It seemed we had uncovered a lost generation of readers, whose formative years had been shaped by videos, videogames and computers. At a later meeting to discuss the research findings, the tale was told about the shoe salesman who discovers a country where no one wears shoes (or reads comics) and returns to say, 'I have found a new market for our product!', only to be told by his superiors that it is obviously the other way round, that no one in the country he has just returned from feels the need to wear shoes (or read comics). I got the impression the latter opinion was holding sway among the directors. I could see their point: the dummy had no mega-brand behind it and would have cost a fortune to establish as an item of interest in the mind of the average 8-12 year old. *Earthside 8* orbited the office for a few months more and was then discreetly switched off.

As the twentieth century drew to a close, I realised that my time in editorial was also drawing to a conclusion. The publishing landscape was as different to when I had started as Mars is from Earth. Children's titles no longer appeared each week; their frequency was fortnightly or even monthly. The paper they were printed on was glossy and expensive, not the pulp newsprint of yesteryear. Whereas a free gift had once been an occasional sales tool, one was now presented with each issue. Picture strips were gradually being replaced by quizzes, spot the differences and wordsearch grids. Each title was still staffed by a team of four, but now the editors and designers were being trained in their readers' capability to complete the aforementioned puzzles. Columns of text were judged trying to the youthful eye, so any copy accompanying a feature was turned into petal-shaped islands of text, dotted around the page, allowing the reader's eye to flit from one to the other like a demented butterfly. The description of periodicals for children as 'children's comics' was slowly replaced by the term 'children's magazines'. The readership was obviously still children, but now the market was aged 5-8, not 8-12. And the point of sale was not the newsagent any more but the supermarket, where a title would be tossed into a trolley to keep little Jessica or Jack happy without the bill-payer noticing that their remembered cover price of a few pence was now often more than a pound. Encompassing all these changes was the publishing model itself, which had morphed into a marriage between marketing and character licensing, with regular research debriefings being the communication bridge between the publisher and the licensor.

In the first year of the new millennium, the *2000 AD* group of titles was sold to Rebellion Developments Ltd, under whose astute management the brand has prospered mightily ever since. For myself, I chose to take the Long Walk into the land of magazine management, where I was befriended by a tribe who called themselves 'Ratmeekers'. They decorated themselves with brightly coloured plastic baubles, shipped all the way from China, and spoke in a tongue that was unknown to me. They worshipped a great number of gods and goddesses, deities with names like 'Pa Dis' and 'Ma Tel' during long, solemn festivals held every Friday afternoon. Before long I was initiated into the tribe, adopting their mannerisms and even rising to a position of some eminence. I strove manfully to improve their daily labours, producing a tribal bible that was handed to each family and read aloud from reverently every evening by the light of twin, blue moons.

Eleven years later, in AD 2011, I decided to leave the Ratmeekers and head out on my own, seeking employment as a writer at large. Not long after, a thought bubble appeared above my head with the notion that I might just have a comic tale or two to tell. And here, for my sins, is the result.

For his part, Bad Steve was let go after he locked himself in the ladies toilet with his ukulele one afternoon and began singing, 'It isn't over until the fat man swims'. Soon after, he split from me and took himself off to Key West, where he married Bella and together they were blessed with twins Winona and Kayenne, the latter being the feisty one. After two unsuccessful attempts to get elected as mayor, he found a new vocation writing lurid romance novels for the South American market, under the pen name of Henrietta Cortes. For author signings, he revelled in dressing up as Henrietta, complete with Derringer revolver tucked into his pink suspender belt. Bad Steve calls me collect from time to time, and where once I would have moodily declined to talk to him, I now happily accept the reverse charges and revel in his nostalgic recollections of future times past.

POSTSCRIPT

IF YOU CAN find the word 'harass' misspelt in any of the comics I edited, I will gladly let you buy me a drink and share with you some of the anecdotes decorum forbade me from including in this gripping account of my curious career in comics. After all, that's what we comics folk do best: chat in pubs, take the rough with the smooth, and the smooth with a very large, sometimes frozen, but always salty margarita. *Salud* and *Thrashoruns, Squaxx Dek Thargo!*

ACKNOWLEDGEMENTS

MEGA THANKS TO David McDonald for unstinting archive research and general encouragement from across the water. To Glenn Rice for inside information on the West London Set and general encouragement from across the bar table, not to mention contributing 'sci-fidelic' and 'schizo-ethanolic'. The same to Philip Donleavy, for 'rodential credentials' and 'loosening up the infield'. To Owen Leech for Irish road trips and @donlefteri, demon stylist of Triton Square. To Eddie de Oliveira for revealing the scribes' sanctuary that is the London Library, and to fellow members Florence Keith-Roach and Katie Barkes for grammar corrections. Thanks to my Rebellion champions: editor Matt Smith, publisher Ben Smith, and PR whizz Michael Molcher. Above all, thanks to all the editors, writers, artists, letterers and colourists, with whom I had the privilege to work with during the turbulent comics years of 1973-2011.